G000129513

Sacred Theatre

Devised & Edited by Ralph Yarrow

Written by Franc Chamberlain, William S. Haney II,
Carl Lavery, Peter Malekin and Ralph Yarrow

Sacred Theatre

Devised & Edited by Ralph Yarrow

Written by Franc Chamberlain, William S. Haney II,
Carl Lavery, Peter Malekin and Ralph Yarrow

intellect Bristol, UK / Chicago, USA

First Published in the UK in 2007 by
Intellect Books, PO Box 862, Bristol BS99 1DE, UK

First published in the USA in 2007 by
Intellect Books, The University of Chicago Press, 1427 E. 60th Street, Chicago,
IL 60637, USA

Copyright © 2007 Intellect Ltd

All rights reserved. No part of this publication may be reproduced,
stored in a retrieval system, or transmitted, in any form or by any means,
electronic, mechanical, photocopying, recording, or otherwise, without
written permission.

A catalogue record for this book is available from the British Library.

Cover Design: Gabriel Solomons
Copy Editor: Holly Spradling
Typesetting: Mac Style, Nafferton, E. Yorkshire

ISBN 978-1-84150-153-6

Printed and bound by Gutenberg Press, Malta.

CONTENTS

ACKNOWLEDGEMENTS

We are grateful to the following for permission to reproduce material published previously.

Cambridge Scholars Publishing for three chapters from William Haney's book *Postmodern Theatre and the Void of Conceptions*.

The editor of *Consciousness, Literature and the Arts* for the essay on 'Genet's Sacred Theatre: Practice and Politics' by Carl Lavery and Ralph Yarrow.

John Fox, Artistic Director of Welfare State International, for his two contributions in Chapter 9, which are published on his website, www.deadgoodguides.com.

NOTE

Where no author is specified in the text, these sections have been compiled by Ralph Yarrow, usually as a result of discussion with one or more of the other authors and sometimes with direct incorporation of text by them.

PREFACE

This book was always conceived as a collaboration, because it does not set out to present a single or monolithic perspective. There are an unlimited number of ways to approach sacred theatre and experience. You cannot schematize a felt sense of the infinite in the language and categories of the finite. Initially, there were to be three contributors; this has grown to five, and as this has occurred, both the process and the outcome have built on the initial model in developing the dialogic interweaving of voices and the juxtaposition of different kinds of approach. The addition of the two contributors to come on board last – Franc Chamberlain and Carl Lavery – has allowed more perspectives to emerge and has significantly contributed to the extension of the plural or heteroglossic model.

Part 1 asks what the sacred might be with reference to theatre and performance as practice, process and production, and how it may be encountered: so while it attempts to analyse key structural features of the kinds of experience we call sacred, and to suggest some of their vital functions, it also gives space to the personal and experiential. Part 2 deals with ways in which these experiences may be generated in performance by text and by the spectrum of modes of production, reception and effect which text-as-performance incites or stimulates; it consists of a number of chapters which are closer to the conventional critical essay, though the contributions are intended to reflect back upon and illuminate each other. The third and final part examines the nature of some of the key processes by which such experiences may be delivered or accessed for performers and participants, with reference to the contexts in which they arise; it concludes with an exchange of views about issues which the writing of the book has raised, which is intended to suggest some directions for further work. What this means is that the parts themselves work rather differently; so there is no need for the reader to feel that they have to be read either in their entirety, or in the order in which they appear in the book. As Yarrow wrote about the first collaborative work he compiled (a handbook of material about or in response to the French New Novel), 'play is encouraged in this space'.

It's also the case that the argument is not only linear. Topics are taken up by different writers in different ways, and the intention is to produce a process of reflection and refraction, to allow the reader to approach issues from different angles and to accumulate multi-layered and multi-perspectival understanding, rather than to lay out a single track. The writers themselves have experienced the sacred in different ways, conceptualized it according to different criteria and cultural or theoretical preferences, and write about it in different kinds of voice and tone. If that is a mess from the point of view of linear rationality, that is not entirely inappropriate, because the sacred in our understanding is precisely what escapes that kind of tramlining. And they represent different kinds of lived experience. Malekin and Haney are practitioners and explorers of consciousness in refined and subtle modes, who apply to the analysis of theatre in performance an unusual combination of precision and intuitive insight about modes of cognition at the edge of experienceability as interpreted by neo-Platonic and Vedic thought, balanced with recent theoretical models. Chamberlain and Yarrow are performance-makers, improvisers and speculators upon their experience whose approach is often more hazardous and whose language is more imagistic and evocative, and whose understandings are checked out against a continuous and innovative practice of theatre methodologies. Lavery is a restless thinker and explorer of performance dynamics whose acute reading of contemporary theory challenges all forms of practice and the domains in which they operate, with a resolute focus on the politics of personal choice. All of them have written about, performed in, translated and adapted, directed and delighted in theatre and performance.

The book aims to:

- argue that the sacred, as experience, mode of being and perception, is central to theatre practice, which thereby locates a radical refiguring of engagement with the world
- signal that an understanding of the sacred in this sense is a vital part of models of performance theory and practice, and to outline its contributions to these fields
- map sacred praxis across dramatic texts and their effects, actor training and directing method, audience reception
- investigate the implications of the sacred as here identified in and as theatre for ethical and political life
- rescue the term 'sacred' from monotheological and prescriptive use

We want to be clear about this – the notion of the sacred discussed in this book has nothing in common with theological or religious notions of the sacred, which, with the exception of marginalized mystic traditions within them, generally try to 'positivise' the sacred by making it knowable, that is to say, reducible to a set of precepts or commandments. Where theologically based ideas of the sacred all too often result in aggressive forms of religious and political fundamentalism – and we all living through the dangerous consequences of that – our view of the sacred is plural, invisible and essentially unknowable. As we understand it, the sacred is without a positive ground, and, for that reason, it cannot be used to prove the supposed superiority of one's own belief system. For us, by contrast with fundamentalist thinkers, the sacred is primarily scandalous – it interrupts self, ego, language and community. It is a value that resists appropriation by the knowing subject – and that is precisely why, in our opinion, it has the capacity to give rise to new, more politically and ethically generous ways of being. Thus, also, sacred theatre as well as sacred and spiritual experience involves something beyond immediate felt states of ordinary waking consciousness. The goal of sacred theatre and experience cannot be reduced to moments of fulfilled intensity; it's not a matter of becoming an unintended commodity, or something you can possess. In this book, the sacred is what opens us to the Other. This is a recurrent theme in the diverse texts that make up *Sacred Theatre*.

PART 1: BASIC QUESTIONS

Chapter 1

WHAT IS THE SACRED?

This book could perhaps better be called 'the sacredness of théâtre' (le sacré du theatre) or 'the theatreing of the sacred': it is not about sacred drama (dramatic texts within or on the edges of a doctrinally prescribed definition of what the sacred is) or even about theatre as a place/space for the sacred, conceived in that kind of way, to manifest; though it may engage with both of those at times. Rather it tries to see what, in the event-structure called theatre, may generate or open up to something which isn't definable within conventional categories, maybe not within any kind of category; moments when you fall through the interstices of categories and into a kind of amazement. Sacred theatre may be searching for the generators or equivalents of the condition of being 'beyond', 'between', 'outside' or 'before'.

So some of the questions we are going to ask are:

- What is the experience that sacred theatre can deliver?
- How is it delivered?
- What are its effects: in terms of being and knowing (status, function, self/world/other); in terms of psychology, physiology, community?
- How does it relate to contexts and frames – aesthetic, political, ethical, psychosomatic, psychophysiological, psychospiritual?
- Is theatre itself too much of a frame, a restriction, for the sacred – or can theatre in some way match it, reconfigure itself as a viable channel or vehicle to deliver it?

Not all those questions will necessarily be answered directly or in this chapter; the book as a whole will return to them at different moments and in different ways. This chapter describes and evaluates versions of the sacred constructed in various 'languages' and terminologies (e.g. anthropology, sociology, psychoanalysis, aesthetics, theology), though referring back throughout to theatre and performance. It examines paradigms by which the sacred may be thought, and assesses how useful and appropriate they are when set against theatre and what it does.

(i) Overture

Ralph Yarrow

I run a UK theatre company called Sacré Théâtre, which works mainly in French. Its name expresses some of the ambiguous delight of doing theatre, and the wager of doing it in a foreign language. It also incorporates something of what motivates this book: the sense that theatre has the ability always to come up with something unexpected, and that it is important to explore precisely the forms and scope of that unexpectedness. They may be both profound and perverse: after all, those who have speculated about the nature of the sacred in theatre range from Abhinavagupta to Zeami, from Jean Cocteau to Peter Brook, from Antonin Artaud to Shakespeare (not forgetting Maurice Maeterlinck, Aleister Crowley, Rabindranath Tagore, Kavalam Pannikar and Nicolas Núñez).

They will also be diverse. So this book is a dialogue of many voices, and it does not seek to come up with singular definitions; rather to offer a spectrum of reflections and perspectives; the writers include theatre-makers, literary theorists and philosophers, teachers of theatre and performance studies; and the practitioners, writers and work discussed range across many periods and cultures, in an attempt to be as non-exclusive as possible.

There are five different voices here, and perhaps within those voices, dozens of other echoes: we are not seeking to be exclusive or to edit out the differences. We are all asking what the sacred may be for each of us, as experience and in its relationship to what we think of as 'theatre'. We each have a different, though overlapping, spectrum of experience and different conceptions of what theatre is. So why are we chasing this combination down?

Somehow, it seems to us that in the nexus of events called theatre (even if some of us would sometimes rather they weren't called that, or did not conform to some of the expectations the term seems to call up), there is a more-than-ordinary possibility of the kind of experience we call sacred (with the same kind of reservations as before). We do not by any means claim that the characteristics of either or both of these concepts (or better, event-horizons, space probes or agents of origin) have exclusive tenure in this domain; what we want to do is to open up some of the processes, problems and outcomes of this collision.

So the writing of this book, whilst by no means entirely dialogic (it offers space for individual pursuits), builds in a process of exchanges, of interaction and intervention in each other's thinking and expressing. We attempt particularly to bring this out in the final section, though an awareness of what each of us has been writing has also been present at other stages.

Why bother to write about the 'sacred'? Firstly, because there is a substantial, if varied, body of work relating to theatre and performance which hovers around this area, and it is a useful way of bringing much of it together and seeing what it might be about. Secondly, because we need a redefinition of the terms which tend to get used, in order to release the theatre and performance processes relating to this area from claims of exclusivity and ownership by doctrines, dogmas and reified ideologies.

Thirdly, because theatre activates forms of knowing and stimulates ways of being and doing – many of which are currently more specifically approached under the heading of performance.

If there is a sense in which the sacred is an entry to a particularly vital condition, then theatre – as a praxis – is one of the primary sites for its activation, and the forms and methods of theatre may lead to it and disclose what it is.

William S. Haney II, in Chapter 3 of Part 2 of this book, defines the sacred of theatre as a 'voiding of thought' (going beyond pairs of opposites) and a condition of liminality; and claims that the optimal subjective experience of liminality is performance. D. E. R. George proposes that performance needs to be investigated as a particular kind of knowledge, 'an actual way of knowing' (George 1999, 8); and that it offers 'other ways to look at Time, at Space, at Person, at Knowledge, at Experience; which may be closer to both contemporary scientific research (Quantum Theory, Chaos, Complexity) and contemporary philosophical enquiry (Cognitive Science, Process Philosophy)' (9).

To take the receiver out of the ordinary is the task here; not just in the sense of presenting something slightly unusual, but much more 'radically' or fundamentally opening up the capacity for seeing anew, for beginning to get in on the way things put themselves together. To do that, you have to go 'back' to 'before' preconceptions, to a 'place' 'prior to' language, what Peter Malekin calls 'emptiness...devoid of boundaries'. Shock may be one aspect of the process, since it may well be a shock to find oneself 'outside' what one thought of as oneself and the configuration of the known world; it may also be a case of loss or abjection, a sudden revelation of the emptiness of role and identity. However, it may also be a gasp of amazement. The issue here is: how does theatre deliver it?

The opening of Hamlet is one way. It is night. People are 'on watch', but mainly for something intangible, a 'shadow', not a substance, something beyond the realm of the known. Someone, somewhere in the darkness, hears someone else coming: 'Who's there?' The play has begun; and it is a play full of questions which should not or may not or cannot be answered, of grappling with things beyond belief and beyond acceptance; which is why doing anything about them is difficult and clumsy and mostly disastrous. The audience needs, from the first moment, to inhabit (or rather perhaps, to un-habit) this otherworld, to be itself the dark spaces in which these things might appear; so that the question 'who' is addressed also to each spectator. I haven't seen many Hamlets which do that; a pity, because it's Shakespeare's gift to the alert director.

Alain Badiou sees Beckett's work as always seeking to initiate the 'absolute singularity of an unforeseen encounter' (Badiou 2003, xvi). Absolute singularity depends on erasing what went before (word, action, self), achieving a 'break with Cartesian terrorism' (xvi), 'suspending the subject in order to see what happens to being per se' (xix) – where 'subject' can refer both to experience and to experiencer. That is why Beckett's plays could be said to take place – like Comment C'est, the novel Badiou mostly writes about, on 'terrains neutres' or in the 'noir gris' (grey black) which lies between one event/manifestation/word and the next. Here being is about as unconditioned as it gets, and 'thought is reduced to its absolutely primordial constituents' (xxii). It is, like the Vedic pre-linguistic condition para, 'a realm of the thinkable that is inaccessible to the so-called total jurisdiction of language' (Malekin & Yarrow 1997, 129). George says that 'truth, experience are to be found...only ever in the threshold' (George 1999, 54); and 'performances occur on and enable spectators to sit on the thresholds – ambiguous Time-spaces in-between' (21). So what is the nature of the 'event' which occurs whenever form emerges from this condition? For Badiou, 'beauty takes place when the poetic naming of events seizes thought at the edge of the void' (Badiou 2003, 115). I think it is the desire for this kind of 'production' that drove Beckett's well-known intransigent insistence on absolute precision in the materialization of his theatre language through breath, rhythm and tonality.

As Bill Haney puts it: 'sacred theatre, then, may be defined as theatre that entails a voiding of thought, and by implication a shift in consciousness that effects a blurring of boundaries between subject and object, self and other.' And it is clear that, 'in terms of sacred experience, while reading the script can no doubt evoke the liminal, the optimal intersubjective experience of liminality, one that interfuses the verbal and the transcendental, the sacred and the profane is certainly that of the performance itself'.

In what follows, Carl Lavery calls the sacred 'a form of *liminal experience, an empty fullness, a full emptiness*'. He says: 'Suddenly, there was a void, a hole which didn't make sense'. Peter Malekin writes about the 'extraordinary presence of emptiness' identified by Peter Brook and sought by him and Ionesco. Franc Chamberlain describes 'a sense of flowing' and 'a sense of doubleness'. I have often tried to trace it as a kind of gasp or gape, a moment when I seem to move outside known configurations. It sometimes happens in the moment of 'becoming another' in performance, and Chamberlain recalls an experience when working in a mask when this occurred; I also remember as a child of 11 or 12 a sudden loss of myself in the ambiguous mystery or beauty of the figure of Ariel I was watching – from quite a distance – in a school version of *The Tempest*. The sudden realization of the possibility of falling from a high mountain, of not being grounded or simply not being, whilst at the same time aware of the enormous extent of the hills and the sky, is something similar.

Together Haney and George's two criteria approximate to the condition known in Vedanta as *turiya*, a consciousness of being conscious without any particular object of that consciousness. George identifies the need to use the phenomenological *époché* in order to understand how we access knowing in performance. He says: 'As we step from one reality (the academic...for example) into others (reading, listening to music, watching or engaging in a play) we reformat our consciousness in the sense of altering radically our expectations of the kinds of experiences and knowledges we are turning to.' (George1999, 6) The *époché* (in which we 'simultaneously engage in each reality but at the same time observe ourselves doing so', (7) may permit us to be aware of this transition; and it looks as though, if we accept Haney's argument, performance itself provides access to *époché*. For both George and Haney, the liminal moment frames a knowing of knowing, which precedes new experiences and knowledges; though the moment of framing is an *aporia*, an un-or-not knowing. In order to access the genesis of performance and know that we are experiencing it, there may also be a sense of a conjunction of stillness or consciousness-without-an-object and an intuition of the emergence of form; potential and kinetic energies operating together. George points out that 'the criterion of a thing's existence in Buddhism is not some moment of pure being but the performance of generative actions' (George 1999, 50). It will therefore be important in this book to identify processes of cognition/creation.

The way in which many recent theatre practitioners have articulated their goals suggests that there is something similar worth tracking down. The sacred of theatre may be its capacity to activate a particular quotient of energy, a form of active and holistic knowing, qualitatively different from 'normal' discrete subject/object cognition. George points to quantum physical models which give precedence to energy-events rather than matter as the fundamental constituents of 'reality' (which is always in process, not a static given). Theatre as practice, more than as text or institution, with both of which it can however work – and which it is also always liable to inflect, to shift – is always a doing, a setting in motion, a mode of creation in which what is created identifies itself as and how it emerges, rather than reproducing already existing things. In this usage, 'theatre' includes rehearsal, ritual, production, reception; its resonance is much closer to many eastern than conventional western modes, it is not confined to texts and buildings; it is a form of cultural dialogue and personal deployment; extending, as Franc Chamberlain discusses below, to new kinds of knowing of self. Lavery's examination of Agamben, Genet and abjection also suggests the function of the sacred as a kind of limen to social orders, to the construction of self and other.

Grotowski speaks of holiness, so does Brook, seeming to target a kind of charged alertness for performers and receivers; Grotowski of sacrifice, Schechner of ritual and transformation, Barba of the 'extra-daily' energy of performance, suggesting the occurrence of extensions of being; Artaud seeks a real 'beyond language' sensed in Balinese performance and, like Núñez 's 'anthropocosmic' quest, as a function of Mexican rites. Other books and articles have specifically referred to theatre practices defined as holy or sacred, often in ways which are tangential rather than parallel to conventional uses of these terms in a western theo/sociological context. Many others (among them Mnouchkine, Lecoq, and specific raiders of the eastern ark like Zarrilli, along with Schechner, Barba, Brook and Grotowski) look to theatre practice to provide an entry into kinds or conditions of physical, imaginative or psychobiological conditions which lie in some way beyond or outside 'normal' daily functioning.

> For Grotowski, Schechner, and to a considerable extent, Peter Brook, 'holiness' and 'wholeness' signify a dimension of experience of intelligence and feeling beyond the limitations of normal activity. The individual performer and/or spectator feels 'complete' in the sense of being in command of and able to call upon an extended range of thought and action, less confined to the everyday level of perception, understanding and expression. Mind and body, left and right hemispheres of the brain, sensing and comprehending, work together instead of blocking each other, as frequently happens when the internal censor is on the job. However similar aims sought by Copeau, Lecoq and Keith Johnstone are not characterised to the same extent by terminology of religious derivation. (Yarrow 1997, 26)

It looks then as if these 'western' practitioners of the period between 1930 and 2000 in some way lay claims for an 'otherness' of theatre which they often describe in a vocabulary which draws on or implies the 'sacred'. The vocabulary is shaped by their contexts and intentions; but their use of it, and the practical work which they attempt both to describe and to produce through it, indicates that theatre in this period and in the activity of many of its most significant contributors has been perceived as an encounter with dimensions both beyond the everyday and in some way incorporating an extra or 'plus-value'. The profit however – which may be more about locating a resource than capitalizing on individual assets – is closely linked to something like a process of loss, in terms of conventionally valued attributes or appellations. If eastern forms of actor-training (and to quite a large extent, the training of the spectator's sensibility) involves a devotional or ascetic commitment, many of the analyses of performance and reception processes discussed in this book, whether derived from ancient eastern metaphysics or contemporary western post-structuralist theory, engage with experiences and concepts which deconstruct the places and spaces in which our thinking and being occurs. That, however, is precisely why it is worthwhile exploring them. It's also why this book does not offer instructions for performers or performance-trainers. There are no simple models, and reading what we say about forms of training, about ritual, about working on performance deconstructively, about neutrality, may help to make this clear and at the same time to provoke practitioners imaginatively. But as Chamberlain points out later, working towards the unknown requires a peculiarly precise and honest kind of ethics.

Frank Kermode indicates two modes of time: *chronos* (linear/historical); and *kairos* (significant): which suggests that some non-linear mode of consciousness is needed to illuminate the merely historical. That seems to align with the 'two time frames' Peter Sellars says theatre can operate, i.e. historical sequence and the moments of recognition of what that sequence means. We have to live in and through history; but if we do not understand it we simply live as its prisoners, seeing only the reflections of its shadows on the wall of our cave. The sacred of theatre is the moment or motion of levitation, the *époché*, of that understanding. 'Theatre' is a place and a way of entering, accessing, stimulating this occurrence. Sellars says: 'The practice of theatre is... connected to spiritual practice' (which is concerned with 'how to sustain [the] instant [of realization]'). Importantly, theatre is concerned with 'how...you put that in your body' (Sellars 2005, 50). So what is meant by 'theatre' here? Clearly a lot more (or less) than a building, or a set of conventional representations of the accepted reality of a particular time frame which takes place within that building or the cultural matrix it signifies. More like a moment or condition: an 'eventing' (*pace* Whorf on American Indian languages, whose grammars embody the notion of some kind of process equivalence with cosmic orders, rather than a fixing (fixating?) of cultural or psychological capital). What can happen in theatre like this, or as this, is an unmaking, a realization that the world isn't like this, like we thought or hoped it might be, and that most of all 'we' are not at all the sort of relatively secure and knowledgeable monads we thought we might aspire to be; and that this realization occurs, as Artaud would have wanted, through psychophysiological rather than merely 'intellectual' means.

So the sacred of theatre (which could happen anywhere, but might have some specific determinants nevertheless) is the opening into the fact that we are not only our everyday selves bounded ('cabined, cribb'd and confined') by the Wittgensteinian limits of logic and language, and the constructs of a psychosocial preservation-mentality. It is, most centrally and specifically, the moment at which all that flies out of the window, or perhaps becomes the window out of which we fly. That means that it has to be able to occur anywhere for anyone – provided certain conditions apply, and those conditions will have to do with the honing of the quality of receptivity and 'participation', which might well equate to an ability to abandon whatever concepts and anchors about one's own boundaries one might have been inclined to fall back on prior to the event called theatre.

So the process of 'theatreing' will be a way of easing us out of those parameters, those protective reflexes: it is a performative movement outside the known configuration of self and world, and who is to say that it cannot occur in reading or internalizing, in spectating or envisioning, in performing or embodying, in making or producing, or even in analysing or understanding the transitions and border crossings which can occur. Centrally, the key moment is epochal: when you come out of the clouds you have walked through for an hour or more and suddenly see the view all around the range of mountains, you lift off.

We are going to circle around this key moment of opening and loss, and the implications it harbours. We're going to be looking at it from the angle of performer training, spectator experience, textual suggestion and so on. But it's worth saying now that this is something common to all processes of theatre. They may not – for quite specific and valid reasons – have in any way shared the kind of terminology we are using or discussing – but they are concerned with what makes working in theatre exciting and potentially transformatory or liberating. We are quite probably going to have to admit that 'theatre' – certainly in a limited (western) historical or architectural sense – is by no means the only domain in which this kind of event can occur; but what we need to be concerned with is whether there are significant characteristics of the events called (loosely) theatre, which can particularly assist the occurrence of such a situation or phenomenon. So, yes, it does have something to do with how and why I 'get a buzz' out of my engagement in theatre – sometimes as a performer, sometimes as a director, sometimes as a spectator; and it also has something to do with why and how that process is performative – not necessarily, however, 'performance' as opposed to 'theatre', but rather performance in or as theatre (or vice versa). For Augusto Boal, the business of becoming conscious of and recognizing that one has a potential for action within one's position as a citizen in a so-called democratic system is essentially enacted through theatre – not simply as the transmission of the message that this is politically desirable, but as the process by which it is potentially and hence politically attainable. If this doesn't appear initially to have anything to do with what we have been postulating as the sacred so far, it's useful to think about the possibility that the moment of embodying (for the performer) and recognizing (for the spectator/spectactor – Boal's notation for the member of the audience who is motivated to intervene and propose an alternative sequence of events, to change the narrative or 'plot' which appears to have been dictated by events, i.e. by economic and political circumstance) means that the époché has occurred in the terms outlined above: in other words the historical determinism of events has been both perceived and superceded, the recognition of a capacity to be and do otherwise has been engendered.

As he approached his seventieth birthday, Eugenio Barba recalled not only forty years of work with Odin Teatret but certain theatrical moments (Brecht's *Die Mutter*, *Kathakali* in Kerala, Grotowski's *The Constant Prince*) indelibly imprinted on his memory which typified for him that strange encounter with the ineffable:

> Similarly, in an unexpected and involuntary way I have experienced and still experience Disorder while working with my actors. From the very beginning, certain designs of their physical or vocal actions, continuously repeated and refined, leap into another reality of being.

I have personally witnessed it: a denser, brighter and more incandescent body than the bodies we possess emerges in the theatrical space from an elsewhere which I cannot place. This body-in-life irrupts, regardless of good or bad taste, by a combination of chance and craft or because of an unforeseen event in a highly structured calculation.

Today it is clear to me: theatre has represented a precious tool to make incursions into zones of the world that seemed out of my reach. (Barba 2005, 60)

Barba adds:

What has the training of my actors been if not... an opening for the irruption of an energy that shatters the limits of the body?

Theatre can be the craft of incursion, a floating island of dissidence, a clearing in the heart of the civilized world. On rare and privileged NEW occasions, theatre is turbulent Disorder that rocks my familiar ways of living the space and time around me and, through bewilderment, compels me to discover another part of myself. (Barba 2005, 61)

In the following, Carl Lavery brings some important questions to bear.

(ii) *Writing the Sacred*

Carl Lavery

In an e-mail, Franc Chamberlain suggested that we talk of *our* experiences of the sacred. His intent was, I think, to find a way of communicating a sense of the sacred rooted in auto-biographical experience, an attempt, then, to make the book concrete and grounded.[1] It's hard to dispute his logic. As I read through my own writing and the writing of others, it does appear that Franc is right. We've made the sacred into a concept or category, a kind of abstraction. While this is perhaps unavoidable, we've overlooked the opportunity to engage in what the US theorist Peggy Phelan has called performance writing, a type of criticism that celebrates the body, the singular experience of the critic writing about performance (Phelan 1993).[2] What follows then is my attempt to redress the balance, to communicate my own lived sense of the sacred. The writing is necessarily aphoristic and speculative, and there is no attempt to develop an argument or idea. Rather these little blocks of text should be seen as provocations, paragraphs that try to give an impression of the sacred. It goes without saying that I recognize my failure in advance, especially on the semantic level.

For me, the sacred is – and this in keeping with my attempt to theorise it – a form of liminal experience, an empty fullness, a full emptiness. When I encounter the sacred, I'm taken outside of time, outside of myself, outside of consciousness. But I'm still aware of my own separateness, or at least something in me is. *This* is not indifference and *this* is often accompanied by anxiety. Fear? Perhaps. But not fear of something – this is not to do with objects. Rather, it is fear in general: nebulous fear, pure fear. Death on the horizon. And yet in this dislocation, or rather because of this dislocation, I get a sense of my world, and of my place in it. The sudden vertiginous rush that I'm here and that this is this.[3]

After my father died unexpectedly, I was overcome – that's the right phrase – with a sense of vertigo. I couldn't settle. I was restless, nothing was stable. I couldn't sleep. The world seemed strange. Suddenly, there was a void, a hole which didn't make sense. There was a lesson in that, a happy lesson, and a kind of drifting, and a body in space, and a sense of distance.

There are moments, particularly when I'm walking, when I get a sense of my own separation – the fact that I'm here and in this place. This is a concrete experience, a sense of astonishment, a sense of strangeness. I guess you could call this a cosmic moment, a moment when I'm aware of my being and the being of the world.

The sacred, for me, is associated with drunkenness, sex, drugs – what Bataille calls experiences of pleasure and expenditure. In these acts, I lose all interest in economic value. I'm pure enthusiasm. Or to put this another way, the sacred is a value that disputes value. That, perhaps, is its scandal. I don't know why but it also suggests, perhaps, why the sacred is so bound up with childhood – at least in my experience of it.

I have experienced the sacred in the strange stare of animals – their sense of presence, their mystery.

I have experienced the sacred when Melanie gave birth to Immanuel, our son, in our living room in Norwich. When his head was out of her vagina and the rest of his body was in hers, Melanie, so it seemed to me, had lost her humanness – or perhaps attained it completely. At any rate, she appeared as a monster.

I have experienced the sacred while looking out of a third floor window somewhere on the campus of Lancaster University and realising that there was nothing more to the world than this. That my thoughts couldn't go any further, and there would always be a limit to my understanding of things.

As I read this, I'd say that my personal understanding of the sacred is governed by an experience of dislocation, of being in two places at the same time – in other words, a no-place. In this in-betweeness my ego, my familiar self, is displaced and, to a certain extent, emptied. This form of dispossession, of not being at home, allows something else to emerge – something that resists and defeats language. Although it is in no way a substance, it fills the void of self – the void left by the sacred. I often think that the no- thing that fills the emptiness is love, for it is what brings the Other into proximity, and reveals the singularity of everything. I have no purchase on this experience. Like the world, it escapes me. But, at the same time, I know that it exists, I've felt it.

Here then are Franc Chamberlain's reflections on what draws him to this investigation:

(iii) *Where to Begin with Sacred Theatre?*

Franc Chamberlain

I don't come from a religious family so I don't have stories of being involved in rituals or other sacred performances when I was a child, nor did we go to the theatre. There aren't, for me, the early experiences and intensities of sacred performances that echo through my life in the way the Easter celebrations of Eugenio Barba's childhood in Gallipoli reverberate through his career even after he has left behind the 'culture of faith' (Barba 1995, 1) or the performers' 'living offerings of their own energy' remembered by Núñez from the sacred performances of his childhood (Núñez 1996, 26). There are no reverberations of lost sacred intensities for me to project onto the theatre in the hope that it will return them somehow cleansed for use in today's world.

I did, as a child, develop an awareness of a world of dreams and visions that were to be important to me, but without a connection to theatre. As an adolescent, though, I discovered both theatre and something of the sacred as my drama teacher was also a spiritual teacher who ran separate classes. A small group of us would explore out-of-the-body experiences, visualizations and basic meditations. Reincarnation was one topic and I remember one evening, sometime in the spring of 1974, in the middle of a conversation, feeling my left arm move with an unfamiliar quality, and then the awareness that the others were seeing someone else sitting in my seat and I became aware that my body felt very different to me. There was a sense of doubleness in this moment, a sense of distance, where I was not identical with the person that was seen by the others, and that I could sense in my posture and gestures. In that moment the teacher's interpretation of what was happening was that this figure was a manifestation of a past life. I was less certain, but one thing which was interesting to me was this emergence of another character; someone who shared the same space as me but was not me and existed nowhere else.

Bates (1987, 27) would call this figure a 'spirit', something which he goes on to describe as an 'emanation from our unconscious', which sounds rather reductive in general, but perhaps appropriate in this context. It is the function of actors in traditional societies, according to Bates, to 'mediate' these spirits to the community.[4] Whether we call this figure spirit and/or character, the experience is of another presence in the room, something which wasn't there before and the figure was being mediated through me.

It is important to note that this figure didn't arise as a part of a theatre process but it does raise questions for the theatrical process, about the relationship between character and actor. In the moment I was observing from one part of my consciousness as a character/spirit manifested herself in the room through another part of my organism. Neither person was in full control and I wasn't skilled enough as shaman or actor to be able to select from the possibilities that might have otherwise been available to me to allow a fuller manifestation, for example, or to join in with the character and follow along with her, not being possessed in the sense that the individual consciousness is taken over by the spirit, by collaborating with it and sensing what wanted to manifest in that moment. Michael Chekhov writes about his exhaustion, his inability to get in the way of the process of playing Skid one evening, and thus to become a spectator of his own acting. When this happened he was surprised by what the character was doing, and also by how his own thoughts and feelings affected the character. When he came to the latter awareness, he realized that he had to be responsive to character and situation, exercising aesthetic judgement.

> Now I was able to conduct Skid's acting. My consciousness had split into two – at one and the same time, I was in the auditorium and standing beside myself and in each of my fellow actors on stage and I knew what all of them were feeling, wanting, expecting. (Chekhov 2005, 144)

This is a very different experience from my own described above, not least because it is a description from a brilliant actor at the height of his powers. It also makes a direct connection to the theatre. Chekhov had been rehearsing Skid, so the appearance of the character wasn't a spontaneous manifestation but something prepared. The preparation for Skid, however, also included the years of training and performance that Chekhov had undergone. On the other hand, it's the awakening of the 'witness' that surprises him, and this transforms his relationship with the character, the audience and the other actors. His training enabled him to welcome the opportunity and make the most of these changed relationships.

A number of questions emerge from this kind of experience, one of which is the difference between the spectator and the actor's perspectives. Chekhov, for example, sees Skid from the point of view of the audience, but he doesn't offer evidence of what any particular spectator's experience was. Roughly a decade after my experience I was in a workshop with Clive Mendus and Dick McCaw struggling with a mask. I was failing miserably when I was told to leave the stage. Initially I refused and then, when either Clive or Dick, I don't remember which, came to escort me off, something moved. My body, which had been stiff, suddenly became exceptionally fluid and, for one of the other participants, 'Franc' was no longer there and this was something that she found terrifying, whilst for me it was intensely enjoyable and liberating. This stiffness in the actor's body, a freezing where old habits are no longer functional, is a coming to the edge of the known in an 'awkward but essential' moment (Yarrow 1994, 223).[5] In order to progress, the actor has to be able to let go of the 'deadness of habit' (Malekin and Yarrow 1997, 19) and take a leap into the unknown.

In this moment I had more of a sense of flowing with what was emerging, keeping it company, not controlling, but again not possessed or at least not possessed to the point where a witnessing consciousness disappeared. There were no fears of betraying an identity in either of these instances in the sense that Schechner writes of his concern that he might be 'betraying' his Jewishness by converting to Hinduism (Schechner 1995, 3), it is closer to his sense of the character being 'not-me' and 'not-not-me'(Schechner 1985, 123). I had used masks in training and performance before and understood that it was not simply a case of putting a mask on and being transformed or liberated from self-consciousness (see Saint-Denis 1982, 170). Extended mask work frequently leads to altered states of consciousness and adjustments of self-perception but these changes can be for a variety of reasons. Mary Wigman, for example, writes of how one mask she wore affected her breathing and how this alteration led to a change in consciousness (Wigman 1974, 34), but others occasionally edit out her performer's perspective in order to evidence a link between masked performance and trance (Sorrell 1973).

In 1988 whilst participating in a mask summer school hosted by Pan Project in London, I had the opportunity to discuss the question of trance and possession with performers from Bali, Zambia, Japan, and China, and I felt that there was a rough consensus that mask and spirit possession didn't go together in theatre and it was precisely the issue of control, or performer's technique that was focused on. The problem with trance possession, according to Mpopa M'Tonga was that you would have no control over which spirit appeared and what it would do – which pretty much puts paid to any play as the 'monkey spirit disappears up a tree' (his example).

Keith Johnstone, in *Impro* sees the mask as vehicle for entering trance or for ensuring possession. He gives one example of a possessed actor, where in the middle of a Theatre Machine performance, a masked actor threw a chair at him and later had no memory of the event. This is very different from my experiences and that of Michael Chekhov described above; in this example from Johnstone the witnessing consciousness, what Rilke called the Zuschauer,[6] is absent. The fascination with being possessed by the character, of being so 'involved' that the individual actor disappears in the character, is a thread that runs through discourse on acting and the theatre. Possession, in the sense used here, means a loss of the witness or metacommunicator,[7] and so the possessed person has no memory of what occurs. The issue here is not whether or not masks are used in sacred processes which lead to possession by a spirit or a deity, they clearly are, but whether 'possession' as defined here is compatible with theatre, and whether masks themselves have a necessary or simply a contingent relationship to trance and possession.

The actor in Johnstone's story was Roddy Maude-Roxby who, in the mask classes I attended with him in the 1980s, was very careful to give an instruction that people were to remove the mask when instructed to. I understood this to be his way of checking that there was still a distance between actor and mask, that the actor was still able to metacommunicate. An actor who has lost this ability to witness and intervene in the actions of the character and who throws chairs at people is a danger to self, colleagues and audience. Chekhov discusses a version of the Master and Servant game that he used to play with Vakhtangov to while away the time whilst on tour. On one occasion they both got 'carried away' and Chekhov, having subdued Vakhtangov, relaxed a moment and 'by chance' noticed that Vakhtangov had 'turned black and was gasping for breath' (Chekhov 2005, 67).

Dating his interest in mask from his time at the Royal Court, Johnstone writes about a mask demonstration by George Devine where he, Johnstone, saw a "toad-god"

> He retired to the far end of the long, shadowy room, put a Mask on, looked in a mirror, and turned to face us – or rather 'it', 'the Mask', turned to face us. We saw a 'toad-god' who laughed and laughed as if we were funny and despicable. I don't know how long the 'scene' lasted; it was timeless. (Johnstone 1981, 143)

Johnstone puts a lot of emphasis on this moment even though Devine was sure that the demonstration had failed. Again there is a distinction between what the audience perceives and what the performer perceives. As in the above example, a spectator, Johnstone, sees the disappearance of the actor but that isn't mirrored by dissolution of the actor's consciousness. Devine, for example, is presumably witnessing the demonstration and recognizing that there is more possible than is occurring, hence his sense of failure. Johnstone's position here is akin to that of the spectator/student for whom 'Franc' was no longer there, but with two differences: Johnstone suggests that his experience was a shared one and, unlike 'Franc', Devine didn't experience a shift in consciousness. It is perfectly possible for the spectator to witness the appearance of a figure that is then attributed to a transformation in the actor's sense of self rather than simply to a change in the actor's appearance.

The actor may be aware or unaware of the significance of the figure that is manifested in a particular context. Devine was clearly unaware of the significance of the toad god for Johnstone. On the evening of 24th February 2001, for example, I was in Kasaragod, Northern Kerala, and set out from my hotel to walk to a performance of A Midsummer Night's Dream directed by Habib Tanvir and performed by his Naya Theatre Company of Bhopal. It was a beautiful evening and, walking in the general direction of the theatre, I heard the sound of chenda drumming, I supposed, to summon the audience for the beginning of the play. Immediately I began to see an outdoor performance of the Dream in my imagination. I turned down a small, dark, tree-lined track and headed for the sound. I arrived at a small temple dedicated to Shri Muttapan where about twenty men, women and children were both surprised and pleased to see me and invited me to join them to eat. I said that I was on my way to the theatre but they tried to persuade me to stay, telling me that there was a procession to another temple where a Theyyam festival was about to begin. It eventually became apparent to me that I had unknowingly entered a symbolized matrix where the very fact of my whiteness performed a function within the semiotic economy of this sacred event. The drumming was not simply to alert people, but to call the powers, the gods and ancestors. My appearance, not as myself, but as what my colour represented, was regarded as a good omen. I was being woven into the emerging texture of the performance. I was warmly related to by the other people and wasn't simply treated as a symbol but as a participant in the festivities. Throughout the several days of the festival at the Pulikkunnu Temple, I was treated generously as a guest and not required to take on any role other than to be a respectful witness to the events. I watched the devas manifest through the performer, noting the different stages of the process of arrival. It was much more gradual it seemed to me than the usual interpretation that the performer sees himself in a mirror and the shock causes him to jump into the 'character'.

When Kali was manifested at the festival, 'she' took a black cock to be killed outside. I followed but missed the actual slaying. As Kali returned through the kitchen area I was caught up in the energy field surrounding her. I dashed to the other side of the structure and saw the assistant carrying away the head and body. As I turned I heard people laughing and saying: 'Kali! Kali!' I can remember the altered nature of my consciousness at that moment, but somehow I wasn't really aware of it until I rejoined some friends and they noticed the change. I sat for a while until it passed, but I had been touched by the dark hand of Kali, like the shadow of a giant wing passing over me. My hosts were clear that this was Kali and I was not to regard the manifestation as the work of an 'actor'. I have no idea whether there was a witnessing consciousness in the body that was hosting Kali, or any of the other figures, but clearly Kali not only has the power to kill, but uses it in the ceremony. The killing, however, follows the score. Kali doesn't go berserk and kill the participants. This can't be regarded as proof that there is a witnessing consciousness that knows the appropriate actions, it could simply be a case that the conditions for manifestation are known so well that the performer can be carried away by the event, something of which Stanislavsky might have approved. This flowing with a well-prepared score, however, is different from the moments of possession mentioned earlier where there is a loss of awareness.

At Pulikkunnu I saw firewalkers. I watched the wood stacked, saw it lit and burn; I stood as close as I could to the flames, there was an intense heat. I have no idea how the firewalkers didn't burn their feet. It was suggested to me that it was because they were in a trance and so weren't aware of the pain, or that they had a special ointment on their feet. Not long afterwards, in rural Northamptonshire, I had the opportunity to firewalk. The heat was intense and as I was walking across, a self-conscious internal voice made itself heard: 'Wow! I'm walking on fire!' At that moment I felt a sharp pinch on the sole of my foot as it blistered. I restored my focus and returned to the flow. When I got to the end of the walk I returned to the start and did it again, like an actor in rehearsal.

The actor's way is different from the way of the spectator. The actor walks on fire, the spectator watches. Both may have their theories about what's occurring, but only the actor experiences the walk. There is a mystery in the walking on fire, but also an art (techne), and it's the technique that gives access to the mystery. Fire is both a good example and metaphor for this process as Eliade refers to the 'mastery of fire'[8] as one of the key skills of the shaman, the 'technician of the sacred' (Eliade 1968, 92). Bates argues that the actor's way leads to the relativizing of self and 'takes away blocks, restrictions, fears, boundaries and conventional views of self and experience' (1987, 202).

One of the key questions for a sacred theatre, if it is not simply to be the repetition of sacred texts, is how the spectator becomes a participant in the mystery. [RY: see Peter Malekin in Chapter 2 (iv) below on Greek mysteries.]

Experientially the work with my drama teacher, Muriel Hayden, constituted my first conscious engagement with issues of the sacred in my life and they can't be reduced to the manifestation or otherwise of spirits or characters. Gregory Bateson catches something of my perplexity when confronted with these experiences that occurred in different contexts and settings, indoors and outdoors, in relation to art, architecture, nature, in relation to others and on my own. Bateson writes: 'The sacred (whatever that means) is surely related (somehow) to the beautiful (whatever that means)' (Bateson 1980, 228). There is something in the use of 'whatever' and 'somehow' that offers a kind of dislocation that prevents a closure and keeps the sacred and the beautiful undefined, as well as the relationship between them. There is always something that exceeds what we can say about it. The difference between Lavery's sense of dislocation, which includes a sense of not-being-at-home and mine is that I feel that the sacred adds another dimension which brings a sense of being more at home. The dislocation is an unfixing from my everyday perspective and a re-entry into a deeper flow of experience.

Bateson's later remark: 'To be conscious of the nature of the sacred or of the nature of beauty is to be guilty of reductionism' (1980, 229) implies more than simply that our consciousness of the nature of the sacred cannot be fully articulated, but that there is always an element of the unconscious, something which is beyond consciousness in our experience of the sacred. Lavery writes of being 'outside of consciousness', yet I'm not sure this catches it for me, there's something about being embedded in a continuum of consciousness that includes indeterminable resonances.

Shortly after the work with my drama teacher I developed an interest in Zen and Taoism. On one occasion I was sitting in a park with a cherry stone as an external focus for my meditation. I experienced an intense vision of a Buddha in a cherry stone, but in the moment remembered the story of the Zen student who ran to his teacher excited about the vision of the Buddha and the teacher replies: 'Keep meditating and it will soon go away'. I continued to meditate without becoming fixated on my 'vision'; I was interested in finding out more about the ground/void/emptiness that underlay this and all phenomena. Yet this formulation of an 'underlying emptiness' was to shift to a sense of form and emptiness being interwoven in an ongoing process with all stasis as relative rather than absolute.

From Taoism I took the idea that everything emerges from the Tao and is therefore sacred in some way – and that the Tao itself was in continual motion and creative flux. I read Capra's *The Tao of Physics* in 1976 and was inspired by the combination of Buddhist, Taoist and Hindu thought with atomic physics, not simply in an abstract sense, but quite sensually in the way Capra himself linked these different ways of thinking to an embodied experience:

> Five years ago I had a beautiful experience which set me on a road that has led to the writing of this book. I was sitting by the ocean one late summer afternoon, watching the waves rolling in and feeling the rhythm of my breathing, when I suddenly became aware of my whole environment as being engaged in a giant cosmic dance. (Capra 1976, 9)

Capra's sense of a 'giant cosmic dance', the dance of Shiva, opens out to the aesthetic, but at this time I had little sense of how to bring this sense of the cosmos, which I would call sacred, into the theatre. Capra's story involves a shift from the cognitive knowing of the dance of atoms, to an embodied knowing which adds another dimension to his experience of the world. There are clearly different levels of significance possible here and not every shift from the cognitive to the experiential is experienced with the same intensity or significance, there needs to be this unfolding into another dimension where the cosmos is experienced as a whole, whatever the starting point.[9] This shift has affinities with the processes of acting as the cognitive understanding of the text becomes an embodied understanding but it would be mistaken to simply fix it in this linear way.

The impact of *The Tao of Physics* on me, not least in its presentation of Chew's bootstrap theory which proposed that all symbolic systems, all models of the cosmos were necessarily incomplete, has stayed with me for the past thirty years, even though I have written next to nothing on it. Since 1976, for example, I have always had either an image or small bronze sculpture of a dancing Shiva, wherever I've lived. But the key point is in the link between contemporary science (first physics, then chemistry and biology), Hindu, Taoist and Buddhist philosophies and somatic practices, and the environment in its broadest sense. A sacred cosmology that meant that Lovelock's Gaia hypothesis made intuitive sense when I encountered it in the early 1980s. The experience that Capra describes might be considered an example of what Zaehner (1961) called 'panenhenic', a sense of oneness with the cosmos that is significantly different from the encounter with the Other articulated in works such as Otto's *The*

Idea of The Holy, and from the mystical sense of inner communion. Zaehner coined the term panenhenic because he considered it to be a more accurate description than pantheism.

Smart (1997) considers the numinous and the mystical as two poles of the sacred (for him religious) experience and discusses the panenhenic as a third type that sits along the continuum between the other two. He also considers the importance of shamanism as holding an experiential dimension that encompasses both poles, and this hints at something that's important for the theatre and for the actor: that it focuses both inwards and outwards simultaneously. At the moment I'm interested in whether the concept of the panenhenic provides a way of thinking about the sacred dimension in theatre that works for me, and includes the shamanic without reducing the sacred in theatre to the shamanic. Also Zaehner's rejection of pantheism as an accurate term was because there was no 'god' in it and an atheistic sense of the sacred, an a/theology, is more useful in trying to understand what we mean by sacred theatre.

This is a book that refuses to allow the reader to treat it as Holy Writ; it is a fractal, if not fractious, volume. Like any text it has more going on than the authors can explicitly state because it has its own intricacy and complexity. Dewey suggests that thinking requires some difficulty to get it started and we hope there are sufficient difficulties to stimulate a variety of readers to engage with the topics here. Hillman reminds us that

> To 'explain' means etymologically to remove the folds, the complications, by laying out smooth and flat. Explanation is served well by two-dimensional models, whereas complex models [...] do not yield satisfactory explanations (Hillman 1992, 30n)

And that 'definition settles unease by nailing things down' whereas the psyche and in this the case the sacred,

> May be better served by amplification, because it prises things loose from their habitual rigid frames in knowledge. Amplification confronts the mind with paradoxes and tensions; it reveals complexities (1992, 31n)

When even Richard Dawkins finds the concept of the sacred meaningful (Dawkins 2004) there can be no easy answers and no reductive explanation of the sacred as a religious category.

(iv) *Performance and Knowing*

Ralph Yarrow

Can the experience of the sacred be approached through, or in some degree equated with, the mode of *performance*, in George's sense? It may also be helpful to bring in here Zarrilli's consideration of the kinds of knowledge (knowing might be a better word) which performance constitutes, generates, invites, requires (Zarrilli 2001). George sees performance as both a recognition of transience and a location of the point of deconstruction and reconstruction, falling apart and coming into being; similarly, for Zarrilli, it is rooted in experience, but should precisely because of that be understood as a process of knowledge, a 'double consciousness' in which a 'non-ordinary state of awareness' is engaged. Zarrilli suggests that certain kinds of 'extra-daily' (Barba) practice are necessary to develop this through a process of 'training... the bodymind in order to become accomplished in attaining a certain specialized state of consciousness, body, agency, power, etc.' (Zarrilli 2001, 33–4); and to attain the 'state of responsivity akin to that which is ideal for the performer – a state of total engagement in the moment' (39). In this context, 'extra-daily practice' includes ritual, martial arts, meditation, as well as the detailed and extensive training for some Asian performance forms.

If one key aspect of the sacred as we are approaching it in this book is its status precisely beyond configuration, beyond the known in conventional terms, it looks as though these understandings of performance are targeting something similar. Zarrilli defines extra-daily practices as 'intersections where personal, social and/or cosmological experiences and realities are negotiated' (34). For Zarrilli performance is a way of confirming that the self is not a stable location or transcendental essence (32). George confirms this view that it is in two senses utterly 'change' – the force for change in its nature as potentiality, the mode of change in its performative interaction. In the sacred moment I am unravelled and knitted up; it is not simply a site of wholeness and stasis, but rather of contestation, of passing through and becoming other.

It is also (pace Blau) 'that aspect of the experience [of theatre] which is not capable of being measured because it always seems to be going out of sight' (quoted in Zarrilli 34).

This formulation suggests the process of transcendence: the object of awareness is gradually reduced in dimensions until only the process of attending, not any object of attention, remains: so the 'aha' is 'ah I see', but not 'ah I see this or that': it is the recognition that I am the capacity for 'pure' seeing, seeing without the requirement for there to be an object which determines or circumscribes the seeing.

Zarrilli seems to be grasping for this when he talks of performative knowledge involving 'subjects looking, highly critically, at their own experiences'. By 'looking critically' he does not just mean analytically, but also understanding as a result of passing through a sequence of training and experience which produces 'sedimentation, assimilation, quickening and activation' (Zarrilli 36) – different strategies and kinds of knowing from the merely intellectual or cognitive, but not excluding these. There is a parallel here with the development occurring through repeated exposure to single moments of knowing, in part suggested above, whereby a more extended state of 'double consciousness' might properly be claimed. And, as I have consistently pointed out (Yarrow 1986, Frost & Yarrow 1990, Malekin & Yarrow 1997, Yarrow 2001), such a more 'holistic' kind of knowing requires at a critical juncture some kind of 'unlearning or deconditioning' (Zarrilli 40). Zarrilli cites Grotowski's via negativa and Stanislavsky's instructions to wipe away 'bad habits' – in order to access what Austin calls 'a strong break from other states of perception or intuition' (Zarrilli 34) – which are also for performers, states of being and doing; Copeau's and Lecoq's approach to the neutral mask involves a similar process central to improvisatory practice and the spontaneity Clive Barker calls 'body/think'. Austin indicates that there is a state in which one does 'not have to think to be conscious' (Zarrilli 39); Blau, rather like Keith Johnstone before him, suggests that it is important to 'discover how not to do' in order to sideline the blocks to performance. The crucial issue here is that the performative mode itself offers a route to locate this situation; but it has to be engaged with. Zarrilli is right to stress performance and extra-daily *practice* and to reject any reification of some essential value to 'experience', the body, subjective consciousness and/or 'self'. There is work to be done to access the modes of these phenomena described here; they are not simply given, out there waiting to be accessed. The work itself is the process by which they are reconfigured; and it requires initially the volition to begin and carry it through, a subtle but powerful mode of intention/attention; subsequently 'such "intuitive" abilities are *only* gained...through the tempering work of psychophysiological discipline, whatever form that might take' (Zarrilli 44).

In case it looks as though the scope of reference of the book might be limited to these twentieth-century orientalist excursions, which have of course been rightly scrutinized from a number of perspectives, including that of cultural politics (see Bharucha 1993), it is worth pointing out that subsequent sections and chapters will also interrogate evidence from other periods and cultures (e.g. classical Greek, Elizabethan, European modernist); the next chapter will specifically consider a variety of approaches to 'sacred' experience.

In the light of these findings, Part 3 explores the dynamics and mechanics of theatre as a poetics and a transforming practice in order to discover how the sacred works and what it produces. Here the concern is with the biodynamics and psychobiology of performance (for performer-participants) and with the aesthetics of reception (for receivers): in both cases, considerations of place, space, event-structure and artefact-structure, process, rhythm and semiotic transfer will be relevant. The chapter also indicates and analyses how theatre practice has been seen to relate to these frameworks across various cultural contexts and periods. It further opens up some of the debates which are signalled above, about the sacred as a politics, an ecology and a phenomenology, and suggests that they might be fit subjects for further debate. This part of the final section is constructed as a debate in order precisely to indicate that here are a number of avenues which stimulate reflection and engagement from a number of perspectives which intersect profitably with the concerns of contemporary performance-makers.

The intervening Part 2 looks at relevant playtexts and playwrights, attempting, however, to engage with as many aspects of their translation into and operation as performance as possible. Although Brook, Grotowski, Barba, Mnouchkine and others frequently commission or create event- and site-specific work, they also operate in an age in which Beckett, Genet, Ionesco and Pinter have foregrounded the uncertain and undermined the familiar; in addition, Brook has turned to Shakespeare, Schechner to Goethe, Kantor to Witkiewicz. In all cases the intention seems to be to grapple, even in 'traditional' or 'canonic' cultural artefacts, with what is strange and to find performance forms which can engage this. Not just in the sense of exploiting the exotic, but as an aesthetics which is also a praxis: the sense that the business of art itself is an encounter with what may appear unfamiliar (Russian formalism's *ostranienye*, Brecht's *Verfremdung*), in order to challenge the limits of the 'known', the accepted, the comfortable; and that to accept this challenge both defines 'art' as a two-way and participatory activity, and situates it as a process of transformation which has both ethical and personal consequences. The chapter does not, however, only look at work which overtly foregrounds strangeness, but explores instances of more 'traditional' theatre practice as well in order to see if they can also provide access to the experiences described above.

Many of these practitioners have intuited, explored and articulated the sense that in pursuing this engagement, theatre and performance most fully justify their existence and deliver their potential; in this they parallel claims for the profound or illuminating or enlivening quality of many art forms, although there are specific distinctions to be drawn.

There are a number of big questions about what the book sets out to explore.

- Does this quality or mode of experience, or whatever it is, really exist as a separate condition or experience, or is it inextricably entwined with other aspects of aesthetic operation?
- Is there a condition 'beyond' or 'between' thought, a mode of unmediated experience, a possibility of direct intersubjectivity?
- Is there such a phenomenon, or zone, or nexus of energy as an hors-texte?
- If so, since it cannot logically be spoken of, isn't it a case of the Emperor's clothes?

In what follows we will endeavour not to duck these.

Chapter 2

TERMINOLOGIES AND CATEGORIZATIONS OF THE SACRED

The first two sections of this chapter confront definitions of the sacred as totemic and/or taboo, as a hedging off or reserving certain kinds of 'knowledge' – thereby opening up questions about what, precisely, might constitute knowledge and how those models which operate taboo and totem categorize it along an intuited>spoken>written/authored/authorized spectrum.

One function of this section therefore is to problematize the notion of the sacred, to propose it as a dialogic tool rather than a given category. This then opens up the possibility of exploring subsequent definitions in the same light. The sacred may helpfully be approached as a form of personal and social difficulty, a not-quite-fitting-in, *un sentiment d'étrangété*. It also helps to establish that although the focus of the book may be on an otherness, it is an otherness which nevertheless has to do with bodies, with social relations and forms of behaviour, which operates from within – although also on and across the borders of – our being in time and space. Theatre, in fact, in one sense can be seen as precisely the confrontation of these temporal, spatial and ontological limits.

(i) *Modern Views of the Sacred*

Carl Lavery
In general, the sacred is subject to three different interpretations in modern culture: secular, theological and a/theological. In its secular definition, the sacred is devoid of transcendental value: it is a structural principle, a way of distinguishing one realm of values from another. According to Emile Durkheim in his celebrated sociological study of the divine, *Les Formes élémentaires de la vie religieuse: le système totémique en Australie* (1912), the sacred acquires meaning and definition in and through its dialectical relationship with the profane: 'Les choses sacrées sont celles que les interdits protègent et isolent; les choses profanes, celles auxquelles ces interdits s'appliquent et qui doivent rester à distance des premières' (Durkheim 1979, 56). As we can see from Durkheim's comments, there can be no sacred without the profane and vice versa. For if everything were sacred, value would cease to exist. This operation of dividing the world into two distinct hemispheres conditions Durkheim's definition of religion:

[U]ne religion est un système solidaire de croyances et de pratiques relatives à des choses sacrés, c'est-à-dire séparées, croyances et pratiques qui unissent en une même communauté morale, appelée Eglise, tous ceux qui y adhèrent. (Ibid., 65)

Although Durkheim speaks of the sacred as a religious phenomenon, his idea of religion does not, as Michèle Richman points out, 'imply any intrinsic property or transcendental quality' (Richman 1995, 65). Durkheim's view of religion and, by extension, the sacred, is positivistic. He searches for the origins of religion in the human community rather than in any outside force. Accordingly, he understands the sacred in secular terms:

[L]a cause universelle et objective [...] dont est faite l'expérience religieuse, c'est la société. Nous avons montré quelles forces morales elle développe et comment elle éveille ce sentiment d'appui, de sauvegarde, de dépendance tutélaire qui attache le fidèle à son culte. C'est elle qui l'élève au-dessus de lui-même: c'est même elle qui le fait. (Durkheim 1979, 597)

Examining Durkheim's essentially positivist/humanist view of religion as a structure of negative prohibitions and positive precepts, it is possible to say that the sacred is not just divided from the profane: it is, moreover, divided in itself. The sacred is a liminal phenomenon, a logically impossible place where two opposing forces meet in a synthesis that is characterized by disjunction. Durkheim defines the disjunctive duality of the sacred in terms of totem and taboo. Where the totemic sacred refers to the sacrosanct quality of both the moral law and the social order, the taboo sacred is equated with those 'self-altering' drives and phenomena (sexuality, violence, etc.), which transgress the law and disturb the sacredness of social identity. According to Durkheim, if society is to keep its shape and perpetuate its order, neither the taboo nor the totem can be touched or dislodged by the profane.

In *Totem and Taboo* (1913), Freud uses the same double-edged version of the sacred to account for the origins of collective society. According to Freud's mythological account, the earliest form of society is the 'patriarchal horde', a rudimentary, violent social order in which a 'primal father', ruling by force over his subjects, 'keeps all the females for himself and drives away his sons as they grow up' (Freud 1990, 202). In Freud's imaginary story, the mastery of the primal father is broken when the sons join together and murder him so as to gain access to the women: 'One day the brothers who had been driven out came together, killed and devoured their father and so made an end of the patriarchal horde.' For Freud, this murder and cannibalism of the Father 'was the beginning of [...] social organisation, of moral restrictions and or religion' (ibid., 203). Freud's theory contends that as a result of guilt for their actions, the fraternal group establishes the dead father as a sacred, venerated object: 'The dead father became stronger than the living one had been' (204). He is transformed into a totemic figure, a presence that manifests itself through various emblematic figures, such as animals and other phenomena that are set apart and are supposed to possess *mana*, divine power.

Paradoxically then, the presence of the dead father acts as a unifying force in the new social organization: the clan of the brothers. According to the logic of totemism, to touch or kill the sacred object is to destroy the foundations of the social. Such an act results in chaos, the war of all against all: 'The new organisation would have collapsed in a struggle of all against all, for none of them was of such over-mastering strength as to be able to take on his father's part with success' (205). Freud argues that in order to protect the sacred quality of the totem, and thus the social order, 'two fundamental taboos' were born: 'not to kill the totem and not to have sex with a woman of the same totem' (192). Interpreted in this way, what Freud is offering us in *Totem and Taboo* is a mythical explanation for the origins of the sacred that, as in Durkheim's model, centres on the consecration of social life and the ethical law.

Though there are important differences separating Freud's account of the sacred from Durkheim's, the essential point to bear in mind for this study is the way in which psychoanalysis and sociology perceive the sacred as a phenomenon that is bound up with questions of individual and collective identity. In both disciplines, the sacred, as its etymological root in the Latin *sacer* implies (*sacer* refers to what is frightening and holy, demonic and divine at the same time), has a dual meaning. Where the sacred in its positive totemic guise founds social identity, the sacred in its negative taboo guise negates social identity. Such a negation occurs when the boundaries separating the sacred and the profane are transgressed. At such moments, the sacred dissolves the identity that it was originally designed to protect. In contrast to Durkheim who traces this 'sacred' crisis to the moment when society loses its 'religious belief' structure, Freud argues that the sacred dissolves identity when the paternal law is unable to enforce castration and is challenged by the maternal.

Unlike sociology and psychoanalysis which understand the sacred in materialist and functional terms, theological discourse grants the sacred holy or transcendental significance. According to a religious sensibility, the transcendental is a value or 'truth' that has no origin in human history. As a consequence, although the transcendental can be 'experienced' by a human agent, we can never know its origins. Such 'holiness' exists outside of our world: it is an uncaused cause. Like the horizon, it is always beyond our reach in some 'noumenal' elsewhere.

In the three major monotheistic religions, the radical alterity of the sacred is communicated by the presence of a God or divinity, who, despite transcending the world, is 'known' through his commandments and through his works. Mark C. Taylor supplies an excellent definition of the monotheistic notion of the sacred in his book *Erring: A Postmodern A/theology*:

> God, who is the original source, groundless ground, and uncaused cause, is both "spatially" and temporally present. In most cases the identification of God with Being and presence does not lead to belief in divine immanence. To the contrary, God is consistently regarded as radically transcendent. The Creator is other than, and separate from, the creation over which He exercises omnipotent rule. As a result of this transcendence, divinity is, in some sense, inaccessible to humanity. (Taylor 1984, 36)

Like Rudolf Otto, the author of the influential book *The Idea of the Holy: An Enquiry into the Non-Rational Factor in the Idea of the Divine and its Relation to the Rational* (1917), Taylor argues that one of the dangers of this monotheistic model of divinity is found in the way it reduces the otherness of the sacred to an anthropocentric deity or Creator figure, whose nature or will can be understood in a rational fashion, via a study of the attributes of theism. Hence, the reason why, Taylor concludes, Christian theology has allocated such importance to the *logos* or word of God. For Taylor – and this repeats Otto's critique of Christian 'rationalism' – language tempers the 'unknowability' of the sacred by providing concepts and ideas (Otto

1973, 3).[10] It replaces what is radically incommunicable with what can be mediated and thus proved. Taylor notes à propos of Christianity: 'The transcendent God, who can never be fully known in Himself, must be known indirectly, through a mediator. For the Christian, the divine *logos*, Christ, effects this mediation' (Taylor 40).

In Taylor's reading, the emphasis monotheism places on the mediating role of the *logos* is reflected in the emphasis it places on the study of Holy Scripture:

> Page by page, and chapter by chapter, the Book weaves the unified story of the interaction between God and self. Since the logic of this narrative reflects the *logos* of history, Scripture, in effect, re-writes the Word of God. (Ibid., 7)

The Bible, as Taylor describes it here, is not, for the believer in God, a mythological narrative, as Durkheim and Freud claim: it is, on the contrary, the text by which the subject is able to understand the ways of the divine; it reveals the 'truth' of creation by providing a sense of certainty. Studying the 'Book' allows the subject to attain a sense of self-presence. Unlike the mystic who loses himself in what Otto refers to as the numinous and/or the *mysterium tremendum*, the student of the logocentric concept of Scripture shares in the transcendental project of a thoroughly rational God (see Otto, 5–30). When the monotheistic subject encounters the sacred he feels no sense of lack and loss; rather he transcends his limitations as a differentiated subject. In this rationalized and logocentric concept of religion, sacred transcendence results in redemption. Paradise is regained through fidelity to the conceptual truth inherent in, and mediated through, the word.

In contrast to the sociological and psychoanalytical models of the sacred, this rationalized model of monotheistic theology, as understood by Otto and Taylor, is devoid of ambiguity and ambivalence. It is pure and uncontaminated by difference or division. Subsequently, the sacred is gentrified and 'cleaned up'. The subject identifies with the divine rather than being altered by his encounter with it. One of the consequences of this interpretation of religion is to reduce existence to a search for unity and comprehensibility, as opposed to an adventure in otherness and inexplicability. From an ethical perspective, as I will discuss later in this book, such an ontology of oneness is inherently problematic. By prioritizing homogeneity, it violates heterogeneity, both in the self and in the subject's relationship with others.

Like Otto and Taylor, thinkers such as Mircea Eliade and Georges Bataille believe that this logocentric understanding of the sacred negates the defining feature of sacred experience: cosmos and continuity. According to Eliade, Christian monotheism is a flight from the sacred. For where rationalistic theology sees God as a Being whose presence can be known in and through conceptual understanding, Eliade sees the sacred as a force that exceeds all thought and scriptural definition. In sacred experience, according to Eliade, there is no distinction between subject and object. Words no longer function and we experience a transcendent plane of being in which the subject and the universe or cosmos are as one. We literally step outside of secular and/or punctual time. Speaking approvingly of sacred transcendence as understood by eastern religion, Eliade says:

On arrive au commencement du Temps et on rejoint le Non-Temps, l'éternel présent qui a précédé l'expérience temporelle fondée par la première existence humaine déchue. Autrement dit, en partant d'un mouvement quelconque de la durée temporelle, on peut arriver à épuiser cette durée en le parcourant à rebours et déboucher finalement dans le Non-Temps, dans l'éternité. (Eliade 1994, 111)

For Eliade, when the subject experiences 'non-time' he does not encounter himself as he really is. He is altered: he sacrifices his individuality and participates in the endless cycle of rebirth and re-generation. He becomes a part of the cosmos. In his analysis of the shaman's ecstatic voyage back to the authentic mode of communication that used to exist in *illo tempore* between Heaven and Earth, Eliade says that the laws of time and space governing the profane world are annulled. In this negation, the shaman exists in sacred time.

Eliade's a/theology attacks monotheistic rationalism for being too profane. Unlike the shaman and the pagan, Eliade contends that the logocentric subject knows nothing of the transformative ecstasy of the sacred. He always remains within his profane limits; he resists 'othering'. In his book on Eliade, Thomas Altizer provides a good explanation of monotheistic theology's perversion of sacred experience:

In choosing to understand the world as creation in a rational sense, theology transformed faith's understanding of the world as profane [...]. The necessary consequence of this transformation was that the sacred could no longer be related to the world, or rather, the sacred could be related to the world only by the rational idea of God [...] which at bottom was the projection of man's *understanding* of the world [...]. Consequently [...] theology cannot bear witness to the presence of the sacred... (Altizer 1975, 40)

Like Eliade, Georges Bataille sees theology, particularly Christianity, as the antithesis of the sacred (Bataille1973b, 38). For Bataille, Christian theology lacks the characteristic feature of authentic sacred experience which, as he sees it, is synonymous with eroticism. To assent to eroticism is, in Bataille's opinion, to assent to death. In the erotic, we sacrifice discontinuity (our differentiated identity) for continuity (non-differentiation).

Toute la mise en œuvre de l'érotisme a pour fin d'atteindre l'être au plus intime, au point où le cœur manque. Le passage de l'état normal à celui de désir érotique suppose en nous la dissolution relative de l'être constitué dans l'ordre discontinu. (Ibid., 24)

In Bataille's explanation, the sacred is thus radically opposed to what he considers to be the spirit of Christian theology. For where Christianity attempts to produce a situation in which 'cette continuité [...] fit entrer dans le cadre de la continuité', the sacred is pure continuity (ibid. 133). It negates, in other words, what Christianity attempts to safeguard: the individuality and immortality of discontinuous beings. For Bataille – and he is close to Otto's notion of the *mysterium tremendum* or 'wholly other' here – the sacred is like a volcanic eruption, it dissolves our being (Otto 27).[11] In Bataille's a/theological understanding of the sacred, we are altered: we lose the self and experience a different register of being, which, for Bataille, explains the sacred's relationship with death: '[A]u- delà de l'ivresse ouverte à la vie juvénile, le pouvoir nous est donné d'aborder la mort en face, et d'y voir enfin l'ouverture à la continuité inintelligible, inconnaissable, qui est le secret de l'érotisme' (Bataille 1973b, 31).

Although Bataille rejects, like Eliade, the definition of the sacred proffered by the rationalising element inherent in the monotheistic approach to the holy, he offers a different explanation for this occurrence. Where Eliade, for instance, traces Christianity's loss of the sacred to the moment when cosmic time was replaced with historical time (this would occur in Eliade's thinking when Christianity divorced itself from archaic religion by embracing a linear notion of time), Bataille believes that Christianity negates the sacred by denying ambivalence. Mirroring the duality of the sociological and psychoanalytical understanding of the sacred, Bataille contends that: 'L'ensemble de la sphère sacrée se composait du pur et de l'impur. Le christianisme rejeta l'impureté. Il rejeta la culpabilité, sans laquelle le sacré n'est pas concevable, puisque seule la violation de l'interdit en ouvre l'accès' (ibid. 134).

Bataille's reference to the notion of violation is important here. For it indicates that sacred experience is not simply to do with holy or divine things; rather the sacred can be aroused by other less desirable aspects of existence such as violence, sexuality, sacrifice and death. This means that the sacred, as understood by Bataille, avoids the standard binary opposition Christian theology makes between good and evil. In Bataille's model, the sacred, as the word *sacer* intimates, is an amalgam of pure and impure; it is linked with sin and transgression: 'La transgression aurait révélé ce que le christianisme voila: que le sacré et l'interdit se confondent, que l'accès au sacré est donné dans la violence d'une infraction' (ibid. 140).

Bataille's insistence on divorcing the sacred from the '[L]e Dieu du Bien, dont la limite est celle de la lumière' changes the significance of transcendence (137). In this reading, transcendence can be brought about by any experience sufficiently powerful to transgress the boundaries of the subject's profane sense of self (that is, his rational and logocentric understanding of the world). In this indifferentiated oneness, Bataille's subject uncovers an alternative register of being based on silence and a mysterious and intimate kind of communication known as inner experience. Inner experience, in Bataille's opinion, endows the subject with:

> [La] communication, par la mort, avec un au-delà des êtres [...]: non avec le néant, encore moins avec une entité surnaturelle, mais avec une réalité indéfinie (je l'appelle, quelquefois, l'impossible, et c'est: ce qui ne peut être saisi d'aucune façon, que nous ne pouvons toucher sans nous dissoudre, qu'il est asservissant de nommer Dieu [...]. (388)

Bataille and (to a lesser extent) Eliade's a/theological version of the sacred combines what the secular and theological notions are concerned to separate: the totem and taboo. In keeping with sociological and psychoanalytical interpretations, Bataille and Eliade perceive the sacred as a territory of radical difference. In their view, the sacred has nothing to do with redemption and understanding; it is a space where the subject is altered and 'othered'. In the presence of the sacred, the subject leaves behind his profane, differentiated identity and uncovers a dynamic continuum. Unlike Freud and Durkheim, however, Bataille and Eliade – and here again they are indebted to Otto's work on the 'spectral' or 'uncanny' nature of the holy – do not believe that this continuum is devoid of meaning. Where Eliade contends that this experience of indifferentiation reveals the ahistorical movement of the cosmos (the continuous cycle of death and rebirth), Bataille maintains that it results in the intimate communication of 'inner experience'.

From what I have discussed, it is evident that the sacred is an elastic concept whose meaning is dependent on the discourse used to interpret it. Where Durkheimian sociology and Freudian psychoanalysis see the sacred as a secular construct aiming to safeguard communal and individual identity from anarchic dissolution, the rationalistic or logocentric viewpoint of monotheistic theology perceives the sacred in transcendental terms as the space where God reveals himself through language. According to the mystic a/theism of Taylor, Bataille and Eliade, sacred transcendence is an irrational cosmic truth that is prior to God. In their versions, the sacred has more in common with eastern mysticism and archaic religion than with any logocentric deity. For Bataille and Eliade then, sacred communion is radically heterogeneous. To experience it, we have to sacrifice our individuality and accept the dissolution into oneness and indifferentiation.

(ii) *Giorgio Agamben and the Politics of the Sacred*

Carl Lavery

Some of us talk in this book about a politics of the sacred, a politics of alterity, of engaging with and respecting the Other. We theorize this sacred politics in a way that will certainly be familiar to anyone interested in post-structuralist philosophy. We use, at times, Bataille, Derrida and Kristeva, and we discuss how the subject's reaction to unknowability, to the impossible, articulates his/her politics. We propose that allowing oneself to fall apart is a good thing. We discuss, in a positive light, a politics of letting things be. For us, this is where the liberation of the sacred resides, and, ultimately, where its moment of transcendence is found: that is to say, in the realization that ethics and politics are located in a value that transcends value. However, this value is not necessarily transcendental; it is not, for instance, traceable to a god or theology. Rather, it is immanent to our being in the world. We have the potential to experience it in moments of disjuncture or dislocation.

The transcendent and optimistic notion of sacred politics that we offer is at odds with the Italian philosopher Giorgio Agamben's view. In his influential text *Homo Sacer: Sovereign Power and Bare Life*, Agamben offers a depressing and sobering view of sacred politics based on what Michel Foucault in the final stages of his career tentatively called biopower, an intense form of disciplinarity in which all of life, and, in particular, the body, is enmeshed in circuits of power and discourse. In his reading of what he refers to as 'sovereign power' (various forms of social government: the king, *polis* or state), Agamben reconfigures Foucault's original notion of biopower in terms of 'the politicization of bare life' (1998, 4). According to Agamben, bare life or zoe is biological life – life that has no meaning other than its own brute materiality. Agamben starts *Homo Sacer* by showing how bare life (zoe) has been excluded from all conventional political definitions of the subject that have been in existence since Aristotle:

> The Greeks had no single terms to express what we mean by the word 'life'. They used two terms that, although traceable to a common etymological root, are semantically and morphologically distinct: zoe, which expressed the simple fact of living common to all living beings (animals, men, or gods) and bios, which indicated the form or way of living proper to an individual or group. When Plato mentions three kinds of life in the Philebus, and when Aristotle distinguishes the contemplative life of the philosopher (bios theoretikos) from the life of pleasure (bios apolaustikos) and the political life (bios politicos) in the Nichomachean

Ethics, neither philosopher would ever have used the term zoe (which in Greek...lacks a plural). This follows from the simple fact that what was at issue for both thinkers was not at all simple life natural life but rather a qualified life, a particular way of life. (Ibid. 1)

As Agamben has it, politics and culture (the stuff of the *polis*) are based on the transcendence of language (the *logos*), since the *logos* is what separates human life from bare life. For Agamben, this separation produces the binary oppositions so cherished by western metaphysical thinking:

> The living being has logos by taking away and conserving its own voice in it, even as it dwells in the polis by letting its own bare life be excluded, as an exception, within it. Politics therefore appears as the truly fundamental structure of Western metaphysics insofar as it occupies the threshold on which the relation between living being and the logos is realized. In the politicization of bare life – the metaphysical task par excellence – the humanity of living man is decided. (Ibid. 8)

In Agamben's view, the *polis* creates itself as *polis*, that is as *bios*, by differentiating itself from bare life (zoe), the life of animals and the body, the life of death (if you will indulge me the pun):

> The fundamental categorical pair of Western politics is not that of friend/enemy but that of bare life/political existence, zoe/bios, exclusion/inclusion. There is politics because man is the living being who, in language, separates and opposes himself to his own bare life and, at the same time, maintains himself in relation to that bare life in an inclusive/exclusion. (Ibid.)

Agamben's reference to the paradoxical notion of 'inclusive/exclusion' is crucial, for it explains the ambiguous role that bare life (zoe) plays in the constitution of any political community. In his lengthy and brilliant treatise on the juridico-institutional frameworks of western politics from the Greeks to the present day, Agamben is concerned to show how bare life, an apparently inferior and derogatory term, actually founds all supposedly superior forms of culture and politics:

> [T]he inclusion of bare life in the political realm constitutes the original – if concealed – nucleus of sovereign power. It can even be said that the production of a biopolitical body is the original activity of sovereign power. (Ibid. 7)

Agamben's thinking here is reminiscent of the post-structuralist notion of politics, which highlights the foundational role played by the supplement or parasite in the production of any type of proper identity. However, Agamben's aim in *Homo Sacer* is not so much to deconstruct binary oppositions (although that, of course, is part of it). Rather he wants to show how 'inclusive exclusion' discloses what western political theory is so concerned to repress: namely, that all politics, including contemporary politics, are based on irrationality and violence: the exclusion of bare life, or what he goes on to call the sacred. In order to advance his version of sacred politics, Agamben teases out the connection between the *arcana imperrii* or sovereign ban and power:

Placing biological life at the center of its calculations, the modern State therefore does nothing other than bring to light the secret tie uniting power and bare life, thereby reaffirming the bond (derived from a tenacious correspondence between the modern and the archaic which one encounters in the most diverse spheres) between modern power and the most immemorial of the arcana imperii. (6)

What is the *arcana imperii*? And how does it operate? As Agamben explains it, the *arcana imperrii* is essentially the right of sovereignty (political power) to exercise the right of exception, and thus suspend all taboos on the act of murder, which in Bataille's study of the sacred is the most powerful of all forbidden acts. By using the right of exception, the sovereign places himself above the law – as a matter of fact he negates it – and thus exonerates himself and his community from punishment for murdering a fellow human being. In the state of exception, the victim loses his *bios* and becomes pure *zoe*, an example of bare life. According to Agamben, when this dispossession occurs, the subject is transformed into *homo sacer*, that is to say, into someone who may be killed but whose life is not deemed worthy of sacrifice. In the context of *Homo Sacer*, Agamben notes:

> The protagonist of this book is bare life, that is, the life of homo sacer (sacred man), who may be killed and yet not sacrificed, and whose essential function in modern politics we intend to assert. An obscure figure of archaic Roman law; in which human life is included in the juridical order [ordinamento] solely in the form of its exclusion (that is, of its capacity to be killed), has thus offered the key by which not only the sacred texts of sovereignty but also the very codes of political power will unveil their mysteries. (8–9)

Agamben's study is important within the context of this book. Because he collapses conventional distinctions between the sacred and the political, Agamben not only legitimates the notion of sacred politics, more to the point, he shows that the two cannot be separated. That much cannot be denied. Nevertheless there are crucial differences between Agamben's theorization of sacred politics and the versions that some of us advance in *Sacred Theatre*. In general, Agamben sees the sacred as a juridico-political fiction, as something that it is imposed by whatever sovereign power happens to be in governance at the time. In his view, there is nothing transcendent about the sacred. Rather, in a tradition that goes back to Durkheim and Freud, he believes that the sacred fulfils a socio-political function by allowing the proper community (initially the city, and now the state) to establish itself contra the claims of others who are defined as *homo sacer* and, thus, not worthy of sacrifice: slaves, criminals, outsiders, foreigners, etc.

Agamben's disabused reading of the sacred is easy to understand in the light of recent and current history. Agamben completed his study during the Balkans War in the mid-1990s, and the death camps of the former Yugoslavia haunt his thinking (176). The tragic geo-political events that have followed the bombings of the Twin Towers on 11 September 2001 only serve to reinforce the correctness of his thesis. Indeed when forced to confront the reality of Abu Ghraib Prison or Guantanamo Bay, or in less dramatic terms, the experiences of countless Muslims as they go about their daily lives in the UK or US, it appears that history has endowed Agamben's book with the gift of prophecy. Agamben's notion of the sacred is apparent everywhere today. Throughout the world, supposedly civilized states are invoking the state of exception and stripping citizens of their basic human rights. Routinely, and much more than we think, the 'terrorist' is reduced to zoe, *homo sacer*, a subject who can be executed but not sacrificed.[12]

While we agree with some of Agamben's insights, and certainly endorse his version of contemporary history, we also think that it is possible to maintain a different, more optimistic sense of sacred politics. As we argue throughout this book, the dislocation brought about by the sacred allows another dimension of being to emerge, and a different kind of *polis* to exist. In our version of the sacred, the subject is not a victim, but rather an ethical and political agent, a being who opens himself/herself to the Other (see *particularly Lavery's section on Theatre and the Wound in Chapter 9*). For us, the state of exception or sovereign ban (which forms the basis of Agamben's theory) ceases to exist in the sacred, since sacred experience is what causes the subject to discover the Other in self – the sense that we are all *homo sacer*. This is not intended to correct or dissent from Agamben's functionalist reading of the sacred; rather, we simply want to offer an alternative notion of the sacred and, by extension, an alternative politics. Whether this is regarded, on account of the current state of the world, as hopelessly naïve or utopian is beside the point. It is crucial to bear in mind that different models of sacred experience exist. We are just as interested in tomorrow as today.

(iii) *Ritual*

Ralph Yarrow

Peter Malekin writes below about sacred drama and early Greek ritual forms, but makes it clear that the sacred does not 'exist...in subject matter...but in a mode of being'. We will examine the processes involved in accessing such a mode more fully in Part 3; here we attempt to outline some of the parameters and perspectives through which ritual has been approached, in order to see how it impacts on understandings of the sacred as and in performance. It is useful firstly to bear in mind the catagorizations of the sacred outlined above by Lavery; to an extent, the same parameters apply to ritual, which may operate as a conservative or potentially transgressive mode. From one point of view, ritual is a highly repetitive form of performative behaviour which leads to an 'accumulation' of identity, as noted by Paul Allain and Jen Harvie (Allain & Harvie 2006, 24). From another angle, or at another point on the spectrum, it may function as a *limen*, an opening into otherness, an opportunity for transcendence or transformation. We are more concerned with this latter capacity, although we need also to be aware that in practice, ritual is not always as liberal or liberatory as it seems.

In *Performance Studies*, Richard Schechner proposes that play in ritual 'gives people the chance to temporarily experience the taboo, the excessive, and the risky', and to 'become selves other than their daily selves' (Schechner 2002, 52). He indicates that ritual can be approached from four angles, in terms of structure, function, process and experience (ibid., 56). In this section we consider more the first two of these; the last two are dealt with in Part 3.

Schechner follows Victor Turner in pointing out that ritual can be social, religious or aesthetic in mode and context. Social(izing) ritual is common to animals and humans, and is largely regulatory or boundary-drawing in function, operating to bond groups within a social or spatial nexus; religion and aesthetics involve reflexive consciousness and are exclusively human; in terms of functional operations such as transcendence, transportation and transformation, both may claim to afford access to these processes, but both may also in fact either operate a politics of exclusion – in which they are reserved for a select (powerful) group – or frame them within a restrictive discourse so as to recuperate them to reinforce the status quo.

Some key characteristics of ritual process include a 'heightened sense of drama' (Gould on Aboriginal ritual), a (symbolic) patterning of movement (Lorenz on ritualization), a location in which '"otherness" [is] explored, explained and contained' (Montelle on 'Paleoperformance'), and a condition in which 'imagination is at ease' (Durkheim) so that it 'integrates thought and action' (Bell). d'Aquili, Laughlin and McManus elaborate this in biological and cybernetic terms as the ability to 'facilate both intraorganismic and interorganismic communication' – similar perhaps to the 'flow' condition highlighted by Czikzentimihalyi (all quoted in Schechner 2002, 56–60).

From both an anthropological and a psychosocial perspective, performance can function in ritual as the confrontation of temporal, spatial and ontological limits in, for example:

- attempts at 'cosmocisation', including trance and shamanic practice
- engagement with or initiation of 'transformation'
- negotiation of participant/witness and of individual/community thresholds

The term 'cosmocisation' is used by Kapila Vatsyayan as a descriptor for the aim of much traditional Indian performance which seeks to negotiate or extend the limits of the individual and/or the community across and against elemental or transindividual forces perceived as existing 'beyond' or 'outside' those frameworks whilst impacting decisively on human affairs. In some Indian forms, and in others in, e.g., Bali, Mexico and West Africa, performers and participant-spectators may apparently enter degrees of trance in which they release kinds of behaviour outside their everyday spectrum and may believe themselves to have become other entities; or, like shamans, acted as a conduit for the transmission of particular kinds of knowledge. Luiz Fithur Nunes presents a clear introduction to two forms which offer a process of initiation for someone who wants to be initiated into a modality where the initiate recognizes the forces at his/her core and where 'liturgy, ritual practices and ceremonies converge on a fundamental purpose: to attain that state of trance or possession in which the deities manifest themselves through the body of the believers' (Nunes 1989, 18).

Ritual events of this kind often mark temporal junctions in the life of individuals or groups – harvest, rites of passage; they are, in Schechner's terms, efficacious rather than merely entertaining, in that they are intended to produce certain outcomes, and central to their process is a degree of transformation of role, status, capacity or mode of operation for some or all of the participants. Their structure frequently moves from a recognition of 'crisis', or junction-event in which the status quo is temporarily suspended, to a situation of 'reincorporation' in which the new order is accommodated to the old.

In all these uses, there is a move 'outside' the borders of the current state of things, although not necessarily – indeed necessarily not in some instances – outside the borders of the social world as currently constructed (e.g. rites of passage shift the hierarchical position of the individual but confirm the hierarchical structuring within the social group); hence, although ritual appears to embody an attempt at transcendence (Artaud certainly thought of its functional capacity as that), it may in fact effect no such thing; it may confirm the sealed nature of the social envelope. In practice, what may appear as radically destabilizing acts (manifestation of spirits, demons, embodiments of death or plague, unsettling 'attacks' on the spectator-participants) may be ways of safely containing any psychosomatic or political attempts at evasion within the theocratic framework which polices the taboo; rather like carnival, are these sorties authorized by the ruling powers? What is 'ritual' anyway? Its very name suggests an adherence, not an escape; a repetition, not a reconfiguration, a particularly conspicuous example of 'restored behaviour' (Schechner). (Yet, of course, in juxtaposition with this, every performance is also a unique and instantaneous event.)

In interrogating other forms of 'ritual' which claim to engage with something 'beyond' – which, however, are often used to legitimate the 'within' of social or cultural convention – we need to ask to what extent such a mode of being does in fact offer a way out of any or all cultural preconditioning or rather only a cunning duplicity which reestabishes its dominion.
In many cases it is clear that participants do experience marked alterations of perception, behaviour and status. To what extent, however, is this brought about by inculturated expectation, by hallucinogens, by rhythmic or other physical stimuli? How do the following impact?

■ cultural determinants (moral and social codes, sanctified images of good and evil, iconic representations)
■ psychophysiological operators (fatigue, stimulants, peer-pressure, collective hysteria)
■ temporal and spatial dynamics (architectural and environmental influences, event-structure and place in time-frame)

It is likely that in most cases, some or all of these exert very powerful influences, particularly in 'hot' situations like voodoo ceremonies, the Balinese kechak (monkey-chant) and so on. Any experiential shift is thus open to extreme manipulation by entrenched religious, social and economic hierarchies.

However, despite all this, we need to ask what, if any, moments of époché may occur. It does appear that ritual performance quite consciously seeks and claims access to perceptual and entity-changing modes, even if the force of social conditioning may reclaim any aberrant experience within its totemic protective fence or excommunicate it as taboo. Turner's 'liminality' is like death, being in the womb or darkness; it is a state of being 'not-this-not-that', 'open to change' (Schechner 2002, 66). Such a suspension of role and identity seems often to involve a reduction or cessation of the egoic, a kind of egalitarianism which may characterize the experience of 'communitas'.

If this phase really does engage a mode of being distinct from the acculturated social model, this must be, even if only briefly, inaccessible to language, thought and learnt bodily habit: in other words, it must be literally and phenomenologically inconceivable. It has to start 'before' thought. As noted above, there is (impossibly and inappropriately, of course) an Indian term for this locus: para – and its emergence as/into pashyanti – discussed by Peter Malekin and myself in Consciousness, Literature and Theatre (Malekin and Yarrow 1997, 45–48).

Schechner, too, suggests that it is at least worth thinking about whether in more conventional theatrical practice, being between the everyday 'I', a 'not I' (= ideal version of the 'character' one is playing) and a 'not-not-I' (detached awareness that there is some modality of self or consciousness which is neither of the two preceding situations) might be on the track of this momentary but crucial condition. Can it or does it occur in 'ritual' performance? In other words, does the structure allow for or indeed encourage this kind of 'suspension' – it is tempting perhaps to say 'suspension of belief' – in the contours of the known world and self? Does it include built-in 'gaps' or exit strategies? (Turner thinks of communitas as 'anti-structure', which would imply that it has this quality.)

Perhaps yes and no, in that although ritual events do possess a 'safety-valve' quality, but they are also forms of dialogue: even in apparently confirming the limits, the very fact that they posit them offers the imaginative possibility that they could be surpassed. K. Ayyappa Paniker's comments about the function of 'death' in Patayani (a south Indian *Theyyam* ritual form) suggest this kind of interpretation. In the performance, Paniker notes, death is pluralized in the body of a single performer as the death-god, who seeks to take away the boy Markandeya, but is himself destroyed by Shiva (force of destruction and change).The performer/incarnator must enact Death as icon and Death-as-force (the Death-God), potential and real death as event (the story of Markandeya and the death-god), a 'higher' form of Death as part of life (Shiva), and the narrative sequence of killings and dyings (Paniker 1986, 3–4). Death is here multiplied, deconstructed, reformed and reconfigured in and through the body of a performer who must 'become' boy, god, state beyond life and cosmic force. You don't, says Paniker, go to the theatre to 'see' things you could see elsewhere or elsewise: such performance at the very least posits the possibility of working across and 'outside' a whole range of boundaries. In one sense the performer can't 'be' all of these; in another, of course (assuming here a male performer), he does in fact hold within himself all of these positions or potentialities; what performance does is to put them all in play, to realize or activate them all 'simultaneously', i.e. within an identical imaginative space/time frame.

Shifts across the border between life and death, past and present, presence and absence are found not only in exoteric forms like Theyyam or Balinese Calonarang, but also in 'cooler' more esoteric forms like Noh, as I discuss in Part 3. 'Cosmocization', shamanic or paratheatrical practice does quite deliberately seek to extend the experience of individual and collective being beyond the limits of conventional social discourse and, frequently, language. It uses drumming, chanting, dancing, cyclical or repetitive action, tactile sensation, sensory stimulation and/or deprivation in order to 'transport' participants (and sometimes – e.g. in promenade performances or Schechner's 'environmental' theatre – this may include those who would otherwise be more normally categorized as mere spectators) into 'other' mental and/or physical conditions. If these practices frequently at least bracket out the 'everyday' use of language, they do so in order to explore sensations or forms of awareness which may in some way 'prefigure' language. Language may tend to over-define, limit or even rule out these experiences, or that at least is the claim. It is, of course, also the case that many writers have seen this extension of 'being' as a major function of poetry (not least Shelley and Wordsworth); it has also been claimed for music of many kinds. For our purposes here it's relevant that any kind of change operates as physiological modifications in the rhythmic and/or perceptual functioning of the body. Vatsyayan claims that Indian theatre has long been preoccupied, both in theory and as practice, with the use of the body to transcend the body (Vatsyayan 1980, 8); it is worth noting though that many kinds of performance training target a similar process. The structure of ritual often contains escalation and leads to heightened physical behaviour, sometimes to a different kind of operation in which 'something' seems to have 'taken over' the body. It moves and sometimes speaks differently. Different traditions interpret this in different ways, but most if not all acknowledge the co-existence of some form of largely uninvolved conscious awareness or control and some degree of physiological and emotional de-inhibition, fluidity and power. It looks as though in this kind of event, self is both lost and not lost, transformed and reformed, absent and present. This kind of duality or in-between-ness may signal the sacred mode. If such a situation does occur, it necessarily has an impact on and is affected by the parameters of space and time. In what follows, Peter Malekin opens up further angles of investigation along these vectors, starting with a different approach to ritual.

(iv) *The Sacred, Drama, Ritual and the Ancient Mystery Religions*

Peter Malekin

The sacred in theatre exists not in ideas, or subject matter, or form, but in mode of being. Form, subject matter, may lend themselves to this mode of being, or they may not, but the mode of being comes first and they are dependent on it, not the other way round. In principle the sacred does not exclude any subject matter, even though certain types of subject matter would be difficult to accommodate. The sacred lies not in the what, but the how of drama. It does not hive off an area of experience as separate from ordinary life and devote a play to that. Such a procedure can produce religious drama, but religious drama is not necessarily sacred, and the sacred is not necessarily religious. Indeed supposedly sacred subjects may hinder the sacred, presenting conventional ideas in a conventional manner rather than shifting perception, or more fundamentally being itself, the ground consciousness itself of the perceiver. In the sense used here sacred drama gives life to participants by disclosing the transcendent reach of human consciousness and integrating with it the everyday active thinking and feeling surface of the mind. If this integration were complete, everything would be sacred.

As often noted theatre and ritual overlap in that much ritual has an element of theatrical display and participants (including the audience or public) can be moved by ritual at least beyond their everyday frame of reference, in intellect, emotion and feeling-attitude. Like theatre, much, though not all, ritual is a social activity. In non-sacred theatre the social can be almost the totality of the dramatic experience and can, of course, be very good theatre nonetheless. Similarly religious ritual can be predominantly or exclusively social and may remain humanly valuable. But the fullness of human potential will not be evoked by such ritual, any more than it is by the rituals of the state. The rituals of the state at large, of politics, parliament, the judiciary, the military establishment, schools and universities are for the most part intended to assert authority, including authority that is unworthy or illegitimate. They can become a means of enforcing or internalizing conformity. They can also foster group belongingness, which is valuable if the group itself is valuable and if membership of it does not conflict with respect for the free will of all those who respect the free will of others.

The potential for disclosure of the sacred in drama plus its power to realize myth and project dogmas palatably have meant that it has tended to go hand in hand with religion, for in the very long run it is such sacred disclosure that also lends status to religion, even though most religion seeks to maintain itself by asserting dogma, employing social and psychological persuasion or intimidation, invoking distinctness of cultural and group identity, and, at the all too common worst, instigating or practising persecution, torture, war and murder. Drama on the other hand also has a tendency to undercut falseness in convention, religious or political. There is, thus, a fraught tension between drama and religion, drama often undermining political and religious establishments, religion tempted to censor and control drama on dogmatic grounds, the more puritanical forms of religion trying to suppress it utterly.

In western traditions the link between drama, religion and ritual goes back at least to the Egyptian drama of Seth or Typhon, though the primary source of early western theatrical traditions is Greek, and more especially Athenian. The Athenian festival of Dionysus was at once political, civic, dramatic and religious, linking foundation myths with the practical functioning of society. It was also both celebratory and mocking. Conversely, the ritual enactment and ceremony of religion have also remained close to drama, from the ritual dismemberment of an animal and the chewing of raw meat in Dionysian worship, a participatory remembrance of the dismemberment and resurrection of the god, to the similar ritual symbolically present in the mass and eucharist services of Christianity. The Eleusinian mysteries reputedly contained a more overtly dramatic element, the history of Demeter and Cora being performed for the initiates (according to Still this is partially re-enacted within *The Tempest* when Ceres blesses and grants fertility to the marriage of Ferdinand and Miranda (*The Tempest*, act 4, scene 1). Ritual, drama and religion all have elements of spectating, participation, enactment and direction (even if only through an inherited procedural script, set of oral instructions, or learnt praxis), the balance varying from instance to instance. Religion, with its extended regulation of the conduct of life by taboo and moral code, is both an enslavement and a liberation, creating space to live in, and also pointing beyond the immediate space-time world and sometimes beyond space and time altogether. Through ritual its participants may at times pass into that beyondness.

The most startling effects of ritual usually arise in initiatory traditions, and the initiates have often undertaken prior disciplinary praxis. Such rituals can cause profound spiritual experience and a complete change of consciousness. At least the psychic or psycho-spiritual levels of effect can also be produced by art – drama, statuary, sculpture and painting – and by chanting. This is an assertion, but one can speak in these matters only from experience, often experience confirmed by the accounts of others. I have known the heart chakra to be activated by Noh drama, and by ancient Egyptian and Indian statues, and all the chakras to be fired by the chanting of the *Rig Veda*. How widespread this effect is, and widespread among what groups, I have no means of knowing, though I have had the effect of Egyptian statuary confirmed by members of my own family. There are now many groups that have concerned themselves, successfully or unsuccessfully, with these matters and some among them have the benefit of belonging to well-established traditions with ancient and tried knowledge – such groups are, however, seldom concerned in the first instance with the chakras or with art. Nonetheless, the triggering of such experience by the arts should not be entirely uncommon. Even its possibility implies a need to rethink aesthetics, and much else, from the ground up. Since such experience lies beyond the dominant paradigm of science and modern society, little official attention is paid to it and it is not allowed to lead to questioning of the foundation of the modern western world-view. The most important potential of ritual and the arts is for us shrouded in darkness.

The potential of art, like ritual, to develop consciousness has, however, been central to the major aesthetic traditions of the East (Taoist and Buddhist in China and Japan, Vedic in India). Something of the kind may also have been known to the West. D'Alviella, writing of Eleusis, notes that:

> Philosophers of the Graeco-Roman period were overwhelming in their praise of the extent and influence of the Mysteries. 'It is said', relates Diodorus of Sicily, 'that those who have participated in the Mysteries are more devout, more honest and better in all respects. Isocrates, Cicero, Plutarch and Porphyrus did not differ. (D'Alviella 1981, 34)

This certainly suggests that the mysteries were much more than religious 'cults' or a kind of ancient Masonic society, the view that D'Alviella himself and many other moderns take ('cult', of course, is a loaded word used exclusively of other people's religions – all religions were once cults). The few statements that have come down from Eleusinian initiates themselves, rather than Church enemies, mention or intimate a number of intriguing factors, the descent to the underworld, the emergence into the bright light of 'the splendour' (D'Alviella, 21) and the sacred drama. Michael Srigley cites one of Plutarch's general descriptions:

First labyrinthine turnings and arduous gropings, various unsuccessful and perilous passages in the darkness. Then, before the rite itself, all manner of terrors, shuddering and trembling, silence and terrified amazement. After this a wonderful light bursts forth, friendly meadows and landscapes receive us, voices and dances and the splendour of sacred songs are disclosed to us. (Quoted in Srigley 1985, 75.)

It is not clear from this whether 'the rite' is to be equated with the encounter with the light, meadows, dance and song, or whether these completed the preparation and the rite proper then followed. D'Alviella alludes to Plutarch's claim that the experience of the initiatory process was similar to the experience of the soul at death (20). He also summarizes Plutarch's account of the impact of the final stage: 'It is there, writes Plutarch, that a man, whose initiation has made him perfect, liberated and truly master of himself, speaks with righteous and pure spirits' (22). D'Alviella adds:

> It is certain that there were apparitions and stage effects which suggest a rather complex mechanism. Does not Plato compare the beholding of the Ideas by the disembodied spirits with the shades which are revealed in the Mysteries? [referring to the Phaedrus] (22)

This presumably equates the final stage of initiation with the visual and auditory experiences. Except for the 'wonderful light' the first passage from Plutarch could suggest stage performances, though the meadows and landscapes would have strained contemporary technology; however, a stage performance is, alas, unlikely to make a man 'liberated and truly master of himself', nor does it enable him to speak 'with righteous and pure spirits'. Moreover it is common for souls immediately after death to experience the inner light, the light of what Plotinus knew as the noetic cosmos (in 6.9. he describes the difference between the transcendent One and nous, as a light shining within itself compared to a light shining outwards); they can in fact be accompanied through death by the living, if the latter are given the appropriate training, and various records of the process are now published in the *Tibetan Book of the Dead* and in other works, and are known in some oral traditions. Something more than theatrical performance is at stake and something more seems to be happening, though what is not clear – unsurprisingly, since all reconstruction of a secret initiation is undertaken by surmise based upon the inevitably limited world-view and experience of the surmiser.

According to D'Alviella, the final 'degree' of perfection, that of an epopt or seer, also involved 'the communication of symbols and formulas, if not dogma' (26). These communications are also usually taken to be the equivalent of modern Masonic passwords and the display of 'cult' objects. However, both visual symbols and verbal formulae can function very differently, as is now well known in the modern West from, for instance, Vajrayana Buddhist initiations and meditative practice, and also from the practices of the meditative tradition in Advaita Vedanta, though the element of empowerment in these traditions is not separately itemized in the Eleusinian references. Such practice can certainly shift consciousness itself, not merely give an emotional high or supply information, occult or otherwise. Such practices were known to Plato at least as a devotional discipline and possibly as a meditative or contemplative method, for in the Phaedrus 252E–253C he mentions the lover perceiving his own particular god in the person of the beloved (again the image of a deity specific to the worshipper is used for meditative practice in Vajrayana Buddhism). In *Enneads* 6.9.11, 548, Plotinus describes the 'ascent' of the mind of the philosopher 'beyond knowing', i.e. to pure consciousness, consciousness devoid of egoic subject and devoid of object, devoid of empirical content. It is, Plotinus says, like the progress of a worshipper entering a temple; the last thing perceived before entering the sanctuary is the image of the god, which is left behind as the worshipper enters the emptiness of the sanctuary itself. On returning from the sanctuary the first thing encountered is again the image of the god. At their fullest these techniques do produce a 'seer' in the precise sense of someone whose awareness spans the range from infinitude to surface subject-object relations and can therefore directly witness the arising of the subject/object worlds out of ultimate reality, which being totally unbounded is not an object of knowledge/perception, as Plotinus pointed out, but rather 'the first self, transcendently The Self' (6.9.4, 539–40, together with 6.8.14, 527). In another passage, speaking of Beauty, associated with manifest nous rather than the unmanifest One, he describes the vision of such beauty as identification with it in its radiance and adds that 'this identification amounts to a self-knowing' (5.8.11, 422).

Unitive mind, passing 'beyond knowing' (6.9.4, 540), i.e. into the 'empty' no-thing-ness of the sanctuary, is associated by Plotinus with the mysteries (6.9.11, 547). So also is the 'vision' of the Good, though this vision is still on the verge of the final stage (1.6.7, 52). This 'vision' is the vision described at length in 5.8.11, 422. Since neither the vision nor the unknowing would be at all likely to be produced by drama, the Eleusinian mysteries would appear to have involved much more than dramatic performance or stage trickery.

The passage in 6.9.11, 547–8 seems to indicate that Plotinus himself was an initiate of the mysteries. If so, then his remarks about unitive noetic consciousness and ultimate unknowing, both associated with the mysteries, would at least reflect back on the long accounts of the universe as itself a cosmic drama in 3.2.15–8, 150–6 and 4.4.33, 320. Since the point of acting in the cosmic drama is to use role to transcend role and arrive at identity beyond the subject-object divide in our time and space, then what Plotinus is saying could have a bearing on twentieth-century and contemporary practices in actor training. For instance, Lecoq and Copeau used neutral mask exercises in actor training in twentieth-century France, in order to free the performer from attachment to everyday habit and to begin to locate a starting point prior to 'knowing what you want to do'. These masks are, of course, different in context and purpose from anything envisaged by Plotinus, for they do not use the image of a god, nor move to pure consciousness, nor do they have any initiatory empowerment. However, in other mask traditions (Balinese, Tibetan, etc.) the actor identifies with the mask before putting it on, using a technique that Brook learnt from an eastern actor. Other experimental work using masks with resonating chambers has become quite common (recalling the functioning of masks in Greek theatre) and in some cases has involved the projection of pure vowel sounds whose meaning is their impact. These developments could represent the coming together once more of religious impulse, ritualized practice and initiatory potential. Perhaps the achievements of the Greeks have not been entirely lost, or are being recreated through the mutual influencing of western and eastern theatre, of the modern and the ancient-rooted traditions. Some western theatre was once, after all, a theatre of epopts.

[RY: Neutral mask work may enable the performer to 'fade out' everyday personality and behavioural modes. It can thus (dis)place her in a condition of alert but unengaged awareness of what is about to be perceived. The preparation for other kinds of masked or transformed embodiment – as in Noh or Kathakali – may pass through a similar stage. This condition of readiness is usually not precisely identical with the turiya or époché described by Haney and George, but it may momentarily touch it and will certainly approach it relatively closely.

Malekin now moves on to suggest some implications of this for the fundamental parameters of performance.]

'The sacred is either present at all times, or it doesn't exist.' (Brook 1993, 59)

In a kind of dialogue with one of Peter Brook's works, this section moves through a consideration of space, time, consciousness and mind, following on from the above discussion of the relatedness of the sacred to drama, ritual and the ancient mystery religions. Only after this is it possible to speak clearly about specific dramas, and in a later chapter move on to Ionesco and the instance of The Chairs, and Pinter's play Ashes to Ashes.

(v) Space

Peter Malekin

Brook has written eloquently about the acting space as empty space, a void that the actor has to fill by his imagination, craft and, perhaps, craftiness. The emptiness is void, devoid of boundaries, an abnegation, therefore, of our 'identity'. It thus poses for the actor a threat, a potential of dissolution or failure. The practical answer is, according to Brook, to rest in and then work from inner emptiness. 'In the theatre one can taste the absolute reality of the extraordinary presence of emptiness, as compared with the poverty-stricken jumble in a head crammed with thinking.' (1993, 22)

Both acting space and actor are here being spoken of in terms of consciousness, and emptiness is not altogether empty. Space, empty space, does not in itself pose any threat. It becomes a threat because of our limitations, physical and mental, and in the case of an acting space because of the demands it makes on us, or we make on it – it is there for us to act in. For some, or for some of the time, it requires us to 'fill' it, to 'expand ourselves' to more than we ordinarily are, to begin to 'signify something'. It makes demands on our consciousness. It can, however, be experienced as an objective embodiment of the absolute silence at the base of our own individualized consciousness, a silence which needs no filling because it is already full. Empty of particulars it is free of boundaries. Empty of action it is a source of inexhaustible energy. It is 'dynamic silence', a phrase used in the West by Plotinus and in the East by the Vedic tradition of India. It is, in Jacob Böhme's phrase, 'freedom'. If the acting space triggers a recoil of the mind into that freedom, then the space itself becomes an objective embodiment of such freedom, as it were a field of possibilities from which all things may emerge given an appropriate stimulus that we are free to choose, a field of play. If this happens then the actor rises above himself, his mere ego is an irrelevance, or rather a means, a tool. On stage new egos arise, the actor is more and other than himself. In ordinary life the nearest equivalent is the forgetfulness of our limitations, our idea of ourselves, in some greater action, and we are in truth never an idea, but holders of the idea.

Space, useful and defined, as in a building, exists on the basis of space extended, undivided, undefined. The same is true of consciousness, as Brook suggests by his parallel between an outer empty space and an inner emptiness. Space as physical extension can only be grasped or imagined by being made a mental object that becomes manifest through other objects located in it. It must extend outwards from the point of 'us', our locus, or it must have a boundary, or it must have objects as points of reference within it. To participate in extension as it is in itself is to move out of ourselves, our space-time consciousness, and become a field stretching to infinity devoid of point of reference, devoid of our point of view. Take this one stage further and extension is no longer extension, there is nothing to extend. Space is no longer a union of subject and object. The field is no longer a manifest field. Space has merged back into undifferentiated consciousness, and consciousness is no longer what we normally call consciousness, con-scious-ness, with-knower-ness (con-scientia, 'Be-wusst-sein', 'med-vetande', 'con-science', all our western languages seem to limit consciousness only to the surface level of the mind). Awareness without any subject-object changes its nature, re-becomes what it always was. In this process our ego too and personality are in abeyance, have disappeared.

To lose the threat of space is to lose the threat of our own ego. It is this loss that enables us to achieve the impossible, 'to taste the absolute reality of the extraordinary presence of emptiness'. But here yet another situation has arisen. Here awareness retains its unconstrained nature yet objects are present and so are we. Yet objects and ego are transformed. They have begun to take on the unconstrained nature of undifferentiated awareness, they are becoming an interplay of subject and object united by a common field awareness that is liberated from the constraints of the ego. The ego too becomes a kind of object. Thus, it is that we, as subjects, 'taste', through our physical senses, the 'reality', absolute and unqualified, of an emptiness that was only empty from our previous point of view – for emptiness can only be emptiness of something, exists only in a world of limitations and expectations. When this phenomenon occurs, then the sacred is in a world and minds in flux, in our world of forever becoming.

(vi) *Time*

Peter Malekin

The present moment is astonishing. Like the fragment broken off a hologram, its transparency is deceptive. When this atom of time is split open, the whole of the universe is contained in its infinite smallness. (Brook 1993, 81)

Certainly if we could penetrate to the very core of a moment, we would find that there is no motion, each moment is the whole of all possible moments, and what we call time will have disappeared. (83)

'Whenever, being in motion, it comes to a rest, and whenever, being at rest, it changes to moving, it must itself, presumably, be in no time at all.' – 'How is that?' – 'It won't be able to undergo being previously at rest and later in motion or being previously in motion and later at rest without changing.' – 'Obviously not.' – 'Yet there is no time in which something can, simultaneously, be neither in motion nor at rest....So when does it change? For it does not change while it is at rest or in motion, or while it is in time.' – 'Yes, you're quite right.' [–] 'Is there, then, this queer thing in which it might be, just when it changes?' – 'What queer thing?' – 'The instant.' (Plato 1996, 156c-d, 163)

Ordinarily in our culture time is perceived as a sequence, often thought of as a series of 'moments'. But within time there is no moment, just what is happening, to all appearances seamlessly linked to time before and time after. Even intervals of quietness, waiting and adjustment link in this way. Something seems somehow wrong, missing, from such a sense of time, and the nature of time puzzles. Eliot pondered it in *Burnt Norton*. A. J. Ayer analysed the problems of past, future, memory and causality in *Problems of Knowledge* and came to startling conclusions:

The reason...why we do not allow ourselves to conceive of our actions as affecting past events is, I suggest, not merely that the earlier events already exist but that they are, for the most part, already known to exist. Since the same does not apply to the future, we come to think of human actions as essentially forward-moving: and this rule is then extended to all other cases of causality. Thus our reliance on memory is an important factor in the forming of our idea of the causal direction of events. (Ayer 1956, 175)

He also notes that if we did know the future outcome to which our actions stood as necessary causes,

We should not credit [those actions] with the same dynamic quality; we should regard them rather as elements in a pattern. Our attitude, even towards our own behaviour, would tend to be that of a spectator. (Ibid.)

The discussion of time here is inevitably also a discussion of consciousness, for time registers only in consciousness and in my view exists only in consciousness. Past, present and future are not what they seem in our culture.

In some ways Ayer, in the passages cited, goes beyond Brook and Plato and begins to approach various eastern perceptions, for instance, the role of memory, the cosmic *smriti*, in the Vedic account of creation, or, via his insistence on the impossibility of proving through logic that the past ever happened or exists except in our minds, the idea of the universe as a kind of misconception, which is an aspect of the notion of *maya*. He also impinges on Plato's famous definition of time as a moving image of eternity, explained further by Plotinus as the subsuming of time space and movement as aspects of being within the eternal noetic intelligences. Plotinus's position is potentially open to partial or total verification; while in ordinary life we are within a space-time framework, as the mind moves to subtler levels of consciousness time and space change, becoming subsumed within consciousness and ultimately disappearing beyond the noetic level in undifferentiated consciousness. In Plotinus indeed the noetic intelligences are one intelligence: 'Each of them contains all within itself, and at the same time sees all in every other, so that everywhere there is all, and all is all and each all....Each there walks upon no alien soil; its place is its essential self...there is no distinguishing between the Being and the Place; all is Intellect.' (5.8.4, 414)

In discursive cause and effect and in our fleeting sense of time, it is the patterning that is a memory of eternity: if the effect, as A. J. Ayer argues, is the cause of the cause then the future creates the past. Even in everday life the past is created by memory, imagination and interpretation. Memory is creative; you can remember things that 'never happened'. Some new 'fact' can instantly change all that has happened, so that the past you thought you had becomes a lie. What you understood to be 'the case' was an understanding. The actors also move on (or move out, according to your understanding of life). The father that is no longer there is no longer the 'person' (itself a dubious concept) who was your father. What you call your father is a memory – or in some cases an absence of memory. If you look at a photograph of the world you knew in childhood it seems unreal. It has a quality of goneness which is very close to never-been-ness. It is less real than a dream. Experience in time is elusive and the experiencer in time itself changes as it fleets. The certainties arrived at by naturalist drama or the law courts are elusive and slippery.

There remains the question of other modes of time, often acceptable to contemporaries only in the contexts of quantum physics and relativity theory and abandoned everywhere else. In the *Tractatus* Wittgenstein remarks that

> If we take eternity to mean not infinite temporal duration but timelessness, then eternal life belongs to those who live in the present. (Wittgenstein 1961, 72)

This also seems to imply that the present is not what it appears and perhaps also that human consciousness has a capacity to be both inside and outside time, for timelessness is not 'an eternal present', since the present is defined by past and future. Without past and future time ceases to be time and there is no present nor absence of presentness: such categories no longer apply in a different reality. To be in and outside time would also change the perception of time and perhaps the way of functioning of time itself on our 'level' of existence. In one of the passages cited above Ayer comments that a knowledge of future outcomes would produce in us the attitude of a spectator. Gaudapada in his commentary on the *Mandukya Upanishad* posits a kind of spectating, a witnessing devoid of identification, caused by the transmutation of time and consciousness through direct being in timelessness. Plotinus, of course, like Plato, ascribes three levels to time, ordinary time, noetic eternity and timelessness. Böhme uses a similar threefold categorization of time. The analytical aspect of the Vedic tradition speaks of a great range of time perceptions from the timelessness of *Brahman nirguna*, or without attributes, through to the 'now' of our lives. The most extraordinary thing about the modern philosophers cited is the way in which, through sheer logical power, they leave the limitations of Logical Positivism behind and approach the perceptions of thinkers from radically different backgrounds and traditions.

Even in ordinary life changed experiences of time can and do occur. I can give an instance from my own experience. Flying with Ralph Yarrow round the stacks of rock that tower up from the floor of the Grand Canyon, I noticed gigantic niches eroded along a level stratum round the side of one of the massive columns. The thought flitted through my mind, 'Thrones for the gods', for many of these columns had been named after Indian deities. Perception of the Grand Canyon disappeared and I found myself suddenly in what I can only describe as geological time. It moved with unbelievable slowness, stretched back and back, and forward and forward. In retrospect I was puzzled by two things. First how did I know that time had changed, since there seemed to be no point of reference by which to gauge it. Secondly I felt that geological time had a direction, and it seemed parallel to the direction of ordinary time. I could not understand why time or times should have this sort of flow. Long afterwards it dawned on me that I knew time had changed because time exists in consciousness. As for the direction, I concluded tentatively that it derived from a pull in all things back towards their ontological origin in spaceless and timeless reality (reality since it is potentially accessible from any point in space or time, whereas all things within space and time pass away). The universe is a weird place and time or times are one of the weirdest things about it. So far as I can see, the universe is a process of occlusion and disclosure that we are part of, whether we like it or not.

I mention this experience and cite various thinkers from different cultures not to foist my ideas or experience on others, but to make it clear that the states of consciousness mentioned are not culture-bound and that we do not all live in the same world. Our awareness of it indeed differs even in the course of our own experiencing and awareness can reach beyond it. The nature of limited consciousnesses, even in the case of one individual life let alone the consciousness of the human race, also changes the world that is perceived. The idea that we have only one shared experience of the universe, from which we can ratiocinatively derive a single total objective truth explaining all things, is untenable, whether the derived intellectual framework is that of science, or political philosophies like Marxism, or the various religions. Such truths are always limited by the experience behind them and by the metaphysic and values of its processing ('metaphysic' in the sense of an a priori and ultimately unprovable theory of the relationship of mind to matter). Therefore intellectual censorship, whether in the name of science, or religion, or political conviction, or the peer group pressure of a not-to-be-questioned consensus, is to be resisted.

Brook, working from experience as an actor, and Plato, writing a treatise on dialectic as transcendent of logic, both conclude that time and its 'moments' are not the mere sequence they seem. The instant for Plato lies outside time, but the direction of the apparent flow of time emerges out of it. For Brook each moment contains all time and there is at its heart a stillness beyond all times. Instead of time as a simple forward movement it thus becomes a kind of pulsation out of timelessness into all times as a whole and then into the 'this time' from which it is being considered. In the Parmenides as I read it Plato was pushing philosophy towards a realization beyond propositions and logic. From a very different philosophical basis A. J. Ayer was moving in a somewhat similar direction. Brook is pointing to such a realization as direct experience, the great experience of the sacred in theatre. 'Sacredness' thus becomes not a matter of surface awe or intellectual convictions, but the experience of what Böhme called 'an eternal beginning', the arising of now out of timelessness. The experience is a transformation. If time is not what it seemed, then neither is the world.

Like space, time is here being discussed in terms of consciousness. Space without consciousness is unimaginable. Time without consciousness is unimaginable. Time and space are held in consciousness, not the individualized consciouness with its before and after, but consciousness in itself, innocent, unbounded, as it were 'transparent' so that it evades objective search. This too is barely imaginable, its emergence in surface consciousness dependent on the individual mind becoming free from space-time entanglement. Such an experience is one of liberation. Liberation in this sense is some or total freedom from the constraints of time and space that characterize ordinary everyday human consciousness, a liberation that affects potentially the whole of human experience and the whole of theatre experience and dramatic performance, including language, timing and relationship to role.

(vii) *Performance Factors*

Peter Malekin

Language, timing and relationship to role are all vital factors in performance, but their use, understanding and impact depend on the condition of consciousness of both performers and audience. They are also related, especially in the case of language, to the author and the author's text, and in the modern western theatre to the director's treatment of the text, and to the actors' range of interpretations of the text. In addition there are performance constraints and opportunities from current fashion and sometimes manias, inherited cultural ways of moving and using the body, current references and preoccupations, performance norms prescribed by tradition and varying ideologies, audience expectations, audience language use and theatre technologies. These factors therefore make sense as part of a whole in performance rather than as isolated and abstracted factors. The comments immediately below are, therefore, cursory and general.

Language can, of course, convey and organize information, but that is not usually its main use in drama. Its affective use on the emotions tends to be more important. At its crudest, as in demagogic speech, it evokes the emotional response of our pack animality, primarily our oneness with the pack and our hatred or suspicion of the outsider or anomaly. It can also evoke subtler and delicately nuanced feeling. Beyond the emotional it can do at least four other things. It can evoke an intuitive sense of something which may not yet be within intellectual reach. It can move cast and audience alike towards an experience of the holistic level of thought preceding discursive verbalization, a level that Ralph Yarrow and I have discussed in connection with the Vedic linguistic category of *pashyanti*. (This level has organizational advantages as sequential parts change their nature in a whole.) It can activate the subtler levels of the human physiology associated with the kundalini system. It may even on rare occasions move the perceiver's mind into spaceless, timeless, undifferentiated consciousness, perhaps while awareness of the performance continues. This last phenomenon must be extremely rare, but its potential effects are far-reaching. Returning to the everyday we would carry as it were the memory of light in the darkness, for the everyday is a condition of constraint, as the Daughter points out in Strindberg's *A Dream Play*:

Poet. What did you suffer most from down here?

Daughter. From – existing: from feeling my sight made weak by an eye, my hearing dulled by an ear, and my thought, my bright aerial thought bound in the labyrinthine fatty convolutions of the brain. Of course you've seen a brain...what crooked paths...what secret ways...

Poet. Yes, and that's why all straight-thinking responsible citizens think crookedly!
(trans. Malekin 1986)

If that constraint is broken and the mind moves into freedom, then anamnesis begins to overthrow memory even while memory is being used and some degree of liberation has been attained.

Relationship to role is primarily but not solely the concern of the actor, but that relationship will be sensed by an audience. Many have commented on the dual awareness open to an actor, both identified with and unconstrained by role, within it and outside it. The role can be articulated as part of a greater whole and the actor's awareness of this whole transmutes the quality of the played role, deepening and enriching it. It is thus distinguished from hypocritical pretense in everyday life, where role and situation are narrowed down to specific purpose only. Similarly timing articulates meaning and plays on suspense in obvious ways, heightening emotions of dread, fear and anticipation or providing a source of humour, but it too can participate in giving a significance beyond the overt meaning of text and performance. An experienced troupe can time performance with total cohesion, so that an effect occurs somewhat akin to the patterning discussed above. Pattern can either bind, as in repetitive behaviour, or if it arises together with non-attachment it can be a freeing from the bondage of time. Silence and stillness are either vague and empty, or are charged with emotion, or resonate with life's fullness. In the latter case they become a kind of alert rest in which a regrouping, a redisposition of intellectual and emotional forces, again arises together with a degree of non-attachment. If this occurs they become part of the performance rhythm of the whole play, action and participatory audience moving towards rest, and towards Plato's instant, and re-emerging from it with new force and direction. The performance breathes with its own life. Silence and stillness joined with movement, language and patterned role evoke the drama in a coherence, not usually sensed in the bittiness of everyday living, that transforms the quality and feel of each component factor. There is an expansion of vision and an intuitive resonance of feeling.

To provide even a glimpse of life's deeper levels through theatrical performance is a great achievement. To evoke anything like a full sense of life as potential in freedom is an even greater one. Such achievement is not the only thing that theatre provides, but it is the most important thing that it can provide and it is what spiritual theatre must provide. The spiritual, as Brook said, is either present at all times or it does not exist. It is not a category of living, but the innermost nature of life itself.

> [RY: Malekin is here drawing on the definition of spirit given in Consciousness, Literature and Theatre: 'spirit is not mind and it is not matter...it is a potentiality out of which intelligent activity arises' (Malekin and Yarrow 1997, 8–9). If the sacred is the moment of suspense (voiding of thought, which implies all kinds of perceptual and conceptual frameworks), then spirit is what allows the possibility of sacred experience.]

(viii) *Aesthetics*

Ralph Yarrow

If the aesthetic means (for producers and receivers) grasping some distinguishing criterion of art, it is as experience, as process, as transaction, that it must occur. Grecian urns and recollection in tranquillity have perhaps suggested the opposite, but there are many approaches which engage with its phenomenological and performative nature. They permit a dynamic grasp of the aesthetic phenomenon/moment rather than static 'contemplation'; mimesis and repetition need to be understood as performative processes in time, but which also have the capacity to reshape time.

Perception in phenomenology is conceived as a grasping towards which engenders relationship, an 'X-ray'level of volition which senses the possibility of shape, as Heidegger writes about the intuitive drive of the potter's hand in shaping the hollowness of the pot. A holding moment in which Langer's proposition of the 'feeling of form' becomes available: the sense that there is something on the verge of emerging; that fractional suspension or hiatus in which I know I am about to 'see'. Clov, typically, 'nails' it ironically with 'we're not beginning to...to...mean something...?' (Beckett 1964, 27). 'Not beginning to' is, as usual with Beckett, both a throw-away formula and an absolutely precise pinpointing of a moment or state just prior to expression. It's all in the not of being about to: once you do mean something, you're back in the old story, the old bag of tricks, the old routines. Throwing away formulae is the only technique that will serve, just as Krapp goes on rejecting past versions of his own big moments and Mouth insists that the subject of recall is 'she', not 'I'.

This excavation charts further the topography of the crevasse we have been peering into for some time now. Like the 'quantum state' I identify in Beckett (Yarrow 2001a, 82), which maps out the contours of identity and world in the moment before they are crystallized, and like the extraordinarily acute tracings of Vedic linguistics, which identifies distinct modalities of pre-verbal language, what is here revealed and required is the recognition that the 'void' conceals at least three phases. At its centre there is only absence; no parameters, no co-ordinates, only the in-between: but, crucially, the awareness of that in-between-ness. The moment when sense is on the verge of being made is crucial in Japanese Noh: listening to the pauses in between the notes, seeing the not-quite-moving, intuiting (stretching the awareness towards) the sources or antecedents – ghosts, ancestors, dreams, desires –, that which is not-quite-formed. On either side is the going in and the coming out; the losing and the gaining, the de- and the re-. If the experience of Existentialism marks most often the falling into or away (see below), aesthetic agency signals the climb out.

George wants 'performance to claim its place not only as a legitimate field of inquiry in its own right but as a primary phenomenon' (George 1999, 11). What he means here is that the well-known ephemerality of performance, for him better characterized as 'work-as-process' (Connor) or 'event' (Crohn Schmidt), is closer to the (quantum) nature of reality than the apparently coherent constructs of the scripted dramatic text, the theatrical representation, or – to an even greater degree – the 'objective' reality we think we live. He uses a line from *The Tempest* as one of the epigrams for his first chapter: 'We are such stuff as dreams are made on': a Shakespearean version of the Indian concept of *maya*. The apparently solid is transitory; the self-evidently and self-consciously transitory (Shiva, destroyer-creator) puts into play (*lila*) the only permanence, which is the energy of the generative (Brahman). As George later says: 'theatre-people...always knew that their worlds were "unreal", the product of their wills, consciousness, perceptions, sensations, desires, that they had no substance, had no "self"' (George 1999, 35). Re-production is all; and performance (we would rather say the sacredness of theatre) allows us to act from that before-moment and, like a Beckettian character, to keep returning to it (they are always seeking to retreat, if possible to before they were born: their syntax and their behaviour directly inscribes and enacts their 'intention', precisely the reverse of a Stanislavskian 'through-line'). (See, in particular, Chapter 7 on Genet and Beckett for further elaboration of how this works in practice and how the theatricality of theatre is used to explode rather than confirm any 'objective reality' of social or ideological 'character' or life.)

So here we are targeting the aesthetic as the process of production, the being-about-to-produce. Iser, in *The Act of Reading*, identifies 'gaps' as the junctions and sutures in a text which offer the reader the chance to enter: in so doing s/he discards the position as consumer/lecteur and takes up the role of producer/scripteur (Barthes). The gaps are not infrequently places where reading (or listening, seeing) is *détraqué*, where you jump the points: an exclamation, a caesura, an enjambement, a non sequitur; hiatus, suspension, holding the breath are the physiological markers. They trip you up, trick you and realign you so that you are present in and to the process of living the emergence of form. Then, according to Zen, 'perception is...related to a certain unique-particular which is devoid of all the qualifications...which the intellect foists on it after it has been apprehended by the sense' (Vyas 1991, 93). If there is fullness or 'beauty', it emerges from here, not from or as confirmation of accepted models.

So it is not surprising that analysis of E. M. W. Jephcott's categorization of 'privileged moments'(Jephcott 1972) – moments of heightened awareness for writers and protagonists in the symbolist/modernist tradition, of an intuition of extension of being, consonance with the rhythms of nature, increased sensitivity, sense of ease, change in the relationship between 'self' and 'world', etc. – suggests that crucial to the acts of cognition, formulation and decoding is a passage through a kind of 'neutrality', a wiping clean of consciousness so that impression and expression arise on a new basis as fundamentally generative processes (in line with George's suggestion about époché mentioned earlier). This passage (which operates via 'defamiliarization and hesitation') moves through 'suspension or extreme refinement of physical activity, suspension of judgment...and consciousness of being conscious (meta-awareness)' towards a 'sense of unity or wholeness..., modification of evaluation of self..., awareness of multiple possibilities' (Yarrow 1986, 3).

The latter situation is also implied in the concept of *rasa*, posited in the fundamental Indian performance manual *Natyasastra* and subsequently repeatedly discussed as the fulcrum of all acts of aesthetic reception in literature and the arts, as what performance is understood as intending to produce: it is, thus, both a process and 'a psychophysiological condition in performers and receivers which marks a transformation of behavioural state' (Yarrow 2001b, 115; see Haney on this in Chapters 3 and 5 below). This condition of full 'tasting' of all the levels and possibilities of significance mediated by interaction in and as performance is seen as the result of a process of cultivation of sensibility functioning at increasing degrees of subtlety and precise focus. According to Bharucha, South Indian dancer Chandralekha sees it as having the capacity to '"recharge" human beings' (Bharucha 1995, 129). *Rasa* is, however, in some sense an esoteric experience for adepts, and the performance forms it is normally associated with (highly compacted poetry and highly crafted theatre and dance) operate in a temporal and spatial zone suspended in-between the business of everyday life (for dance-drama, traditionally during the hours of darkness). The shift from daylight to another kind of illumination is marked by the presence of a burning lamp at the front of the performance area, in part an index for Agni, the 'god' or energy of fire and transformation, the phoenix-sign of transition and transformation. Situating the action in this liminal space-time is a way of indicating the need for 'extra-daily' functioning and emphasizing the charged or concentrated quality of focus required: the performative mode is a transference and transposition of modes of knowing. As in Japanese Noh, disruption is deliberately employed to '[upset] the normal dimensions of natural perception' (George 1999, 193) and generate, through *hana* – the 'moment when the flower blooms', 'pure Feeling that transcends Cognition', the possibility of a 'small satori' (George, 200). It is worth noting too that the 'instantaneous and immediate nature of satori requires that any experience contain implicitly all experiences' (George, 149).

(ix) *The Absurd*

Ralph Yarrow
Existentialism can be seen as a sensual metaphysics based in 'shocking', self-voiding-and-vindicating experiences, and also as an attempt to explore the physical nature of thinking the void – as absence of given meaning; this attempt becomes an ethical obligation in order to accept the responsibility of each act and each new configuration. The 'Absurd' enacts, refocuses and sharpens such points of censure, seizure and scattering. We shall look in more detail at the kinds of theatre practice and process which operate here, and can be seen as part of the set of moves and production of experiences we are calling 'sacred', in the following chapters. It is important here to ask in what senses the terminology of the 'absurd' initially suggests that this exploration is justified and to place it in some contexts.

The occurrence of both Existentialism and the Absurd mainly – though not exclusively – in the Europe of the 1940s and1950s can be situated historically as a political and existential crisis, which emerges as forms of deconstruction (one of its major impetuses is Nietzsche's 'God is dead'), frequently involving a passage through motifs of death or unknowing against the background of war; it refocuses the perennial problem of meaning, epistemological and ontological doubt; the 'fall' (a term variously used by Kafka, Rilke and Beckett) from certainties and systems. From our point of view here, it is tempting to view these phenomena as a kind of 'fisssure', a tearing apart of language, culture, identity and a confidence in history or grand narrative, a fall into an economy of uncertainty which matches the claims we have made for sacred moments in these opening chapters. However, if it is such a 'moment', it is either a recurrent or a prolonged one, and not very precisely locatable in chronological terms: not necessarily an embargo, given other aspects of our argument, but at least a motive for caution.

Nonetheless, Existentialism particularly illuminates the crisis of recognition that 'I' am not what I might have thought I signified: a moment at which, therefore, 'I' step outside the systems of signification which purport to define who/what I am and what I 'ought' to do. It is in one sense a quest for experience prior to language, even though its delivery is for the most part unable to escape it, as in Sartre's ironic attempt in La Nausée. Philosophy attempts to grapple with non-being via a series of extended koans (Sartre's L'Etre et le Néant is one example, but much of Heidegger would qualify too); Beckett, particularly in Murphy and Watt, takes up the game and adds a condensed hilarity which acts physically like the mechanics of farce to push the reader beyond what s/he can rationally comprehend. Where much existentialist drama remains stuck in the toils of exposition, the absurd takes the hint and aims to subvert, invert, obvert and derange: it operates a de-and re-construction of form, which radicalizes Existentialism's more rationally mediated grappling with the sense of coming apart. In so doing it frames the following kinds of question:

■ Theological: what is my origin?
■ Psychological: what is my identity, consistency?
■ Linguistic: what is my discourse, how can I say?
■ Epistemological: what do I mean?
■ Ontological: what is my being, who or what am I?
■ Ethico-political: what is my value?

A significant feature of much theory which accompanied or succeeded the high points of absurd practice (Heidegger, some writing about the Nouveau Roman, Derrida, Cixous) is its attempt to transmit some of the koan-like or playful 'strangeness' of the works in its own use of 'difficult' or neologistic forms of writing, as though seeking to engage more directly than its own articulation of the inevitable representative status of language would allow. The absurd – where corpses grow and proliferate (Ionesco, Kantor) or fall out of cupboards (Orton) is a zone where entropy undoes orders of all kinds and all pretensions to sense are, as Gombrowicz puts it, 'honeycombed'.

The 'absurd' is a declaration of crisis, an articulation of the ungraspable, an incitement to enter the unknown. It highlights the moment of/as experience of 'crisis' or loss, but also as the necessity to 'void' the overdeterminism of tyrannical systems and imposed meanings (Ionesco, Gombrowicz, Rozewicz, Simpson, Orton); it works frequently as a sudden (and essentially ludic) recognition of the ludicrous, an unravelling of the 'tissue of overlapping fictions' (Sukernick) which compose our 'realities'. In all these contexts it operates as a defecation, a disorientation, a losing (or loosing) of the solid and the structured, a falling apart. The absurd in theatre is a machine to produce the explosion of all known categories, systems, limits, modes, forms and frames, and leave you in the resultant void/vortex/vacuum.

So the absurd is also a kind of sacred wound, a tearing apart or splitting open, in and from which the freedom to make anew is engendered. Characteristics also include explosion, implosion, epiphany, ecstacy. It operates:

- as playful explosion of the pomp of image and role
- as scathing denunciation of mindsets (fascistic, narcissistic, aspic)
- as doleful exposure of the banality and deadliness of the quotidian
- as revelation of *maya* and consequent encounter with the void
- as formal deconstruction and meta-tactic.

If its content bewilders, its treatment of its audience frequently seeks to deconstruct the matrix of expected theatrical form. The absurd in and as performance adopts scurrilous, shocking, surprising, shifty and silly tactics to drop us in the real, the moment in time, history and cognition when the shell of habit splits open ('Fear! The crack that might flood your brain with light', as Bill Haney reminds us below, from *Rosencrantz and Guildenstern are Dead*).

This in part is why Part 2 draws mainly on examples from the theatre of the absurd (Stoppard, Pinter, Beckett) and theatre closely affiliated to it (Genet) – other examples from Beckett and Polish twentieth-century drama are discussed in Part 3. It is a form which not only signals what Thomas Mann ambiguously terms 'Durchbruch' (breakthrough) as thematic focus, but also attempts to produce it as its principal outcome.

The next part will look at how sacred experience is generated in and by texts in performance, largely through consideration of European and American modernist and postmodernist work; it also aims to relocate that work in critical reception, and to open up questions which will be returned to later in the book. Haney writes about Stoppard, Churchill and Hwang, with shorter pieces on Ionesco and Pinter, who are considered further by Malekin; Lavery and Yarrow explore the politics and practice of Genet's theatre.

Haney elaborates how the texts he examines produce the sacred as a void in thought, especially in terms of 'gaps' which deconstructive practice opens up between real and imaginary, self and other, and between self as the potential for experience and self as concept ('consciousness' and 'mind' in the terminology of Consciousness Studies). These gaps operate not merely by deconstructing fictional narratives of self and world, but by making available – through shifts of perspective, comprehension, sensation and ontology – that which occurs *between*: a moment and mode of awareness which recognizes that 'I' am not 'this' or 'that', yet there is still something which is 'I'. This is not so far away from the operation of kinds of holes, gaps and liminalities which have been described above by Lavery, George, Malekin and others. They effect a kind of *époché* in and as performance, and locate not simply a Möbius strip of equally inauthentic identities, but the key moment and status as awareness aware of its own being as not any of these but yet as a performative potential for physical action and ethical choice. Through the plays he discusses, Haney identifies a whole range of precise practices whereby the moment of *époché*, the voiding of thought, self, reality and constructed world, is rendered available *as* theatre. He shows how the oscillatory mechanics engendered by verbal play, gender and role juxtaposition and alternation, ethical dialectics on the border of the human and the non-human, patriarchy and subaltern orders and so on, produce again and again the experience of falling into or being abandoned in liminality. This situation is further exemplified and interrogated by material from the other contributors in later chapters.

Notes to Part 1

1. I'm assuming here that Franc is interested in the etymological sense of autobiography, which, as is well known, is often read today as a kind of bodily writing.
2. This reminds me of the term 'everyday life', which in order to be understood is transformed into an abstract category.
3. I'm aware that this writing is remarkably similar to Julia Kristeva's opening account of abjection in *The Powers of Horror: An Essay on Abjection* (1980).
4. Bates makes explicit links between the role of the shaman and that of the actor, as many others have before and since, see, *inter alia* Schechner, 1985, 1988, 1994, 1995; Dodds 1951; Kirby 1975; Frost and Yarrow 1990. Another way of describing what occurred was that an imaginary body had been spontaneously created.
5. 'This awkward hiatus, this standing stock still and not being able to move, locates a moment – awkward but essential, often sought by actor-trainers like Jacques Copeau or Grotowski through improvisation – when the actor does not know what to do next, where s/he cannot fall back on tricks, familiar resources, or even a learned "text" of words or actions. If actors don't get to and through this state, they will not discover how to extend their resources.' (1994, 223)
6. See Malekin and Yarrow (1997, 84–5).
7. Bateson (1980, 129) mentions that he took the term 'metacommunication' from B. L. Whorf's *Language Thought and Reality* (1956). My use of the idea has been informed by the work of Arnold Mindell, see, for example, Mindell (2000, 286).
8. Eliade writes that the 'mastery of fire...renders its practitioners insensible to the heat of live embers' (1968, 92). Clearly something he hadn't experienced by doing.
9. The problem is that literally anything could be the trigger for such an experiencing, which is one reason why I have come to have less interest in the texts of dramatic literature as providing gateways to the sacred dimension, because literally any text can be such a gateway. This is connected to my emphasis on personal experience rather than literary analysis here.
10. According to Otto, the rational element inherent in Christian theology fails to 'do justice to the non-rational aspect of its subject'.
11. According to Otto, the *mysterium tremendum* is the defining feature of sacred experience. Otto defines this incomprehensible experience as a 'peculiar moment of consciousness [...], the stupor before something "wholly other", whether such an other be named 'spirit' or 'daemon' or 'deva', or be left without any name.'
12. As I write this in early September 2006, *The Guardian* newspaper has revealed the existence of CIA-run 'interrogation camps', where those suspected of terrorist activities can be questioned and held for an indefinite period of time. These camps contravene all forms of national and international law, and, in them, fundamental human rights have been suspended. Given the religious backgrounds of those held in the camps, it is ironic that Agamben should have termed the epitome of *homo sacer, der Muselmann*:

   Now imagine the most extreme figure of the camp inhabitant. Primo Levi has described the person who in camp jargon was called 'the Muslim', der Muselmann – a being from whom humiliation, horror, and fear had so taken away all consciousness and all personality as to make him absolutely apathetic (hence the ironical name given to him). He was not only like his companions, excluded from the political and social contexts to which he once belonged; he was not only, as Jewish life that does not deserve to live, destined to a future more or less close to death...Mute and absolutely alone, he has passed into another world, a world without memory and without grief. (1998, 184–5)

PART 2: TEXT AND PERFORMANCE

Chapter 3

THE PHENOMENOLOGY OF NONIDENTITY: STOPPARD'S ROSENCRANTZ AND GUILDENSTERN ARE DEAD

William S. Haney II

(i) *Introduction*

In the aftermath of the post-structuralist deconstruction of the metaphysics of presence, how do we account for the fact that contemporary theatre often seems to manifest and evoke the basic attributes of sacred experience? If a modern play can be considered sacred, one may assume this is because it evokes a subjective experience described as sacred and not because it conforms to a culturally specific, third-person, objective theory of sacredness. Nevertheless, a theoretical framework may be useful to explain what it is like to have a sacred experience in theatre, after the fact. Antonin Artaud, in *The Theatre and Its Double*, famously attempts such an explanation by comparing the avant-garde with 'Oriental theatre,' specifically Balinese dance. In the deconstruction of logocentrism, however, critics have noted the necessary contradictions and paradoxes of trying to explain subjective, first-person experience through objective, third-person analysis. Jacques Derrida, for example, deconstructs Artaud's efforts to create a theatre beyond representation with signs fully present to themselves (Derrida 1978). Nonetheless, Artaud's definition of the sacred, which integrates western and non-western views, still holds currency and may help to elucidate sacred experience.

While the work discussed here bears little physical resemblance to Balinese theatre – with its sacred rites, lofty myths and dance – it does evince what Artaud considers its most significant effects. Artaud claims that in Occidental theatre 'the Word is everything, and there is no possibility of expression without it' (Artaud 1958, 68). 'Oriental' (or, if you prefer, Asian) theatre, on the other hand, has 'its own language' identified with the *mise-en-scène*, one constituted by 'the visual and plastic materialization of speech' and by everything 'signified on stage independently of speech' (68–69). The purpose of this materialization of speech is to restore and reinstate the metaphysical aspect of theatre, 'to reconcile it with the universe' (70) and 'to rediscover the idea of the sacred' (Artaud 1988, 276). Artaud's aim, however, is not a theatre that regresses to a *pre*-rational, *pre*-verbal state in the Freudian sense, but rather one that includes and then transcends language and reason to evolve to higher, *trans*-verbal, *trans*-rational states (see endnote 2). He describes this as 'communication with life,' or 'the creation of a reality' (Artaud 1988, 157, 155). Arguably, the sacred elements found in Asian theatre can also be found in Occidental theatre. Sacred theatre as discussed here relies on ordinary language and the Word, but also produces one of the salient effects of Asian theatre: taking the spectator (and performer) toward a trans-verbal, transpersonal experience. The way Asian theatre does this, as Artaud says, is by

> creat[ing] *a void in thought*. All powerful feeling produces in us the idea of the void. And the lucid language which obstructs the appearance of this void also obstructs the appearance of poetry in thought. That is why an image, an allegory, a figure that masks what it would reveal have more significance for the spirit than the lucidities of speech and its analytics. (1958, 71, italics added)

A void in thought is a state of mind that begins with language and meaning and then goes beyond them through a shift in consciousness. As an unidentifiable emptiness, this void is knowable not through ideas indirectly, but rather through the immediacy of transcognitive, non-contingent Being after ideas have run their course. To experience a void in thought means to experience transcendental pure consciousness. Whatever third-person, objective theory we use to describe it, the subjective 'experience' of the void is trans-cultural, transpersonal and, thus, largely the same in any theatre, whether Asian or Occidental. Theatre induces this experience, which transcends the concept of the sacred, through the unsayable dimension of the text, that is, through the suggestive aspect of language and performance that points beyond language and thought altogether toward pure consciousness – without which the sacred would be nothing more than an intellectual construct.

Sacred theatre, then, may be defined as theatre that entails a voiding of thought, and by implication a shift in consciousness that effects a blurring of boundaries between subject and object, self and other. This theatre is particularly significant in contemporary culture where stage drama and social drama meet in life lived as performance – as Victor Turner, Umberto Eco and others have shown. Stage drama and social drama, theatricality and history, the sacred and the profane converge in a liminal zone of sacred experience, the in-between-ness we transit whenever we encounter and then go beyond pairs of opposites. As neither this pole nor that, the sacred is a void that cannot be defined except in negative terms. As this and the following chapter will demonstrate, in the theatre of Tom Stoppard, Caryl Churchill and David Henry Hwang, the spectator oscillates between opposites toward a sacred wholeness that is not a fixed point of reference, but a spiralling pattern that encompasses the sacred and the profane, ordinary mind (thought) and 'pure' consciousness (a void in thought).

(ii) *Liminality and Subjectivity in Theatrical Space*
As suggested earlier, the shift in consciousness experienced by performers and spectators in sacred theatre is described differently by different symbolic traditions. In the Vedic tradition of India (which recent evidence suggests could be 10,000 years old), this shift is the special focus of the classical treatise on dramaturgy, the *Natyasastra*. This treatise and Indian thought in general have profoundly influenced western theories of drama. Notable examples of this

influence are Jerzy Grotowski's 'poor theatre,' which creates a 'translumination' in performer and spectator (1969), Eugenio Barba's 'transcendent' in theatre (1985), Peter Brook's 'total theatre' (1987), and Victor Turner's redressive phase of social drama responsible for transformations (1998). In a series that includes breach, crisis, redress and reintegration or schism, Turner's redressive phase constitutes a threshold or liminal phase, 'a no-man's-land betwixt-and-between the structural past and the structural future as anticipated by the society's normative control of biological development' (Turner 1998, 65). In contrast to the indicative mood of ordinary life, the liminal constitutes the 'subjunctive mood' of maybe, which includes 'fantasy, conjecture, desire', and can 'be described as a fructile chaos, a fertile nothingness, a storehouse of possibilities' (65). This fertile nothingness is the 'ground' of in-between-ness against which binaries can be distinguished.

Liminality or the experience of in-between-ness has clear affinities with the absolute one of Plotinus, the nondual consciousness as suchness of Buddhist Vijnanas and the Brahman-Atman of Shankara's Advaita (nondual) Vedanta. In Advaita Vedanta, for example, the aim is to establish the oneness of reality and to lead us to a realization of it (Deutsch 1973, 47).[1] This realization comes through the 'experience' of consciousness in its unified level as non-contingent Being. Vedanta explains this 'experience' with reference to the four quarters of mind: the three ordinary states of consciousness – waking, sleeping, dreaming – and a fourth state (turiya) of Atman or pure consciousness.[2] This fourth state, which underlies the mental phenomena of the three ordinary states, corresponds to Artaud's description of a void in thought. As a witnessing awareness immanent within the other states, it constitutes an 'experience' based on identity, unlike the ordinary sense of experience as a division between subject and object.

Liminal interiority in sacred theatre, then, is a void in thought shared by performer and spectator. Not reducible to the mundane, this void lies in the gaps between words and thoughts, in the background of all language and ideas as a silent beyond-ness, and immanently within knowledge as its generative condition of unknowingness. Liminal experience occurs in varying degrees, however, depending on whether the operative medium is the text of the drama, the non-verbal signs of the theatre, or the interaction between actors and audience in the actual performance. As Richard Schechner says, 'the drama is what the writer writes...the theatre is the specific set of gestures performed by the performers...[and] the performance is the whole event' (Schechner 1988, 85). In terms of sacred experience, while reading the script can no doubt evoke the liminal, the optimal intersubjective experience of liminality, one that interfuses the verbal and the transcendental, the sacred and the profane is certainly that of the performance itself.

(iii) Intersubjectivity in Stoppard's Theatre

Stoppard is famous for undercutting preconceptions, treating philosophical and moral issues with a lightness of non-attachment, and innovating a new relation between ideas and farce, all for the sake of entertainment and enjoyment. Against a background of inquiry into basic reality, Stoppard examines how people conduct themselves with one eye engaged in their activities and the other eye observing or witnessing that activity. The gap between engagement and witness enlivens his plays with a unique quality of entertainment and relieves the audience from the pressures of mental agitation. Rather than attempting to solve the problems of goodness and the human condition, his plays invite us to stand back and observe the world from a non-attached, pre-interpretive vantage point – which includes yet surpasses Brecht's 'alienation effect' (Brecht 1964). From this perspective, the vagaries of human existence are seen not as tragic, but as farcical and humorous.

The elements of Stoppard's theatre from the 1960s most relevant to the sacred include brilliant language, absurd yet inspired theatrical ideas, and a frame of reference that escapes the tone of general mockery. These can also be found in his recent plays such as *Arcadia* (1993) and *Indian Ink* (1995). In addition to Shakespeare, the influences on Stoppard's work include Oscar Wilde, James Joyce, quantum physics, Chaos theory and Wittgenstein's *Philosophical Investigations* (Levenson 2001, 160). His most famous theatrical idea was to set a play, *Rosencrantz and Guildenstern are Dead* (1967), within and around the action of *Hamlet*, with the two attendant lords who are marginal in *Hamlet* holding centre stage. Similarly, in a style reminiscent of Joyce's *Ulysses*, Stoppard models his play *Travesties* (1974) on Wilde's play *The Importance of Being Earnest*. The intellectual frame of reference of many of his plays is also striking for his style of rendering translucent the content by revealing the silence or void behind it. However profane the content, it can still evoke a sacred experience.

In *Rosencrantz and Guildenstern are Dead*, characters and audience co-create a sacred space of intersubjectivity. As mentioned in Chapter 1, this space deconstructs the ordinary places and spaces in which our everyday thinking and being occurs. The participants begin with language and interpretation within a specific cultural context, and then cross into a space or 'presence' characterized by the 'absence' of exterior boundaries. As a liminal domain, this presence involves a dis-identification with the profane exterior, including the verbal and conceptual tokens of our interpretive frameworks. Thus the experience of sacred space, which transcends the boundaries of conceptuality, offers other ways to look at space and time. Unlike film and television, which on the whole present more accurate detail with faster cutting than stage realism, theatre has broken free of realism and gathers a live audience to witness a representation not dependent on a full simulation. Theatre spectators, although immersed in the material context of the hall and stage, experience the attenuation of exterior domains in a move toward an intersubjective, non-physical presence constituted by the performance as a whole. This attenuation or fading out of the external, which induces a decontingencing of the historical self, resembles that in meditative quiescence, as described by B. Alan Wallace:

> As long as one is actively engaged in society, one's very sense of personal identity is strongly reinforced by one's intersubjective relations with others. But now, as one withdraws into outer and inner solitude, one's identity is significantly decontextualized. Externally, by disengaging from social interactions, one's sense of self as holding a position in society is eroded. Internally, by disengaging from ideation – such as conceptually dwelling on events from one's personal history, thinking about oneself in the present, and anticipating what one will do in the future – one's sense of self as occupying a real place in nature is eroded. To be decontextualized is to be deconstructed. (Wallace 2001, 211)

This decontextualizing process abounds in Stoppard, most notably in his plays within plays, such as *Hamlet* in *Rosencrantz* and *The Importance of Being Earnest* in *Travesties*.

According to a statement for BBC Television entitled 'Tom Stoppard Doesn't Know', since 1972 Stoppard has suspended the choice between binary opposites that contextualize the world. Stoppard describes a common pattern in himself with the phrase, 'firstly, A; secondly minus A': 'that particular cube which on one side says for example: "All Italians are voluble" and on the other side says, "That is a naive generalization"; then, "No, it's not. Behind generalizations must be some sort of basis"' (quoted in Hunter 2000, 17). Stoppard repeatedly traces such binaries in his writing. Influenced by Wittgenstein's reflections on language, his plays question the functioning of reason and the reliability of philosophical tools like syllogism (Levenson 160–61). 'There is very often no single, clear statement in my plays. What there is, is a series of conflicting statements made by conflicting characters, and they tend to play out a sort of infinite leapfrog' (*Theatre Quarterly*; quoted in Sales 14–15). Rather than pretend to certainties, Stoppard shows how the mind's stream of binary opposites doesn't yield the truth, and that to cling to any one conceptual point or context is to invite falsehood. As a dialectical movement, his 'A, minus A' opposition is not an exclusive either/or system but a both/and system. This style, as illustrated below, has the effect of attenuating social or objective boundaries, decontingencing the historical subject, dissolving the boundary between self and other and creating an intersubjective space – even without sacred rites, lofty myths and dance.

(iv) *Rosencrantz: A Void in Thought*

Stoppard's *Rosencrantz and Guildenstern are Dead* takes two minor characters in Shakespeare's *Hamlet*, which becomes a play-within-a-play here, and makes them central characters constantly on stage. One morning before the play begins Rosencrantz and Guildenstern are called to court by a messenger and given the mission to discover what troubles Hamlet. They have no memory of anything previous to this or any knowledge of how to fulfil their mission, and they mistrust all perceptions and ideas, being certain only of the fact that they were called by a messenger. Another play underlying the decontingencing of the historical subject in *Rosencrantz* is Beckett's *Waiting for Godot*. Both *Godot* and *Hamlet* provide an anti-intellectual framework for Stoppard's work, neither offering a conceptual solution to the problems they pose. Stoppard's Ros and Guil are barely more coherent than Beckett's characters, anti-hero's like Hamlet who in their confused identities question everything, including themselves.

From the opening scenes of *Rosencrantz*, Stoppard undermines the intellect through a series of frog-leaps or ambushes. 'I tend to write through a series of small, large and microscopic ambushes – which might consist of a body falling out of a cupboard, or simply an unexpected word in a sentence' (*Theatre Quarterly* 1974; quoted in Sales 14). These repeated ambushes undermine our naturalistic expectations. The first ambush centres on Guil and Ros' game of heads and tails, with heads coming up over 85 times. The pun on head counting results in the actors metaphorically counting the spectators in a reversal of their traditional roles, with the spectators becoming the spectacle. As Ros says, the repetitiveness of heads threatens to become 'a bit of a bore' (3), a sure sign that the intellect is being diminished in a decontingencing move beyond language and interpretation.

These ambushes combine with Stoppard's 'A, minus A' technique, or 'infinite leap-frog', the arguments, refutations and counter-arguments that never lead to the last word. The audience is teased out of its culturally conditioned habits of discursive thought and into the relative openness of a new intersubjective space. While Ros spins the coins unconcerned, Guil tries desperately to rationalize the spinning after 85 head counts, wondering why Ros has no 'fear' of this uncanny outcome. 'Ros: "Fear?" Guil: (*in fury—flings a coin on the ground*) "Fear! The crack that might flood your brain with light"' (5). His outburst suggests the possibility of a break in conceptual boundaries, a frog-leap beyond the field of 'A, minus A' toward a void in thought. Once performers and spectators approach this void within themselves, they can share it on stage as an intersubjective realm. The power of this experience, which is generated through the 'visual and plastic materialization of speech', serves 'not to define thoughts but *to cause thinking*' (Artaud 1958, 69, original emphasis) – in the sense of taking us to the 'fertile nothingness' (Turner 65) at the source of thought, the void or *turiya* from which thoughts arise.

Each of the four explanations for the succession of heads proposed by Guil in the opening scene, though doubtful, have metaphysical undertones.

One. I'm willing it. Inside where nothing shows, I am the essence of man spinning double-headed coins, and betting against himself in private atonement for an unremembered past. [...] Two. Time has stopped dead, and the single experience of one coin being spun once has been repeated ninety times . [...] Three. Divine intervention.... (6)

Ros, who is Guil's audience on stage, fails to understand as Guil continues to explain with two syllogisms. Gradually Ros and Guil enter a space beyond meaning. When Ros can't answer the question, 'What is the first thing you remember?', Guil says, 'You don't get my meaning. What is the first thing after all the things you've forgotten?' (6–7). But Ros has forgotten everything, every interpretation, even the question. He seems to be content here to drift on the fringes of a conceptual void. When Guil then asks if he's happy, Ros says, 'I suppose so.' And Guil says, 'I have no desires' (7). This condition evokes in performers and audience a freedom from contingency and suggests a taste (*rasa*)[3] of pure consciousness (*turiya*) – a liminal space of a sacred experience.

Stoppard avoids or parodies intellectual investigations because he intuits that the intellect does not hold the solution to human suffering. Comedy, on the other hand, offers greater promise. Humour, which Stoppard exploits, can be said to arise from a distinction between emotion and intellect – or more specifically between mind and consciousness. In Advaita Vedanta and Samkhya-Yoga, which elaborate on the distinction between mind and consciousness, the mind includes the intellect, emotions and all the qualities (qualia) of phenomenal experience: perceptions, memories, sensations, moods, etc. In contrast, consciousness (*purusha*) is distinct from primordial materiality (*prakrti*), which contains 23 components, including mind (*manas*), intellect (*buddhi, mahat*) and ego (*ahamkara*) (Pflueger 1998, 48). Intellect, mind and ego together with thought, feeling and perception are thus defined as different forms of nonconscious matter, all of which make up the *content* of witnessing consciousness (*purusha, turiya*). This tradition underlies the model for theatrical experience presented in the *Natyasastra*. The mind/consciousness distinction, in which both mind and body are unequivocally material, differs from the garden variety of mind/body dualism in western thought (Pflueger 49).[4] The material content of experience related to the intellect, mind and ego comprises only part of experience, which is made whole by the element of consciousness itself. Stoppard's theatrical devices – the leap-frogging of 'A, minus A', humour, dis-identification and unpredictability – serve to heighten the sense of a distinction between mind and consciousness, if only subliminally.

Spectators are encouraged to leap-frog into a trans-conceptual space after language has run its course, to witness the mind reflexively as it plays with logical conundrums. We find the sacredness of Stoppard's theatre, then, in its pointing away from the agitated mind toward the joys of consciousness.

The anthropologist C. Jason Throop clarifies the trans-conceptual by distinguishing two aspects of subjectivity: cognition, which is culture-specific; and non-cognitive direct experience, which is trans-cultural. Whereas anthropology tends to collapse all subjectivity into the cognitive camp, including pre-conceptual emotion, Throop proposes that 'pure experience' is a type of non-conceptual awareness corresponding to pure consciousness:

> While both pure experience and pure consciousness can be considered types of non-conceptual awareness, pure experience as a pre-conceptual awareness corresponds to a view of consciousness that focuses on describing the initial 'stages' of sensation and perception from one moment to the next, while pure consciousness as a trans-conceptual awareness points, on the other hand, to different 'levels' of consciousness that may transcend culturally conditioned conceptual awareness. (Throop 2000, 48)[5]

Pre-conceptual pure experience occurs in the initial stages of perception or sensation before the cognitive function of the mind kicks in to interpret it. Throop suggests that most people are familiar (if only unconsciously) with the pre-conceptual glimpse of an object of perception – the consciousness of an object before habit spurs the interpretive faculty. This pure experience sets the stage for a shift from culturally dependent interiors toward the domain of pure consciousness (*turiya, purusha*), a domain created in the theatrical production of intersubjective presence – a fusion of sacred and profane elements. While post-structuralist/postmodernists hold that the human subject is constructed by the discursive contexts in which it is situated, Stoppard demonstrates how theatre can point beyond itself and allow the spectator to experience subjective awareness in the gaps between these contexts. Stoppard's theatre thus intimates that consciousness is not an epiphenomenon of semiotic materialism.

Ros and Guil live in the present to the point of having no foreknowledge of *Hamlet* – a production that to any western audience, as Jacques Derrida would say, has 'always already' begun (1978, 232–50). In addition to their not being able to enlighten the audience about the anomaly of 92 consecutive heads, the actors are also at a loss about their roles in the play. They have no past beyond the memory that, as Guil puts it, in terms of the law of probability, 'a coin showed heads about as often as it showed tails. Then a messenger arrived. We had been sent for. Nothing else happened' (8). Being summoned to perform their parts in a play they've never heard of, they appear, 'Practically starting from scratch' (10), out of the mystery of a timeless nowhere associated with unicorns and mythology. In one of his philosophical treatises, Guil comments on the unreliable and relative nature of sensory impressions. He speculates on whether an obscure object will be seen as a unicorn or as a 'horse with an arrow in its forehead' (12). According to Throop, this would depend in any ordinary realistic context on the stage of one's perception: a pre-conceptual pure experience, or the consensual agreement of an interpretive community – which may override the pure experience of the thing itself. As the onstage audience, Ros ignores Guil's speculations. While this reaction may reflect the general lack of interest in, or confusion by, the true nature of human experience, Stoppard's audiences are repeatedly confronted by pure experience prior to interpretive agreement.

Throughout the play, Ros and Guil act out their parts as characters in *Hamlet* with a non-involvement that heightens the distinction between mind and consciousness, interpretation and a void in thought. We often find them in a mode of witnessing the Other before reaching an interpretative agreement. Any pre-conceptions the audience may have about *Hamlet* will be attenuated by watching Ros and Guil approach the play with an unintentional innocence of the initial stage of our encounter with the Other. Performers and audience join in reversing the direction of ordinary thought, erasing habitual discursive patterns, even about their self-identity, and co-creating an intersubjective space outside the exterior tokens of linguistic consensus.

Stoppard's characters approach the immutability of Pirandello's in *Six Characters in Search of an Author*, but whereas the six characters know who they are, Stoppard's do not, at least not in any conventional sense. Ros makes the introductions to the Tragedians:

Ros: My name is Guildenstern, and this is Rosencrantz.
Player: I recognized you at once–.
Ros: And who are we?
Player: –as fellow artists.
Ros: I thought we were gentlemen. (13)

Whatever their social identities, Ros and Guil continually act out of character, responding to others in a pre-cognitive sense. At times they fail perversely to get the point, as when the Player covertly offers them sex and violence, 'flagrante delicto at a price.' Like the theatre audience, Guil acts as voyeur to Ros' confusion. When the Player says, 'I don't think you understand' (15), Guil, 'shaking with rage and fright', finally catches on to the offer of Alfred dressed as a girl. But he expected more: 'No enigma, no dignity, nothing classical, portentous, only this – a comic pornographer and a rabble of prostitutes . . .' (18). Guil and Ros are not afraid, however, 'that there might be nothing beyond a purely physical existence' (Sales 24). In fact, they resist the pressure to abandon their purely physical, pre-conceptual existence – a metaphor of the pure, if fleeting, experience of a trans-cultural presence that Artaud finds in Asian theatre. But the performers encounter difficulties, as evidenced by their embarrassed responses to the Tragedians and their inability to undergo change or to take initiative.

Ros and Guil are prone to stagnate throughout the play, especially in act three. Once they bring the spectators into a sacred space, they have merely set the stage for the next level of development. This involves re-entry into the surrounding cultural context in a continual oscillation between the varied aspects of human experience: cultural and material, subjective and intersubjective, contingent and non-contingent, which interact and co-evolve simultaneously. Ros and Guil lead the way in the decontingencing of the human subject through their pre-cognitive reactions on stage, but then leave it up to the spectators to imagine a follow up in real life. At best the characters indicate through negation or non-realization how the audience might realize the benefits of their intersubjective insights. They become catalysts for the audience, both by disrupting discursive boundaries and by embodying the risks of not acting upon their unexpected freedom. This ironic doubling of cultural and trans-cultural states underlies much of the play's comic effect.

Whether or not Stoppard intended to evoke states of pre-conceptual awareness or non-contingent being is, by his own account, irrelevant. As Stoppard says, if a custom's officer were to ransack *Rosencrantz* and come 'up with all manner of exotic contraband like truth and illusion, the nature of identity, what I feel about life and death', he (Stoppard) would say, 'I have to admit the stuff is there but I can't for the life of me remember packing it'; 'one is the beneficiary and victim of one's subconscious: that is, one's personal history, experience and environment' (Delaney 2001, 25; Macaulay 1998, 7). In a related interpretation of the play, Neil Sammells argues that 'The choices faced by the two courtiers, and the pressures that envelope them, are clearly political pressures: the pressures of individuals trying to assert themselves against collectivism' (Sammells 2001, 111). The courtiers do have difficulty making choices and exerting control against collectivism, as we have seen. In viewing collectivism politically as the historical effect of a totalitarian state, Sammells seems to suggest, as I have argued here, that even in their subjectedness, Ross and Guil have the power to act and thereby effect something as autonomous agents. But for Sammells, the agents can never act from their subjected positions with more than a very limited autonomy and power. It seems to me, however, that Stoppard's play suggests the possibility of a more radical freedom from subjectedness. As postcolonial writers have shown, the possibility does exist for a 'historyless' world (Ashcroft et al. 2002, 33) – a world experienced in trans-political, trans-historical terms. We are certainly all subjected to cultural as well as trans-cultural influences, most of which are beyond our control. As Sammells says, 'Rosencrantz and Guildenstern fight to preserve the distinction between actor and agent, to hang on to the short-lived sense of purpose that will give their actions meaning' (110). Another collective force that needs to be considered here in relation to agency, a force universal for all but zombies, is that of the mind's irrepressible flow of thoughts. As anyone who tries deliberately to 'create a void in thought' can tell, no amount of agency or effort as advocated by Sammells will interrupt the stream of mental activity or induce a pure witnessing experience. Effort will only increase mental activity, producing more thoughts, more pressures of all kinds over which we have less control. Ironically, then, to lose control like Ros and Guil suggests in one sense to go beyond control, to escape thought and the pressures of political collectivism – as in the spontaneous experience of aesthetic rapture (*rasa*).

By integrating the sacred and the profane through a transformation of the latter, *Rosencrantz* can be said to enhance freedom by opening an auratic space. Walter Benjamin defines aura as a relation between an artwork (sacred) and its viewer (profane): the viewer looks and the artwork looks back (Benjamin 1969). In looking at something we invest it with the capacity to look at us and produce a transformation. In this process, the viewer's attention undergoes a subtle shift from mind to consciousness. Benjamin believed the loss of aura in art occurred in the middle of the nineteenth century with the development of photography. Because the camera could not see, film was postauratic, yet the emancipatory effect of reproduction compensated for the loss of aura. Theatre on the other hand retains the quality of aura because the performers are influenced by the live audience – just as an actor can be influenced by the camera. In *Rosencrantz*, the spectators look at the actors, and the actors look back, causing the spectators to reflect on their own experience.

In deconstructing the playwright's control over a dramatic text, however, post-structuralists like Gerald Rabkin argue that the script in theatre precludes presence through 'dispersion, discontinuity and dissemination' (Rabkin 1983, 51). Elinor Fuchs, in deconstructing the aura of theatrical presence associated with live actors and spectators, calls into question 'the theatrical enterprise of spontaneous speech with its logocentric claims to origination, authority, authenticity' (Fuchs1985, 172). In its place she posits a 'theater of absence' that 'disperses the center, displaces the Subject, destabilizes meaning' (165). But given the distinction between mind and consciousness, which the vast interdisciplinary field of consciousness studies today has widely accepted (Chalmers; Throop; Wilber), Stoppard's theatrical enterprise simultaneously achieves a theatre of absence on the level of mind, and an aura of presence on the level of consciousness. On the level of mind, *Rosencrantz* destabilizes meaning by loosening the mind's control over pre-cognitive experience and disperses the centre of political hegemony through humour and parody; on the level of consciousness, it displaces the subject(ed) by evoking a liberating void in thought (*rasa*). The cultural materiality of the mind associated with our subjected-ness is temporarily supplanted in theatre by an auratic presence. Both spectators and actors, in their reciprocal looking back and forth, find their awareness momentarily lightened of the discursive frameworks with which to judge their relationship. Even in a theatre of absence, then, a liminal in-between-ness effects a decontingencing of mind toward unknowingness as a void in thought. Stoppard's theatrical devices thus serve to open an intersubjective space, not that of testing or judgement, but of a co-created auratic lightness.

(v) *Rosencrantz: Social Mirrors and Stage Mirrors*

In social mirror theory originated by Dilthey, Mead and others, self-reflection or mirrors in the mind depend on mirrors in society (Whitehead 2001, 3). As Stoppard suggests, self-awareness in both the socially induced and trans-cultural sense is evoked by social mirrors and shared worlds of experience. A dramatic change occurs in *Rosencrantz* just before the appearance of Hamlet when the coin falls on tails for the first time and the play's social mirror suddenly shifts. As Hamlet and Ophelia enter, Ros and Guil witness incomprehensively an ambiguous mime verging on the licentious. Rather than engage in sustained action, they begin to explore their relationships with others. Any determinate meaning they might have found with *Hamlet*, had they remembered the play at all, is ambushed by the unexpectedness of Hamlet's mime, the lack of a famous speech, and the ongoing fluidity of their own identities. Claudius turns to Guil and says, 'Welcome, dear Rosencrantz.' Guil and Ros remain at a loss, Guil managing only, 'We both obey / And here give up ourselves in the full bent / To lay our service freely at your feet, / To be commanded' (26–27). They need their lines fed to them, or mirrored, a theatrical technique that Sammells sees as manifesting political pressure but that Stoppard parodies. In doing so, he mirrors the actors' attenuated mental content as they hover in the liminal zone of a pre-conceptual pure experience – unable to fix on conceptual meaning in their decontingencing lack of memory of *Hamlet* or their intended roles.

As the first act draws to a close, Ros and Guil increasingly enter a space beyond logic, memory and meaning. Guil asks, 'What in God's name is going on?' Ros responds, 'Foul! No Rhetoric. Two-one' (34). As the wordplay continues, Guil seizes Ros violently and shouts, 'WHO DO YOU THINK YOU ARE?' (35), which, of course, has no answer in terms of social appellation.

Ros: It's *all* questions.
Guil: Do you think it matters?
Ros: Doesn't it matter to you?
Guil: Why should it matter?
Ros: What does it matter why? (35–36)

The matter of the play is the play itself, just as the matter of the mirror is the mirror itself, and the matter of awareness is awareness itself, not its content. In the mirror theory of human identity, as Charles Whitehead explains, the content of our reflective consciousness depends on public expression, a shared experiential world, and social reflectivity (28). If this is the case, then we might reasonably extend this theory to include a mirroring of emptiness – as implied above in Fuchs' deconstruction of presence. Instead of reflecting only the content of reflective consciousness, could the mirror not also reflect the emptiness of consciousness, as in the thought voiding state experienced by Ros and Guil and induced in their spectators? Stoppard's theatre, being theatre of theatre, parallels the mirror being mirror of mirror. In social mirror theory, as Whitehead puts it, 'it is only when subjective states are made objective by public confirmation that we can pay attention to them, so making them conscious' (21). Although this typically applies to the content of consciousness, it can also apply to consciousness itself. In watching *Rosencrantz*, our capacity to attribute mental states to ourselves and others, including states beyond thought, is verified by their dramatization. Pure awareness or a void in thought (*turiya*) is not created by social mirroring, not a third-person formulation, but a first-person experience that comes with the territory, something once experienced we automatically know that we know. The mirror of social and stage drama helps us to pay attention to it, and, thereby, to reap its benefits, which include love, freedom and joy.

Ros and Guil, for example, find themselves in situations where they don't so much identify with their own bodies as observe them in action. In this way they cultivate what B. Alan Wallace calls 'a kind of self-alterity,' experiencing their bodies 'simply as a matrix of phenomena, rather than as a self' (Wallace 2001, 214). They break away from a reified sense of identity as being localized in the material domain of their minds and bodies. Observing each other, Ros and Guil perceive certain qualities unique to each as well as qualities they share in common. This common ground includes their feelings of empathy and compassion. As Wallace puts it,

> Is consciousness essentially intersubjective in the sense that the very nature of consciousness, with its own innate luminosity, is constituted by the relation of the self to others? The observation that the *bhavanga* [Sanskrit for the primal state of contentless awareness] is of the nature of love would imply that empathy is innate to consciousness and exists prior to the emergence of all active mental processes. One might infer from this that empathy on the part of researchers must be a prerequisite for any genuine science of consciousness. On the other hand, the assertion that this state of awareness is free of all sensory and mental appearances implies a certain degree of autonomy from language, conceptual frameworks and active engagement with others. This could suggest that consciousness is not really constituted by the relation of the self to others, but rather that it is intersubjective in the weaker sense of simply being inherently open to, and connected with, others. (213)

Intersubjectivity, as mentioned earlier, does not create contentless awareness, but only mirrors it, allowing it to be shared by the inter-subjects. By parodying notions of reality that have become conceptually fixed, Stoppard opens communication out from verbal agreement to a participation beyond discursive constructs. *Rosencrantz* emerges out of absurdism and initially seemed to be an absurdist work itself, but it is generally regarded as more high-spirited, light-hearted, compassionate and gentler than absurdist drama. Stoppard does not succumb to the modernist despair over a lost unity. He delights in providing yet another angle of vision in a series that does not endorse fragmentation, chaos, or nihilism, but leads instead to an empathetic co-creation of a theatre of sacred presence. This presence suggests the contentless, non-contingent dimension of the self, variously known, recall, as the absolute one in Plotinus, Atman or *turiya* in Advaita Vedanta, and nondual consciousness in Buddhist Vijnanas.

In act two, Ros and Guil continue to be at a loss about their dramatic roles and social identities. They test the practical validity of concepts by putting them on performative display, hoping someone will give them a sense of direction by mirroring their expected behaviour. By implication, the absence of social mirrors would reverse the normal acculturation process. That is, without the objectification of our subjected states, we would tend more readily to accept the (liberated) condition of pure physicality or experiential immediacy prior to interpretive agreement. But as Guil says, 'Wheels have been set in motion, and they have their own pace, to which we are...condemned. Each move is dictated by the previous one – that is the meaning of order' (51). In 'The Murder of Gonzago', Shakespeare anticipates social mirror theory by showing how the pretend play's social reflectivity evokes Claudius' and Gertrude's reflective consciousness, and how self-reflection can change the order of meaning and the nature of reality.

When Hamlet arranges for a play-within-the-play to trap his uncle Claudius into revealing his guilty conscience, the audience finds itself watching more actors acting people (Hamlet and Horatio) 'watching more actors acting more people [Claudius and Gertrude] watching still more actors acting yet more people [the Tragedians/Players] acting even more people [Claudius and his queen]' (Hunter 2000, 9) – with the 'onionlike' contexts unfolding all at once in theatrical exuberance. When actors dress up to play characters who put on further disguises, spectators are encouraged not only to adopt a critical distance on the conceptual level but also to engage in the phenomenology of dis-identification. Actors and spectators participate in a space where exterior boundaries dissolve. The ordinary identification between an actor and a role is distanced by the fact that characters are doubly not who they pretend to be. Each layer of disguise unravels before a free-floating witness with none of the tangible roles producing a reliable or fixed point of identity. In the *theatrum mundi*, where in Shakespeare's words 'all the men and women are merely players', the real self behind our roles is not just another in an infinite series of subjected appellations, but the innate luminosity of our contentless awareness (*bhavanga*) – a field of all possibilities for self-formulation. The shifting roles of stage drama, as of social drama, do not leave us in a state of limbo, tossed back and forth between contingent identities, as post-structuralist/postmodernists claim. Rather, if Stoppard's theatre is anything to go by, spectators and performers, engaging linguistic and conceptual tokens from their various context-bound subject positions while instantaneously transcending them, are given the opportunity to relish a void in thought beyond contingency (*rasa*). On this groundless ground, they co-create a sacred space – however nonsacred the play's actual content.

In *Rosencrantz* this process has two components: the dialectical movement of 'A, minus A' and the other devices through which characters and audience reflect on the arbitrary nature of thought; and the aftermath of this reflection through which they slip momentarily into a suspension of thought – a decontingencing of the historical subject toward pure consciousness. The latter, as the ultimate escape from political collectivism, is perhaps also the ultimate form of 'control' – in the sense of self-mastery over the mind's inexorable stream of qualia. In *Rosencrantz* both stages of self-awareness are mirrored in a spiralling interplay of thought and non-thought, boundaries and freedom.

The Player says that when the Tragedians act without somebody watching, they feel humiliated because it means nothing happens (55). Theatrical and everyday consensual reality depend on a reciprocity of social mirrors. To be without an audience, the fourth wall of a stage in theatrical jargon, is like being dead in a box. The audience in this analogy symbolizes the light of witnessing consciousness, without which everything on stage would occur in virtual darkness. Hamlet's pretended madness may seem real because the court spends a lot of time in the dark acting without an audience.

Ros: He talks to himself, which might be madness.
Guil: If he didn't talk sense, which he does.
Ros: Which suggests the opposite.
Player: Of what?

Small pause.

Guil: I think I have it. A man talking sense to himself is no madder than a man talking
          nonsense not to himself.
Ros: Or just as mad.
Guil: Or just as mad.
Ros: And he does both.
Guil: So there you are.
Ros: Stark raving sane. (59–60)

Stoppard's comic treatment itself teases the spectator out of an either/or logic. Again casting about for social mirrors, in this case for dealing with Hamlet, Ros and Guil seek guidance from the Player:

Guil: We don't know how to *act*.
Player: Act natural. You know why you're here at least.
Guil: We only know what we're told, and that's little enough. And for all we know it isn't
          even true.
Player: For all anyone knows, nothing is. Everything has to be taken on trust; truth is that
          which is taken to be true. It's the currency of living. (59)

The Player's advice to act naturally is paradoxical because everything in theatre is artificial. As Sales says, 'the further over the top an actor goes, the closer he gets to acting naturally. Heightened artificiality and theatricality are, or ought to be, natural phenomena in the theatre' (40). But you can also say that the further an actor goes over the top of socially expected behaviour, the closer s/he gets to the edge of thought.

As a theatrical mirror, *Rosencrantz* reflects the courtiers' constantly going over the top as a form of voiding the discursive mind and revealing the non-historical dimension of life in the present.

In trying to act natural by rehearsing their roles, Guil and Ros play a game with the Player who feeds them questions about Hamlet. But the game only leads them over the top, having no rational end other than being an end in itself. The actors and spectators cannot genuinely be who they say they are, not completely. Although Jacques Lacan claims that subjectivity exists in language, that the unconscious mind is structured as a language (Lacan 1978, 188), subjectivity is also consciously aware of language, separated from and extending beyond language. Sammells as noted earlier questions the confusion here between the possibility of a spontaneous act versus a capitulation to collectivism, to a 'logic unstoppable and absurd': 'Are we all just actors in someone else's script – defined not by individual, authentic voice, but by the pressures of collectivism?' (110). Ros and Guil suggest not, for in spontaneously skirting the boundaries of thought they reveal the possibility of also transcending the script. They do this not by dispensing with words, but by using words to open their attention to a realm beyond semiotic materialism. Similarly, they transcend the body/mind not by denying its reality, but by using it as a springboard to higher levels of consciousness. Herbert Blau, who like Rabkin and Fuchs, questions the notion of presence in theatre, argues that the immediate presence of the body on stage is 'ghosted' by the script (Blau 1987, 164). Even without the text, performance seems written because of the semiotics of theatre (171). The body/mind, however, while, of course, still there on stage, is not only ghosted by stage semiotics, it is also ghosted by the leap-frogging from semiotics to a witnessing vantage point. Theatre thereby reveals that although we are both mind and body, we are also consciousness, and that the hard problem of western metaphysics is not how ideas and bodies relate, but more importantly how ideas/bodies and consciousness relate.

In the interweaving of *Hamlet* and *Rosencrantz* leading up to a discussion of death, Ros and Guil are baffled to see two characters dressed like themselves played by the Tragedians, thus heightening the ambiguity over identity and the distinction between reality and illusion. When Ros claims, 'you can't act death', the Player argues that real death on stage, such as the one he was once able to arrange, 'just wasn't convincing! It was impossible to suspend one's disbelief – and what with the audience jeering and throwing peanuts, the whole thing was a disaster!' (77). Significantly, as drama theorists from Diderot to Stanislavsky and Brecht have argued, the performer who holds an aesthetic distance between actor and performance is more convincing in conveying the desired emotion to the audience. On stage, literal identification fails to convince, to swing one over the top of language and interpretation and thereby open a gap between mind and consciousness. The point of theatrical language use is not its referential meaning but its manner of ghosting itself to reveal the underlying self-awareness of performer and spectator.

In act three, Ros and Guil have several opportunities to change their lives and influence the plot, as by preventing Hamlet's death, but fail to exploit them. As Guil says, 'we are brought full circle to face again the single immutable fact – that we, Rosencrantz and Guildenstern, bearing a letter from one king to another, are taking Hamlet to England' (93). Acting naturally, they almost make a difference by opening the letter to discover Hamlet's intended fate. But even at this turning point, they miss their chance to effect change when Guil refuses to rescue Hamlet. In their normative subjected state, their material agency is indeed limited. In a final attempt to discover their identity and purpose, they again prod the Player, but he can only tell them that in his experience, 'most things end in death' (115). He means literally, but the play also suggests metaphorically. What the death of man in Stoppard's theatre suggests is the death of our subjected-ness and a rebirth of the memory of consciousness, as opposed to consciousness itself – which in eastern thought is beyond space/time and thus beyond death and (re)birth. Feeling desperate, Guil snatches the Player's dagger and stabs him in the throat, for the first time taking action into his own hands. But agency must have a purpose beyond physical change. After dying convincingly, the Player gets up and brushes himself off to the applause of his fellow players, with the dumb show of death transforming the tragedy into a comedy. The Player's metaphorical, feigned death opens a space for 'death' as rebirth, as transcendence from the material mind/body condition. In the end, Ros is happy not to have harmed anyone as far as he or Guil can recall: 'All right, then. I don't care. I've had enough. To tell you the truth, I'm relieved' (118).

Does *Rosencrantz* not show, then, that neither thought nor action can provide the answer to identity or freedom? Perhaps one needs to transcend agency into non-contingent being before knowledge becomes true and action effective. As Ros and Guil demonstrate, gaining self-awareness involves putting ourselves in the shoes of what George Mead called '"the generalized other" and from that third-person perspective look[ing] back and observ[ing] [our] own thoughts' (Whitehead 18). In *Rosencratz*, this reflective 'generalized other' has an added dimension: conceptuality (thought) *and* emptiness (non-thought), the duality of otherness *and* the 'witnessing' of wholeness as a space of inter-being. In the latter condition, which Stoppard's theatre induces, the sense of being this or that begins to dissolve, along with the spatio/temporal gaps between the three components of experience – 'experiencer, experience, experiencing' (S. N. Maharaj 1988, 164).

(vi) Conclusion

Stoppard's power as a dramatist derives from his ability to distance his characters and audience from attachment to or identification with our everyday concerns. Instead we glimpse how to appreciate these concerns from a liminal field of pre-interpretive awareness. Stoppard shows how the discordancy of our thoughts, emotions and actions appears farcical in light of the harmony, silence and freedom at deeper levels of experience. His plays expose the discrepancy between conceptual, analytical frameworks on the one hand, and the observing theatregoer who is led to dis-identify with these frameworks on the other. Spectators can laugh at the show and appreciate its illusion in the process of going over the top. We see the illusion as uninevitable, and realize that things might have turned out differently with only a slight change of perspective. Through transcendence and transformation, the spectators co-create with the performers a new space beyond normative frames of reference.

Although *Rosencrantz* ends in a frenzy that apparently achieves nothing, throughout the play the actors and spectators co-create a theatrical space which, as we have seen, has two dimensions. They find their attention moving from meaning to non-meaning, thought to non-thought, contingency to non-contingency, representing two types of intersubjectivity, as reflected in the play's bifocal mirror. Intersubjectivity has been variously defined by theorists such as Jürgen Habermas, Ken Wilber and Christian de Quincey. Rejecting the 'paradigm of consciousness,' Habermas favours a paradigm of 'communicative action' mediated by language and reason (Habermas 1987). He sees language and reason as underlying intersubjective recognition and on this basis tries to integrate the context-bound and the universal. Similarly, Wilber seems to define intersubjectivity as mediated by language and interpretation: 'You will talk to me, and interpret what I say; and I will do the same with you' (Wilber 2000, 161). De Quincey (like Stoppard) recognizes that intersubjectivity can *include* language and interpretation but also *extend* to consciousness by itself. This involves the co-creation of a non-physical presence. He contends that intersubjectivity allows for

> direct interior-to-interior engagement even when contact is made via language – in fact, that is the *only* way people can share meaning and understand each other. But the point is that the actual sharing of meaning is not accomplished by linguistic exchanges, but by the accompanying *interior-to-interior participatory presence* – by true intersubjectivity. (de Quincey 2000, 188, original emphasis)

Although their definitions differ, Habermas, Wilber and de Quincey each accept the importance of intersubjective space, which in *Rosencrantz* includes the exterior and interior, mind and consciousness. Ros and Guil constantly participate in linguistic mediation – the logical ambushes, the discourse of 'A, minus A', the shifting identities, the self-reflection on roles and on theatricality in general – which take them and the spectators to a space beyond language and interpretation. While social mirrors reflect subjective experience as communicated by the physicality of human discourse, Stoppard's theatre dramatizes how they also reflect a direct 'interior-to-interior participatory presence'.

Chapter 4

BETWEEN THE OPPOSITES: GENDER GAMES

William S. Haney II

4.1 CARYL CHURCHILL: *CLOUD NINE*

(i) *Introduction*

Caryl Churchill presents a vision of justice in a theatre that, like Stoppard's, is playful, comic and startling, but also subversive in a manner she intends to be 'not ordinary, not safe' (Churchill 1960, 446). As a feminist artist who experiments with subject, form and style, Churchill departs from the Brechtian technique of distancing the audience and develops a new process of identifying and confronting social problems. She is particularly concerned with gender oppression and the inequalities of capitalism, largely induced by patriarchal ideology. In defining human identity, Churchill shows how the representation of a dramatic work to an audience parallels the way an individual represents the self to society. She exposes the patriarchal definitions of masculinity as dependent on the exclusion of the feminine as 'Other' in a closed structure of oppositions in which the feminine is objectified and women repressed. In her confrontation with traditional male-dominated theatre, Churchill deals not only with stages, curtains, scenes and lighting, but also with the historical and economic conditions that support and legitimize male hegemony. In *Cloud Nine* and *Top Girls*, Churchill links societal change with personal development, showing that individuals can effect significant changes not only in themselves but also in society. The relevance of Churchill's feminist drama for sacred theatre derives in part from its linking of opposites. Her approach to theatre opens up a sacred space between the opposites of male/female, power/powerlessness, subjective experience/historical circumstance. As in Stoppard's theatre, the space she opens between subject and object is the sacred space of empathy and inter-being. Through the unsayable dimension of discourse, the theatrical text and its performance leads the audience toward a sacred space, which as mentioned earlier deconstructs the way we ordinarily look at space and time. Churchill's heady theatrical style, through a juxtaposition of opposites, leads to the self-transcendence of language, a shift from ordinary waking consciousness and language as a system of differences toward pure consciousness where language points toward a transcendent unity-amidst-diversity.

(ii) Cloud Nine: *Player/Role*

Rachel Blau du Plessis has pointed out that socialist/feminists working in theatre have tried to 'break the sentence' of the symbolic order that legitimizes masculine authority (1985). In analyzing Churchill's theatre as a feminist deconstruction of 'the sentence' of patriarchal subjectivity and its institutions, Amelia Kritzer examines the key elements of theatrical representation that Churchill challenges. Kritzer explains that 'the sentence' in theatre consists of four conventions: a) the space accommodating the stage and audience; b) the relation between the performance and the written role of at least one actor; c) the 'density of signs', as Roland Barthes defines it, created by lighting, staging and the actor's physical presence, gesture, vocal tones and costume; and d) time (Kritzer 1991, 8; Barthes 1972, 26). Churchill takes on the first element of space by giving voice to female and feminist viewpoints. This involves breaking down the patriarchal boundaries erected on stage between performers and audience. Churchill 'uses both Brechtian devices (such as seating non-performing actors on stage) and literary techniques (i.e., fragmented narratives and open endings) in her plays to challenge the convention of audience passivity and engage the audience in a relationship to imaginative reciprocity' (Kritzer, 9). The second element, the player/role relationship, has a special significance for feminist theatre. It is based on Barthes' description of theatre as 'the site of an ultraincarnation, in which the body is double, at once a living body deriving from a trivial nature, and an emphatic, formal body, frozen by its function as an artificial object' (Kritzer, 27–8). In theatre, which reflects the social construction of identity, the performer/role doubleness reinforces the masculine/feminine opposition central to a masculine or patriarchal subjectivity. As Kritzer puts it,

> Theater's player/role opposition mimics the division and hierarchization of masculine and feminine. The player is real, while the role makes visible the false man – i.e., the feminine – that must be repressed in the attainment of subjectivity. Stage parlance, which places the player 'in' a role, confirms the penetrable, 'feminine' quality of the role, as well as the unitary, 'masculine' quality of the player. (9)

In this hierarchized opposition between the 'real' man as the unitary player and the 'false' man as the feminized role, the 'false' man position sustains the 'real' masculine subject as a phallic unity by reinforcing the role as the 'other' that threatens masculine unity. The false man of the role position masquerades on stage as the real or true man, who is both comforted and threatened by the role. This doubleness of theatre, which replicates the ambiguity of the subject/object division, can be seen as opening a sacred space in Churchill's theatre within the subjectivity of actors and audience.

The sacredness of theatre, as we have seen, unfolds within the space of subjectivity created by the decontingencing of the subject through a dis-identification with fixed roles. The dis-indentification or decontextualization of subjectivity that begins with the player/role doubleness of representation accelerates when the player is a woman. A 'woman playing a role would be not-man enacting false man, and the reassuring value of doubleness would be lost' (Kritzer, 10), with the effect of accentuating the threat to the phallic unity of the true man, who ironically would be exposed as doubly false. [RY: *Shakespeare knew this: Viola in Twelfth Night refers to men as 'the proper false'.*] For this reason women tend to be cast as ideal feminine objects given to passive acceptance of the hierarchal male/female opposition. Because the patriarchy considers the true woman (player) and false woman (role) to be the same, women are generally denied the kind of ambiguities and fragmentation that construct, but can also deconstruct, social identity. Feminists like Churchill try to express a non-patriarchal subjectivity by answering Hélène Cixous' call for an écriture féminine (1986). This project would help dissolve the male/female opposition and the link between the phallus and the word that marks patriarchal discourse, and substitute a 'density of signs', the third convention noted earlier, based on feminine attributes: breast, clitoris and vagina. According to Kritzer, 'Feminist theatre must attempt to deconstruct the socially constructed wholeness of the gendered subject. To do so, it must break down the masculine/feminine opposition reified in the player/role division, theatricalizing the possibility of a subjectivity based in multiplicity and relationality rather than binary opposition and separateness' (11). This deconstructed place is where women, as Cixous puts it, would make a 'shattering entry into history' (1976, 880). But in fact this entry always already occurs whenever an actor plays a role, as we have seen in Stoppard, for the doubleness of representation can be understood not only in terms of the division between a true man/woman and a false man/woman, but also between the constructed identity of any role and the witnessing attention of the player performing this role. The point is not only 'to deconstruct the socially constructed wholeness of the gendered subject', as Kritzer puts it, not only to fracture the subject into multiple identities, but also to disassociate oneself from all identities in the sacred taste of a void in thought, which is also the fullness of consciousness as pure witness.

(iii) *Identity and Gender*

Cloud Nine, written in 1978 and 79, consists of two acts: the first is set in Victorian Africa and explores the links between imperialism and the oppression of Africans, homosexuals and women; the second is set about a hundred years later in London in the 1970s, where several members of the same family in act one, together with their new friends, try to free themselves from their Victorian heritage. In playing with the element of time (the fourth convention Kritzer identities), Churchill not only separates the two acts by a hundred years while maintaining continuity, but also has the characters – specifically the mother (Betty) and her two children (Edward and Victoria) – age only 25 years. Act one begins with Clive coming home after touring the restless native villages to the care of his wife, Betty, who complains about the rudeness of their servant, Joshua. Betty tells of the unexpected arrival of a widowed neighbour, Mrs Saunders, whom Clive will incessantly pursue, and he in turn tells Betty of the imminent arrival of their friend Harry Bagley, a homosexual with whom Betty is infatuated. As the first act unfolds, the Clives and friends hold a Christmas picnic, hostilities mount and Joshua patrols the compound. Edward is caught playing with his sister's doll, Harry inadvertently reveals his homosexuality to Clive, and in the final scene Joshua aims a gun at Clive as he toasts the bride and groom. In addition to the player/role doubling, we see a farcical clash between outrageous behavior and a Victorian ethical code common in British satire.

Act Two, set mostly in a London park, consists of a series of scenes from everyday life in the 1970s and features both familiar and new characters: Victoria as a middle-class professional and her husband, Martin; Lin, a working-class lesbian who becomes Vic's lover, and her daughter Cathy; Vic's brother Edward, a gardener in the park, and his lover, Gerry; their mother, Betty, recently divorced from Clive and about to become liberated; and Lin, Vic and Edward in a *ménage à trois*. The characters from act one find sexual liberation in act two, but have not completely thrown off the ghosts of Victorianism. In the doubling of roles, none of the characters are played by the same actors in both acts, while one character plays the roles of Ellen and Mrs Saunders in act one.

Churchill, who accentuates the doubleness of theatrical representation by cross-casting her characters, makes these comments in the Preface:

> Betty, Clive's wife, is played by a man because she wants to be what men want her to be, and, in the same way Joshua, the black servant, is played by a white man because he wants to be what whites want him to be. Betty does not value herself as a woman, nor does Joshua value himself as a black. Edward, Clive's son, is played by a woman for a different reason – partly to do with the stage convention of having boys played by women (Peter Pan, radio plays, etc.) and partly with highlighting the way Clive tries to impose traditional male behaviour on him. (1985, 245)

By contrasting two historical periods, Churchill shows how sexuality and power are not fixed attributes; they change over time together with other personal attributes. The fact that the identity of characters as characters continues across the two acts, then, depends not on their roles, genders or any of their changing attributes, but on their witnessing awareness remaining the same, providing a sense of continuity to one's shifting conventional identity.

Against this background of self-observation, which is nonchanging, *Cloud Nine* dramatizes the liberating move from patriarchal domination to greater individual freedom. Clive's role as Cathy in act two highlights the arbitrariness of gender and hegemonic status, as well as the openness and flexibility of human development. As Churchill says, 'Cathy is played by a man, partly as a simple reversal of Edward being played by a woman, partly because the size and presence of a man on stage seemed appropriate to the emotional force of young children, and partly, as with Edward to show more clearly the issues involved in learning what is considered correct behaviour for a girl' (Preface 1985, 246). This cross-casting has the effect of startling the audience out of their preconceptions about human relationships and the distinctions of race, gender and power.

This startling effect is enhanced by the irony of cross-cast performers playing the role of the 'other' they try to deny. Clive as Cathy in act two caricatures his role as patriarch in act one, and despite being black Joshua has a pseudo white-male subjectivity apparent in his contempt for his own race and for Betty, who as a women is oppressed like blacks. Betty in act one is played by a man, to ironic effect when her homophobic husband, Clive, embraces her. She tries to seduce Harry Bagley, a family friend and explorer, who is having casual affairs with Edward and Joshua. Ellen, Edward's governess, lusts after Betty, but is forced to marry Harry, who mistakenly comes on to Clive. In unexpected ways the play shifts our conceptions of space, time and identity in two acts that span over a hundred years. As Joanne Kleine notes, 'the dissimilarities of time, like those of setting, are partly harmonized by contrapuntal situations in each of the acts; thus, the leisure quality of Act One generates frenzy, while the kaleidoscopic pattern of Act Two produces ennui' (Internet). Churchill's aesthetics simultaneously call attention to and undermine the qualities of her fictional world. Her multi-level paradigm and partial discontinuity between the two acts empower the characters to begin shedding their socially conditioned attributes.

In deconstructing gender politics, Churchill makes gender visible by separating it from the body and sex. As the characters are introduced, the incongruities multiple: Joshua, played by a white, internalizes colonial values; Edward, played by a woman, tries to elude the role expectations of his father; and Victoria is at first played by a doll, emphasizing the mindless status of Victorian children. The play begins with the imperialist song 'Come Gather Sons of England', with the characters introducing themselves in the rigid language of rhymed couplets. Betty says:

> I live for Clive. The whole aim of my life
> Is to be what he looks for in a wife.
> I am a man's creation, as you see,
> And what men want is what I want to be. (251)

Even in her adulterous attraction to Harry Bagley, she remains locked in her role as object, unable to become an active agent:

Betty: When I'm near you it's like going out into the jungle. It's like going up the river on a raft. It's like going out in the dark.
Harry: And you are safety and light and peace and home.
Betty: But I want to be dangerous.
Harry: Clive is my friend.
Betty: I am your friend.
Harry: I don't like dangerous women....
Betty: Am I dangerous?
Harry: You are rather.
Betty: Please like me.
Harry: I worship you.
Betty: Please want me. (261)

The degree to which Betty as a character identifies with her role as object prevents her from experiencing her sexuality directly, instead compelling her to experience it through the mediated idealizations of the male: 'You are safety and light and peace and home' (261). And later: 'Betty: Can't we ever be alone? Harry: You are a mother. And a daughter. And a wife' (268). Her immediate experience of sexual indulgence is erased, replaced by the masculine representation of it, which takes primacy over female desire. Moreover, if Betty were played by a woman, her role as a not-man enacting a false man would undermine the reassuring doubleness of representation that preserves masculine identity. But Betty's being played by a man maintains the hierarchized opposition between the true man as the unitary player and the false man as the feminized role. The false man position of Betty as man would thus seem to sustain the masculine subject as a phallic unity by reinforcing the role position as the 'other' that threatens masculine unity. The problem, however, is that the performer, although played by a man, is supposed to be a woman. Does this mean that she is ironically sustained as a masculinized subject with a phallic unity? If so, the gay Harry hasn't noticed, for he resists seduction by Betty as a man, acting a woman, even though s/he supposedly reinforces masculine empowerment. But then, is Harry really a man seeking empowerment himself? In the ambiguity of the pairing of Betty and Harry, they can be viewed as either a heterosexual or homosexual couple, depending on whether Betty is viewed in terms of gender or biology. This complex doubleness in Churchill's theatre, which multiplies the ambiguities of the subject/object division, creates a sacred space in the subjectivity of actors and audience by first scrambling and then emptying out its content. What replaces this content is not so much a Brechtian critical mind but an impersonal, disinterested awareness that witnesses the rapid decontingencing of any fixed or finite sense of conventional identity.

The lesbian Ellen tries to seduce Betty, but she also fails to communicate her feelings directly. She can only express her desire by trying to substitute herself for Harry. But when she says, 'I love you, Betty', Betty responds from an indoctrinated perspective, 'I love you too, Ellen. But women have their duty as soldiers have. You must be a mother if you can' (281), spoken convincingly as a 'man'. Joshua reports to Clive on having spied on Ellen's talking 'of love to your wife, sir', but Clive refuses to take it seriously (285). He does, however, condemn Betty for her flirtation with Harry, which he also hears about from Joshua. No woman in act one has much success in fulfilling her desires. Mrs Saunders tries in vain to fend off Clive, and when she succumbs he can only satisfy himself:

[He (Clive) has been caressing her feet and legs. He disappears completely under her skirt.]
Mrs. Saunders: Please stop. I can't concentrate. I want to go home. I wish I didn't enjoy the sensation because I don't like you, Clive. I do like living in your house where there's plenty of guns. But I don't like you at all. But I do like the sensation. Well I'll have it then. I'll have it, I'll have it:

[Voices are heard singing The First Noël.]

Don't stop. Don't stop.

[Clive comes out from under her skirt.]

Clive:　　　　　The Christmas picnic. I came.
Mrs. Saunders: I didn't.
Clive:　　　　　I'm all sticky.
Mrs. Saunders: What about me? Wait.
Clive:　　　　　All right, are you? Come on. We mustn't be found.
Mrs. Saunders: Don't go now. (263–64)

Though farcical, Clive as the symbolic father imposes his divine right as a colonialist on anyone he pleases, exploiting his linguistic authority and control over language and desire. In coercing his lascivious will on Mrs Saunders, he wields the caricature of a romantic rhetoric: 'Caroline, if you were shot with poisoned arrows do you know what I'd do? I'd fuck your dead body and poison myself. Caroline, you smell amazing. You terrify me. You are dark like the continent. Mysterious. Treacherous' (263). Mrs Saunders, like Betty, is reduced to monosyllables: 'Don't stop. Don't stop.' Clive's discourse, as Kritzer puts it, 'enforces the opposition between subject and object on both women and colonized people, as is evident in parallels between patriarchal concepts of women and Western European concepts of Africa in his speech' (118). Recall the above quotation: 'You are dark like the continent.' Similarly, when he hears of Betty's infidelity, Clive says, 'This whole continent is my enemy....I sometimes feel it will break over me and swallow me up....you must resist it Betty, or it will destroy us....We must resist this dark female lust, Betty, or it will swallow us up' (277).

Although Betty agrees to resist these dark impulses, the play's sexual nonconformity suggests a covert resistance to partriarchal authority. But Betty as played by a man shows resistance not only to male authority – as in a subject/object, male/female opposition discussed by Kritzer – but also to the very constructedness of the personal subject, whether male or female, which is based on our identification with arbitrary attributes. Churchill's overall dramatization heightens our mindfulness of body, mind, thoughts and emotions in a manner that opens a space in our attention between these attributes and awareness *per se*, so that awareness mirrors itself. As we saw with Stoppard, the matter of theatre as mirror is the mirror, just as the matter of awareness is awareness – the mirroring of emptiness.

One of the most comical scenes of the play involves the misunderstanding between Clive and Harry, who mistakes Clive's assertion that 'There is something dark about women, that threatens what is best in us. Between men that light burns brightly', as an expression of homosexual desire (282). Clive is taken aback when 'Harry takes hold of Clive' (stage directions) and says, 'My God, Harry, how disgusting' (283). Forced by Clive to take a wife, Harry first proposes to Mrs Saunders, who chooses to be alone, and then finds Ellen more receptive, though ironically their both being attracted to the same sex offers little prospect of conjugal bliss. Shortly afterwards Betty sees Clive kissing Mrs Saunders and attacks her. Clive springs to the rescue, declaring, 'Betty – Caroline – I don't deserve this – Harry, Harry' (297). To appease his wife, he embraces and kisses her, a show of affection between two male actors who again can be viewed as having either a heterosexual or homosexual relationship.

The basic doubleness of representation we find in act one has long been noticed by drama theorists who describe the paradox of acting in which the performer remains detached from the emotion of a role even while evoking this emotion in the spectator, as in Diderot's paradox between actor and spectator and Stanislavsky's paradox within actors observing themselves. But the paradox now is that roles and emotions are not more convincingly played but more convincingly undermined. As noted earlier, drama theorists point to a state of consciousness beyond ordinary emotion and speech, as in Brook's 'total theatre' which touches on the transcendent, and 'holy theatre' which makes the invisible visible; Grotowski's 'poor theatre' which induces a state of 'translumination' in performer and spectator; and Barba's 'transcendent' as a quality of the performer's presence. Theatre not only engages the critical mind, but also expands consciousness in performers and spectators (see Meyer-Dinkgräfe 2001). In 'Theatre Degree Zero', Ralph Yarrow develops this approach into a 'metaphysics of praxis' (Yarrow 2001a, 90). Thus, as Churchill so aptly demonstrates, self-discovery involves not so much knowing what you are, as knowing what you are not. This entails watching yourself carefully and rejecting or 'zeroing' all that doesn't go with the basic fact: 'I am.' The spectator in *Cloud Nine*, as in any theatrical doubleness of representation, is led away from the identification with 'I am this or that', whether 'this or that' is a performance, a role, a self-image or even a job, friends and family. What remains after racial, ethnic, professional, gender and other attributes fall aside is simply the 'I am' of impersonal, non-contingent being (*turiya*). In this process one goes from knowing and identifying with relative qualities, toward a state of pure knowingness beyond the subject/object duality of conceptual content. Even if distinctions remain in our awareness, sacred theatre can enhance our ability to see them as transitory properties of the mind and body, to witness them from the non-attachment of a qualityless, unidentifiable 'I am', which includes, yet goes beyond, duality. Churchill's feminist theatre accentuates this witnessing attention by deconstructing the oppositions that would preserve the masculine subject, however ambiguously or under threat, and by undermining any egoic identity by revealing it to be an illusion, nothing more than a relational matrix of multiple energies.

(iv) *Mindfulness*

Cloud Nine, therefore, not only challenges, as Brecht does, 'the traditional belief in the continuity and unity of the self' by showing how individuals evolve through different historical contexts (Speidel 1982, 45), it also undermines the notion that these contexts fully constitute the individual. The sacred quality of Churchill's theatre suggests that the individual, not completed by the sum of social fragments, has another dimension: mindfulness or witnessing awareness. The ability to develop mindfulness is part of the Theravada Buddhist tradition. As Wallace explains, mindfulness as a practice entails an observation of

> the body, feelings, mental states and mental objects of oneself and others. A common theme to each of these four applications of mindfulness is first considering these elements of one's own being, then attending to these same phenomena in others, and finally shifting one's attention back and forth between self and others. Especially in this final phase of practice, one engages in what has recently been called reiterated empathy, in which one imaginatively views one's own psychological processes from a 'second-person' perspective. (Wallace 2001, 213)

Churchill's doubling and cross-casting of characters encourages mindfulness, a second-person perspective between player and role, or as noted earlier the third-person perspective of Mead's notion of 'the generalized other' (Whitehead 2001, 18). When the player, such as Betty in act one, is a man in the role of a woman, s/he is spontaneously mindful of his/her multiple identities. The player/role division, far from locking the subject (performer/spectator) within binary oppositions, explodes all conceptual boundaries through a multiplicity that not only deconstructs one's gendered wholeness but also destroys the very concept of identity, whether essentialist or constructed. In breaking down masculine/feminine oppositions, the identities of the player/role mutually negate each other through a multiplicity of the 'I is not I', as Yarrow illustrates in his analysis of Beckett (84–89). Experiencing (non) identity as not this/not that (*neti, neti* in Buddhism) points to the qualityless state of 'I AM', the transpersonal witnessing awareness mirrored by sacred theatre.

(v) *Are We Really Free?*

In act two, as the pace slows down and the language expands to express unprogrammed desires, we see the effect of the power structure on sex and relationships. Clive is gone and with him the authoritative center, replaced by greater freedom and a corresponding uncertainty. Lin as a lesbian mother reverses Ellen's position in act one by making her own decisions without constant self-doubt and feeling the need for patriarchal approval. Scene one begins with Cathy, played by Clive, in a rebellious mood, responding to Lin's suggestions for games to play by repeating, 'Already done that' (289). Her attitude sets the mood of questioning and exploration in which the characters reject normative behaviour. As mothers in a park play centre, Lin says to Vic, 'I really fancy you' (290). In contrast to the first act where the women were usually confined indoors, the outdoor setting here fosters open expression and freedom of choice.

As Vic and Lin talk about their lives, we see their preoccupation with ordinary everyday concerns in which they make their own decisions:

Lin: I've got a friend who's Irish and we went on a Troops Out march. Now my dad won't speak to me.
Victoria: I don't get on too well with my father either.
Lin: And your husband? How do you get on with him?
Victoria: Oh, fine. Up and down. You know. Very well. He helps with the washing up and everything.
Lin: I left mine two years ago. He let me keep Cathy and I'm grateful for that.
Victoria: You shouldn't be grateful.
Lin: I'm a lesbian.
Victoria: You still shouldn't be grateful.
Lin: I'm grateful he didn't hit me harder than he did.
Victoria: I suppose I'm very lucky with Martin.
Lin: Don't get at me about how I bring up Cathy, ok?
Victoria: I didn't.
Lin: Yes you did. War toys. I'll give her a rifle for Christmas and blast Tommy's pretty head off for a start. [Tommy is Vic's son.]

[Victoria goes back to her book.] (291–92)

Lin has rejected certain aspects of her socially constructed identity, but she still craves acceptance by people she likes. The characters break taboos and find new identities, but the important thing in act two is not their new identities, which they eventually transcend, but the process of transformation itself: giving up the familiar world and their status quo as a substitute ideal, and seeking out instead new possibilities for love and happiness. The fact that the characters espouse one sexual preference over another is secondary to the fact that they have begun the process of transformation and self-discovery. The contrast between gays and straights adds another dimension to the doubleness of representation, sharpening awareness of both the arbitrary nature of all social conditioning, and of the need to deconstruct and overcome this conditioning, which gays and women may have more practice in than ordinary males.

Edward and Gerry talk about their different attitudes toward gender roles, with Gerry at one point describing in graphic detail a homosexual encounter with a stranger on the train, insinuating that he's more liberated that Edward. Later they discuss their relationship: Edward says he likes knitting and wants to be married, and Gerry says he doesn't mind the knitting but wants a 'divorce'. Afterwards, Edward discloses his bisexuality to Victoria:

Edward: I like women.
Victoria: That should please mother.
Edward: No listen Vicky. I'd rather be a woman. I wish I had breasts like that, I think they're beautiful. Can I touch them? (307)

By the end of act two, Lin, Vic and Edward have a *ménage à trois* that plays havoc with the doubleness of representation by being simultaneously heterosexual, homosexual and incestuous.

In contrast, Martin can only express a conventional desire for his wife and like most ordinary men feels insecure about discussing his sexual prowess. He talks about his feelings with Vic:

> Martin: My one aim is to give you pleasure. My one aim is to give you rolling orgasms like I do other women. So why the hell don't you have them? My analysis for what it's worth is that despite all my efforts you still feel dominated by me....You're the one who's experimenting with bisexuality, and I don't stop you, I think women have something to give each other. (301)

Martin feels insulted because he thinks Vic hasn't been able to get herself together, but Churchill suggests that none of the characters have succeeded in doing so, that their behaviour will never lead to the desired results. The point suggested here is not only that the characters will find it hard to make changes in their personal lives, to lay to rest the ghosts of Victorianism, but also that they will always face other conceptual or ideological constraints obstructing their happiness and freedom. The very absence of happiness and freedom, however, implies the possibility of their attainment. The performers and spectators intimate this, not by sensing the end of patriarchal hegemony, which they don't, but rather by co-creating an intersubjective space beyond language and the emotions of attraction/repulsion.

Churchill convincingly portrays this absence that leads to presence. A significant example is Betty, who divorces Clive at the beginning of act two in a futile attempt to break her ties with the past. Her children haven't fully accepted her, and she has lost her sense of independence. But finding a job gives her confidence and leads to her experimenting with autoeroticism: 'Afterwards I thought I'd betrayed Clive. My mother would kill me. But I felt triumphant because I was a separate person from them' (316). In an orgiastic ritual when Vic, Lin and Edward try drunkenly to evoke a mythical goddess, Vic says, 'You can't separate fucking and economics' (309). But, with her new job and eroticism, is Betty really fulfilled?

Critics have noted the lack of wholeness or completion in *Cloud Nine*. Act one does not complete the destruction of Victorianism, just as act two does not complete Betty's transformation. It offers only the 'before' and 'during' but not the 'after', which the audience must imagine for itself (Kritzer 129). The play dramatizes the point that 'before' and 'after' are conceptual constructs, that immediate reality is 'during', the on-going process of transformation that voids or zeroes thought. The sacredness of Churchill's theatre unfolds in the experience of 'during' as a space of inter-being that compels us to break out of a doubled reality mediated by representation – even while using representation as a means. The openness of 'during' takes precedence over the closure of 'before' and 'after' by collapsing oppositional structures in the immediacy of a presence between performer and spectator.

4.2 *M. BUTTERFLY*: THE PHENOMENOLOGY OF NONIDENTITY AND THEATRICAL PRESENCE

(i) *Introduction*

M. Butterfly by David Henry Hwang is widely regarded as 'the ultimate postmodern, poststructuralist play', blending periods and styles and suggesting that 'all intimate relationships are determined by politics' (Smith 1993, 44). Hwang himself in his Afterword says that he wanted to write a 'deconstructivist *Madam Butterfly*' (Hwang 1988, 95), to cut through the 'layers of cultural and sexual misperception' and reveal how 'considerations of race and sex intersect the issue of imperialism' (99, 100):

Heterosexual Asians have long been aware of 'Yellow Fever' – Caucasian men with a fetish for exotic Oriental women. I have often heard it said that 'Oriental women make the best wives.' (Rarely is this heard from the mouths of Asian men, incidentally.) This mythology is exploited by the Oriental mail-order bride trade which has flourished over the past decade. (98)

On this argument, the rhetoric of empire inexorably constructs identity. Patriarchy, as the basis for imperial conquest and colonial discourse, has inscribed hierarchical definitions of geopolitics, ethnicity, gender and race that valorize the West as masculine and powerful and denigrate the East as submissive and weak. In *M. Butterfly*, Rene Gallimard, a French diplomat in Beijing now jailed in Paris as a spy, fantasizes that he is Pinkerton in Puccini's opera and that his lover is Butterfly. By the end of the play he realizes their roles have been reversed: 'it is he who has been Butterfly,...duped by love; [while] the Chinese spy, who exploited that love, is therefore the real Pinkerton' (95–96). The play's Orientalism posits a binary through which the West defines itself in relation to the East, its Other, but as Hwang demonstrates masculinity is not an essential attribute of western identity.

The play abounds with alienation devices for deconstructing the notion of a unified subject and fixed meaning associated with Orientalism and its 'violent hierarchies'. But given the popular post-structuralist metanarrative that the self is a reactionary trope, that the metaphysics of presence is 'always already' an illusion, and that the only universality is our socially constructed identities, the question arises, what holds these identities together as dynamic matrices that function coherently within their discursive contexts? How tenable is the constructivist claim that our shifting subject positions designated by power relations are self-sustaining, that the self does not in fact extend beyond narrative conventions and discursive fields?

Post-structuralists argue that *M. Butterfly* reconstitutes identities as shifting positions in discursive fields. As Dorrine Kondo says, 'Hwang opens out the self, not to a free play of signifiers, but to a play of historically and culturally specific power relations. Through the linkage of politics to the relationship between Song and Gallimard, Hwang leads us toward a thoroughly historicized, politicized notion of identity' (Kondo, 22–23). Hwang de-essentializes identity and explodes stereotypical notions of gender and race and the abstract 'concept of self' (Kondo, 26). Kondo asserts that 'Asia is gendered, but gender is...not understandable without the figurations of race and power relations that inscribe it' (24–25). Similarly, David Eng, in his psychoanalytic reading, declares that the 'white diplomat's "racial castration" of Song...suggests that the trauma being negotiated...is not just sexual but racial difference' (Eng,

2), with sexuality and race being 'mutually constitutive and constituted' (5). But even if performers and audience do shift identities by resisting Althusser's interpellative injunction (1971), they would only have switched from one constructed position, one prison house of language to another with its own set of ideological constraints. How tenable is the generalizing third-person theoretical implication that our immediate first-person phenomenal experience outside discursive contexts is nothing but a liberal humanist delusion? I will suggest that in *M. Butterfly* Hwang creates a phenomenology of non-identity and theatrical presence between performer and spectator based on a recognition of self that exceeds and underpins constructed identity.

(ii) *Concept of Self vs. Pure Consciousness*

The demystification of the 'concept of self' refers literally not to a deconstruction of the self, but rather, as the phrase indicates, to a deconstruction of a concept, and the self, as a locus of integrated energy, is for all practical purposes not a concept. If self and concept (or thought) of self can be conflated, as post-structuralists seem to imply, then by inference a concept would be able to engage in thought and simultaneously be aware of itself in the act of thinking. But can thought be aware of itself? By implication the answer is yes if we accept the post-structuralist definition of the subject as a cultural construct dispersed along a chain of signifiers (Lacan 1978), subjugated by relations of race, gender and power. What in that case would distinguish us from zombies, hypothetically perfect physical duplicates who behave like their human originals but lack feelings and inner awareness? Although artificial intelligence or DNA computers, like zombies, can be said to engage in thought, they are not conscious entities, and as some argue may never become conscious. As far as we know, only humans and not machines, as discussed shortly in greater detail, can be aware of the act of thinking and appreciate the meaning of their thoughts. The constructivist fallacy is to conflate self and concept of self in humans, and thereby to implicate thought in the unlikely task of being aware of itself thinking. Kondo is an unwitting advocate of this position in her defence of Hwang's self-proclaimed deconstruction of essentialist identity:

> It [the play] subverts notions of unitary, fixed identities, embodied in pervasive narrative conventions such as the trope of the 'Japanese woman as Butterfly.' Equally, it throws into question an anthropological literature based on a substance-attribute metaphysics that takes as its foundational point of departure a division between self and society, subject and world. *M. Butterfly* suggests to us that an attempt to describe exhaustively and to fix rhetorically a 'concept of self' abstracted from power relations and from concrete situations and historical events, is an illusory task. Rather, identities are constructed in and through discursive fields, produced through disciplines and narrative conventions. Far from bounded, coherent and easily apprehended entities, identities are multiple, ambiguous, shifting locations in matrices of power. (Kondo, 26)

This claim is, of course, valid to the extent that the self identified as a container of substance-attributes is a function of the mind. As a storehouse of phenomenal qualities (qualia) within discursive fields, the mind is typically defined as non-material in opposition to the material body.

As we have seen, this mind/body opposition prevails only in the garden variety of western dualism. In the hard problem of the relation between the human brain and consciousness in cognitive science, the opposition is not between mind and body but increasingly between mind/body on the one hand and consciousness on the other. The mind is characterized by thought and corresponds to our constructed identity, while consciousness in its pure form is beyond thought and corresponds to the trans-verbal, transpersonal self. This self, recall, is what Antonin Artaud, in distinguishing between Oriental and Occidental theatre, refers to as 'a void in thought' (1958, 71). The mind/body and consciousness duality, with the mind/body defined as material and consciousness as non-material, derives from the Samkya-Yoga tradition of India (Pflueger 1998), but is increasingly accepted in the vast interdisciplinary field of consciousness studies in the West (Chalmers 1996; Forman 1998). The missing element in the western literary critical understanding of the self in general, and in the constructivist deconstruction of identity in particular, is an appreciation of the first-person experience of the self as pure consciousness, the void in thought associated by Artaud with Oriental theatre. This self as knower, which Arthur Deikman calls 'the internal observer' (Deikman 1996, 355), complements the third-person concept of self as known, a rhetorical construct or the 'Word as everything' associated with Occidental theatre (Artaud 1958, 68).

M. Butterfly questions the unified concept of self as a function of the mind, but in the process it opens up a theatrical space in which performers and spectators can experience the self as a function of consciousness without qualities (turiya). As Deikman notes, 'we know the internal observer not by observing it but by being it' (355, Deikman's emphasis). William Demastes says that theatre 'forces us to think materially about everything before us, even the apparently immaterial' (Demastes 2002, 42). But as Daniel Meyer-Dinkgräfe notes,

This is incorrect if we consider thinking. The immaterial cannot be thought about immaterially, because thinking is a function of the intellect, and the intellect, on the model of mind in Vedic literature, cannot grasp any more refined levels than itself, and thus cannot grasp the level of the immaterial, which is the level of pure consciousness' (Meyer-Dinkgräfe, 11, original emphasis).

Immaterial pure consciousness exceeds the material mind, just as the actor in entering a dramatic text exceeds the text, adding, as we shall see, the presence of a new life that the text does not exhaust.

(iii) Theatrical Gaps

For constructivists, Hwang powerfully exposes identity as being constructed through 'disciplines and narrative conventions' (Kondo, 26). But the interesting thing about Hwang's characters is that they do not consistently believe in themselves as coherent and easily apprehended linguistic or conceptual entities; instead they acknowledge the fact that their identities 'are multiple, ambiguous, shifting locations in matrices of power' (ibid.). If that is the case, and Gallimard informs the audience repeatedly in his frame rupturing comments that he lives subjectively within his unstable imagination, then which 'concept' is witnessing these shifting subject positions in the mind/body matrix of material power? Hwang's constantly shifting frames of reference and attention on dramatic technique focuses the performer and spectator on the process of re-presentation, on the forms of utterance that subvert iconicity and the illusion of a real or natural performance. This division between referential narrative and metanarrative, histoire and discours (Benveniste 1971, 209), or 'the simultaneous inscribing and subverting of the conventions of narrative' (Hutcheon 1989, 49), opens a gap between subject and object, consciousness and mind.

If Rene Gallimard and Song Liling do not identify with their shifting subject positions, then some modality of self must be witnessing these positions from the gaps in their 'rhetorical identification' (Burke 1966, 301). To see the 'bounded, coherent and easily apprehended entities' (Kondo, 26) of identity as illusory rhetorical constructs, as constantly changing and unreal, implies a non-changing dimension of the self that is possibly real. This distinction between the changing and non-changing, which is ultimately that between mind and consciousness, thought and a void in thought, pervades the play right from the opening scenes when Gallimard retells the narrative history of his relation with Song from his prison cell in Paris.

In deconstructing the axes of gendered, racialized and politicized identity, Hwang opens the dramatic spectacle from several points of view simultaneously, as Kondo, Haedicke, Lye and others have pointed out. The Brechtian practice (1964) of baring theatrical devices by presenting a diversity of visual frames has the effect of exposing monological perspectives as nothing more than competing ideologies. But something overlooked also occurs here. In his prison cell in scene one, Gallimard, downstage with 'a sad smile on his face', gazes upstage at a vision of Song, who appears as a 'beautiful woman in traditional Chinese garb, danc[ing] a traditional piece from the Peking Opera....without acknowledging him' (1). Gallimard says, 'Butterfly, Butterfly', and the audience watches Song dancing through his gaze. Right afterwards, as the stage directions indicate, Gallimard 'forces himself to turn away, as the image of Song fades out' (1), and the illusion of realism in Hwang's theatre – if its theatricality is not seen already as artificial – suddenly dissolves. The spectator's rhetorical identification with Gallimard's unitary gaze breaks up, a rupturing process that polysemously creates multiple points of view, those of performer and audience. The spectator, momentarily put in a self-reflexive state of non-(constructed) identity, must either choose or oscillate between them.

At the end of scene one, Gallimard again disrupts the frame, which by now has become a metaframe: 'With a flourish,...[he] directs our attention to another part of the stage' (2). The audience and Gallimard are now both spectators sharing a distant scene in which three characters on stage discuss Gallimard's notoriety. But instead of perceiving the scene as 'real', our joint spectators perceive it as a mediated doubling of narrative visualities. In a deconstructive interpretation like Kondo's, the disparity between a realistic and mediated frame leads the spectator to perceive any identity as already a social construct. This implies that unmediated subjectivity or trans-verbal first-person experience is an illusion, and that the only 'real' identity is a third-person objective representation of our linguistically splintered subjectivity. As Janet Haedicke notes,

> Gallimard's life story [is depicted] as 'always already' constructed much as Hwang has constructed Boursicot's history [in the playwright's notes]. Gallimard directly forewarns the audience that the illusion of unmediated subjectivity constitutes performance and that the specular eye/ I confuses theatre with history, history with truth, autobiography with life. (Haedicke 1992, 30)

By this account, our immediate first-person experience, as portrayed theatrically through the specular eye/I, confuses performance and history, or a constructivist notion of identity with an essentialist 'concept of self'. But how do these two mental constructs differ to begin with? Who is there to witnesses the shifting constructions of identity in the play's multiplying of narrative visualities along a hegemonic chain of signifiers?

While the constructivist position appears true on the level of mind, what emerges in the gaps between rhetorical identities in these early scenes and throughout the play is a taste of an underlying, trans-conceptual, self-referral consciousness (rasa). To demystify metanarratives and to refuse iconic representation can certainly deconstruct rhetorical identity as a conceptual absolute, but how reasonable is it to assume that this also delegitimates first-person subjectivity or consciousness per se, relegating the human being to the level of a machine? To define essentialist identity as a rhetorically fixed 'concept of self' is to confuse an absolute thought about the known with the knower as a void in thought. In the dialectic between Gallimard and the audience at the beginning of scene 3, act 1, Gallimard does not completely lose himself in the illusions of identity but rather toys with these illusions and bids the audience's indulgence. As Gallimard puts it:

> Alone in this cell, I sit night after night, watching our story play through my head, always searching for a new ending, one which redeems my honor, where she returns at last to my arms. And I imagine you – my ideal audience – who come to understand and even, perhaps just a little, to envy me. (4)

Gallimard enters the scene as one of the spectators, and through empathy the spectators can share his phenomenal experiences as well as the gaps between them. As the play demonstrates, he is not merely a mind/body with thoughts running through it; he is a conscious agent aware of the process of having thoughts. Thoughts about self-identity here coexist with self-referral consciousness, which simultaneously comprehends the value of change and nonchange, boundaries and unboundedness, thought and non-thought.[6] If we accept provisionally the Vedic definition of pure consciousness (sat-chit-ananda: being-consciousness-bliss (Deutsch 1973, 9)), then we are prepared to see how M. Butterfly reveals a presence in the interstices of thought. Gallimard and the spectators break their fixation on any particular role as a constructed identity not through the agency of the mind and its content, but through their presence in a void in thought, the interstices between the mind's rhetorical identifications.

(iv) Identity: Machine or Witness

In her analysis of gender identity in Simone de Beauvoir's Second Sex, Judith Butler writes that for 'Beauvoir, gender is "constructed," but implied in her formulation is an agent, a cogito, who somehow takes on or appropriates that gender and could, in principle, take on some other gender' (Butler 1990, 9). This cogito, which serves as a witness to mental content, remains firmly associated in feminist discourse with the mind rather than with consciousness or an essential self. Butler's only reference to anything resembling such a self is a critique of the sexist conflating of 'the universal person and the masculine gender', in which women are denigrated and men extolled as 'the bearers of a body-transcendent universal personhood' (1990, 9). While cogito can be understood as a representation of pure consciousness as the internal observer, the long association of patriarchy with body-transcendent universals in Judeo-Christian onto-theology has biased critics from recognizing this. They are blinkered from self-awareness by their political/historical preconceptions. Recently, Butler and others sought to redress the criticism made against post-structuralists for failing to take universality into account and for eroding 'its force by questioning its foundational status' (Butler 2000, 3). As a trope substituting for pure consciousness, the *cogito* suggests a capacity to stand outside of constructed identities and enjoy a degree of autonomy over the mind. Without the power of a thought-transcending self-referral, which phenomenological critics such as Georges Poulet discuss in terms of the subject-object division,[7] how would either Gallimard or Song be able to perform as transvestite protagonists?

In a review on 'three books that examine the future of artificial intelligence and claim that the human brain is in trouble', the British philosopher Colin McGinn says,

> Can machines duplicate the external intelligent behavior of humans? And can machines duplicate the inner subjective experience of people? Call these the questions of outside and inside duplication. What is known as the Turing test says in effect that if a machine can mimic the outside of a human then it has thereby replicated the inside: if it behaves like a human with a mind, it has a mind....However, the Turing test is seriously flawed as a criterion of mentality.
>
> (*New York Times Book Review*, 3 January 1999)

The three authors here are like deconstructive postmodernists who equate self and concept of self, subject and object, unmediated and mediated experience, Gallimard's theatrical representations and his first-person experience of life. What McGinn suggests is that human identity cannot be equated with the computational mind: 'It is true that human minds manipulate symbols and engage in mental computations, as when doing arithmetic. But it does not follow from this that computing is the essence of mind; maybe computing is just one aspect of the nature of mind' (*ibid.*). There are many kinds of computational systems, such as silicon chips or DNA computers, that can replicate the mind but have no consciousness. Human beings are distinct from computational systems primarily because of their conscious awareness, regardless of how duped they are about the identification between mind and consciousness. What Brechtian theatre with its narrative discontinuity, refusal of realism, and A-effect attempts to achieve ultimately is not a distinction between one imaginary unity of mind and another, but rather a distinction between mind and consciousness, knower and known. This distinction emerges when the Brechtian *gestus* – 'a gesture, a word, an action' that exposes 'the social attitudes encoded in the play-text' (Diamond 1988, 89) – succeeds in evoking the semiotically invisible; that is, when it directs attention from a self-dramatization to a self-shedding, thereby opening awareness to the coexistence of silence and dynamism, boundaries and unboudnedness characteristic of higher consciousness.

As McGinn notes,

> One aspect of mind wholly omitted by the computational conception is the phenomenological features of experience – the specific way a rose smells, for instance. This is something over and above any rose-related computations a machine might perform. A DNA computer has biochemical as well as computational properties; a conscious mind has phenomenological as well as computational properties. These phenomenological properties have a stronger claim to being distinctive of the mind than mere computational ones. There

is thus no reductive explanation of the mental in terms of the computational; we cannot regard consciousness as nothing but a volley of physically implemented symbol manipulations. (*NYTBR* 1999)

Proponents of artificial intelligence dispute the relevance of the phenomenological features of experience just as constructivist critics dispute the self as unmediated subjectivity. Both define humanity in terms of mental computation, as represented by third-person theoretical models, and question the validity of first-person experience – which in the form of pure witness antedates narrative constructs.[8] Gallimard, as theatrical witness, watches his life stories run through his head in the form of thoughts that Hwang renders to the audience through dramatic narrative. His thoughts depict the phenomenal features of his experience, the content of his awareness centered on his love for Song – however delusional – and his desire for sympathy from the audience as judge and jury. These phenomenal qualities are mental properties within awareness yet distinct from awareness, just as computation as the known is distinct from the knower. From an Advaitan perspective, 'The self is single. You are the self and you have ideas of what you have been or will be. But an idea is not the self' (Maharaj 1988, 188). Gallimard has ideas about the Orient, gender, Song and imperialist power, and as the play unfolds his ideas are debunked, but his witnessing self remains unchanged, until it is fatally overshadowed by the rhetorical identifications of the mind in the final scenes. As *M. Butterfly* suggests, 'The body appears in your mind, your mind is the content of your consciousness; you are the motionless witness of the river of consciousness which changes eternally without changing you in any way' (Maharaj, 199).

(v) *The Actor's Double Entry*
Gallimard dramatizes his own version of Puccini's opera *Madame Butterfly* as a frame to the representation he stages with Song. Haedicke writes that by staging a-play-within-a-play, Hwang displaces the binaries of presence/absence, reality/illusion, perceiver/perceived, subject/object, and thereby 'dismantles the spectator's unitary gaze as Gallimard…[and] attempts to perform another into existence' (31). But dismantling binaries can make a difference only if it shifts the field of perception between play and spectator from ordinary mental binaries to an awareness of the metabinary of the witnessing self as the ultimate frame of thought. Otherwise, the attempt to 'perform another into existence' will produce a mere mental existence, not a living consciousness. In his gloss on Puccini's opera, Gallimard creates a distance to his own rendition, characterizing Cio-Cio-San as 'a feminine ideal', and Benjamin Franklin Pinkerton of the US Navy as 'not very good-looking, not too bright, and pretty much a wimp' (5). Gallimard ends by saying, 'In the preceding scene, I played Pinkerton, the womanizing cad, and my friend Marc from school (Marc bows grandly for our benefit) played Sharpless, the sensitive soul of reason. In life, however, our positions were usually – always – reversed' (7). The play's Brechtian double casting and role reversal demystifies the process of dramatic representation. But the gaze will remain unitary, or a series of unitaries, incapable of dismantling binaries, if the spectator merely exchanges one of Gallimard's roles for another, without an appreciation of the interstices between them.

Critics typically overlook the implication of the A-effect: namely, that spectators cannot step beyond binaries by merely switching between interpellated positions. What happens when performer and spectator become critically aware of dismantling identification, besides shifting between different modes of thought? Arguably, it is not unreasonable to assume that they begin to purge their constructed identities by entering the gaps between them. How else would they elude the power relations latent within the political unconscious (Jameson 1981) responsible for violent hierarchies? Through the A-effect, performer and spectator may avoid conflating actor and role univocally, but to negotiate the play's multiple perspectives implies an awareness of non-attachment to any of them, even while simultaneously the thinking mind continues to identify with them in serial form. In common usage, the phrase 'shift' or 'expansion of consciousness' is used merely to describe a shift in mental content and ignores what the term consciousness potentially implies for a deconstructive theatre. One thing it does not imply, as suggested here, is that the self is fully determined by historical materialism, dispersed along a chain of signifiers.

The gaps exposed by theatrical alienation and historicization between knower and known, actor and character, theatre and history in M. Butterfly can be understood either as being confined within the mind, language and the text, or as opening a window beyond the mind to the freedom of self-awareness. This freedom, which differs from polysemy or textual indeterminacy, has radical implications for theatrical presence. As the play proceeds, Gallimard tends to dwell on the grand narratives of a unified realism based on racist/imperialist illusions about Song, gender and the Orient. After watching Song perform Madame Butterfly at the German ambassador's house, he says, 'I believed this girl, I believed in her suffering. I wanted to take her in my arms – so delicate, even I could protect her, take her home, pamper her until she smiled' (15–16). But Gallimard's desire for an iconic identity that would verify his preconceptions about East-West relations is immediately debunked by Song as a romantic stereotype. She asks, 'what would you say if a blonde homecoming queen fell in love with a short Japanese businessman?...I believe you would consider this girl to be a deranged idiot, correct? But because it's an Oriental who kills herself for a Westerner – ah! – you find it beautiful' (17). If the only thing this scene and others like it accomplish is to make the mind rethink its adherence to racial, ethnic or gender stereotypes, then its impact would be ineffective and ephemeral. Inevitably, the mind, like Gallimard's, would revert back to its pre-established patterns of thought. On the other hand, if the play prompts the spectator to move beyond identification altogether in a trans-conceptual awakening, which may initially go unnoticed by the thinking mind, then consciousness will be expanded. Awareness itself is changeless, and your own changelessness is so obvious you tend not to notice it unless it is brought to your attention. Arguably, Hwang makes it noticeable, aesthetically taking the audience from a Brechtian phenomenology to a taste of going over the top of conceptual boundaries altogether, and back again, until silence and dynamism can be held in awareness simultaneously.[9]

As an actor, then, Gallimard is also a spectator who ruptures the frame by commenting on his entry into the drama at different points throughout the performance. After his rendition of Madame Butterfly, the play-within-the-play, with himself as Pinkerton and Marc as Sharpless, he notes that 'The ending is pitiful. . . .' (15). Later in recounting his own story he says, 'I returned to the opera that next week, and the week after that . . .' (27). At the end of act 2, after his wife, Helga, says, 'I hope everyone is mean to you for the rest of your life', he turns to the audience and says, 'Prophetic' (75). In these entries and others like them Gallimard's reflexive commentaries exceed their conceptual content and open a space in the performance through which the spectator recognizes and identifies with the actor's self-referral posture. In his book

On Drama, Michael Goldman analyzes the process of recognition and identification in theatre, which he describes as 'making or doing identity' (Goldman 2000, 18). Although Goldman defines identity as an aspect of mind, his model touches on my analysis of the self through its emphasis on the 'most inward' part of mind (Goldman, 77) – or pure consciousness in Vedic psychology. Theatre, as Gallimard's performance demonstrates, portrays the confusions of self-identity, but his repeated entries into the text establishes what Goldman calls 'a self that in some way transcends the normal confusions of self' (18). Contrary to the popular post-structuralist view, Goldman defines 'subtext', the 'mutual permeability of actor and script', as not reducible to text (49). An actor's performance can always be treated semiotically,

> But in drama one finds inevitably an element in excess of what can be semiotically extracted—something that is also neither irrelevant to nor...completely independent of the text. No matter how exhaustively one tries to translate what an actor does with a script into a kind of writeable commentary on it, there will always also remain the *doing* of it—the bodily life of the actor moving into the world, at a specific moment in time, to set in motion these words, these gestures, these writeable ideas, this other identity. And, if the doing were itself to be reduced to a text, there would still remain the doing of the doing. The actor enters the text. (50, Goldman's emphasis)

If the actor's physical entry into the text, as subtext, exceeds what can be extracted semiotically, his entry as consciousness exceeds it even more so. Not only does the actor enter the text as Gallimard, he enters it self-reflexively, highlighting the gaps between text and subtext, enhancing for the audience the distinction between mind and consciousness, thought and awareness of having thoughts. In Hwang's treatment of subtext as a double entry, spectators still identify with the actor as mind/body, if only as a hypothetical construct. More subtly, they recognize the entry of Gallimard's trans-verbal, transpersonal self as their most intimate identity, the 'most inward' part of mind. As Goldman says, 'Contrary to Derrida, there is *always* an hors-texte, a place from which someone at some moment needs to enter, even to constitute the text as a text' (51, Goldman's emphasis). As the play dramatizes, there is also a place from which someone at some moment needs to enter the constructed self, which otherwise would languish as nothing more than what Peter Brook would call a 'deadly' text. Spectators recognize and identify with the actors' total entry into the play, 'making or doing identity', by means of consciousness, the non-constructed, non-changing internal observer, as *M. Butterfly*'s theatrical structure demonstrates,

(vi) *Changelessness and Presence*

Noticing changelessness requires the mirror of a theatrical presence, a space through which self and other, audience and performer can recognize their interconnectedness beyond the tokens of language and interpretation. When Song and Gallimard talk after her performance at the Beijing opera house, she remarks on his long absence since their first encounter: 'So, you are an adventurous imperialist?' (21). Although true in one sense, Gallimard denies the accusation, but she insists: 'You're a Westerner. How can you objectively judge your own values?' He replies: 'I think it's possible to achieve some distance', as he has been doing already as we have seen. Song suggests they go outside to escape the stink of the opera house, which he calls the 'smells of your loyal fans'. She retorts, 'I love them for being my fans, I hate the smell they leave behind. I too can distance myself from my people' (21). This exchange accentuates the possibility of standing outside of race, sexism and imperialism altogether, and entering a 'historyless' world, as postcolonial critics would argue (Ashcroft 2002, 33), even though the trans-Brechtian implications of this stance can easily go unnoticed. Two performers claim not to be who they seem to be historically, implicitly inviting the audience to share a dialogical space beyond their constructed identities. The shared space is dialogical because they mutually distance themselves from their respective people, East and West, dissolving into thin air the historical ground beneath them. Although the moment passes quickly, it lingers to the extent that Song asks Gallimard to be a gentleman and light her cigarette, thus reminding the audience that a covert distancing continues between Song as witness and her transvestite facade. Performers and audience share an intersubjective liminality between constructed identities. They embrace simultaneously the constructed and decontextual dimensions of self – contrary to the generalizing discourse that finds only a seamless continuum of interpellated positions trapped within matrices of language and power.

Toulon, the French Ambassador, says to Gallimard that he has noticed a change in him:

> Want to know a secret? A year ago, you would've been out. But the past few month, I don't know how it happened, you've become this new aggressive confident...thing. And they also tell me you get along with the Chinese. So I think you're a lucky man, Gallimard. Congratulations. (37–38)

The obvious interpretation of these remarks is that Gallimard's conquest of Song has given him a newfound sense of masculinity and power. But Gallimard's sense of power may derive not so much from his contact with Song, per se, as from his having intermittently distanced himself from his various constructed identities, to the point where he is no longer cowed by any of them as being irrevocable. Something else lies beyond them, even though in the end he loses sight of this and succumbs to his fixating ideas.

It is not illogical to assume, then, that M. Butterfly, in creating a space devoid of textual identities behind the play-acting, suggests the presence of consciousness devoid of qualities. Performer and spectator may taste this theatrical void (rasa) for only a succession of fleeting subliminal moments, but to deny the intersubjective space of the witnessing observer as a real presence would be in effect to contradict the demystification of unitary, fixed identities. Without this trans-textual self, the deconstruction of stereotypes would leave you with a mere succession of thoughts, each fixed and unitary, however vast the constellation of alternatives. Through the movement of différance Derrida attempts to undermine logocentrism and establish a democracy free of privileged hierarchies: man/woman, white/brown, West/East, powerful/submissive. But as noted earlier, without the controlling influence over thought by consciousness, any dismantled binary will inevitably devolve into another hierarchy by dint of racist, sexist and political forces. While Derrida hopes to resist this trend through constant vigilance, M. Butterfly and history both suggest that without the spontaneous input of the internal observer, the intellect struggles in vain.

Ostensibly, then, a Brechtian, purely intellectual demystification does not liberate Gallimard of his racial stereotypes. We see this failure in the way he repeatedly ruptures the theatrical narrative only to retreat into Orientalist deceptions. Visiting Song who is still offstage, Gallimard tells the audience what he thinks of her: 'She is outwardly bold and outspoken, yet her heart is shy and afraid. It is the Oriental in her at war with her Western education' (27). Later in the same scene, he says to the audience, 'Did you hear the way she talked about Western women? Much differently than the first night. She does – she feels inferior to them – and to me' (31). While the dramatic irony allows the audience to see through the sham, and even to taste the self-reflexive void in thought that Gallimard points to, Gallimard himself is always at risk as he floats in and out of his various roles, intermittently sharing with the audience a liminal presence/absence of the self as consciousness.

This presence/absence underlies Gallimard's realization that his thinking mind is not always in control of his theatrical representations. In act 2, Toulon refers to the gossip of Gallimard's 'keeping a native mistress' (45), and comments approvingly, 'Now you go and find a lotus blossom...and top us all' (46). From the self-referral margins of his constructed identity, Gallimard tells the audience, 'Toulon knows! And he approves!' (46). In this liminal space he feels empowered. But right afterwards when Song appears and Comrade Chin intrudes, he protests, 'No! Why does she have to come in?' (47). The attempt to control the scene suggests that he has already half shifted toward a position of agency, a *cogito* outside of re-presentation and constructed identity. The discontinuity between dramatic frames opens gaps between conceptual reifications, evoking a taste of witnessing consciousness in performer and audience.

(vii) *False Reversals*

Some critics, as Haedicke notes, believe that M. *Butterfly* ultimately posits a fixed subject by simultaneously salvaging the position of 'hero' while attempting to deconstruct it (29). This seems to occur in Gallimard's ritual suicide at the end of the play, when his mind fixates on one of the play's multiple perspectives. Tina Chen (1994) and Coleen Lye (1995), for example, think that M. *Butterfly* fails to achieve a transformation on the spectator because she identifies with Gallimard univocally as a tortured protagonist. In the first half of the play, as we have seen, the Brechtian mechanism demystifies its dramatic representations, setting up for the audience a subliminal distinction between two levels of subjectivity: mind and consciousness. In the second half beginning in act 2, Gallimard and Song compete for control over the play, which retreats to the fixed representation of binaries and their restricting influence on the subject positions of the audience. By this stage, however, Hwang's theatre goes beyond the Brechtian A-effect, revealing the possibility of self-identity devoid of attributes.

By the end of the play, Gallimard suffers a relapse when he cross-dresses into the role of Madame Butterfly after Song discards his own transvestite identity. Although the masculine/feminine and West/East hierarchies seem to be reversed, they end up being preserved instead, at least as discerned by the thinking mind. Throughout act 3, Song and Gallimard repeatedly rupture the dramatic narrative. At the beginning of scene 1 in the courthouse, Song reviews his career for the audience: 'So I'd done my job better than I had a right to expect' (80). His opening re-performance puts the audience at a critical distance from the rest of the scene, which serves as a meta-commentary on Orientalism. In response to the Judge's questions, which centred on whether or not Gallimard knew he was a man, Song demystifies western men in relation to Oriental women, but without satisfying the Judge, or the audience, about what Gallimard may or may not have known. The upshot of his analysis of Gallimard is that when he 'finally met his fantasy woman, he wanted more than anything to believe that she was, in fact, a woman....And being an Oriental, I could never be completely a man' (83).

Like Song in scene 1, Gallimard opens scene 2 by addressing the spectators, again rupturing their uneasy fix on constructed identity. He says that 'even in this moment [of greatest shame] my mind remains agile, flip-flopping like a man on a trampoline. Even now, my picture dissolves, and I see that...witness...talking to me' (84). On Gallimard's cue, two things occur: Song, who is standing in the witness box, turns to address him, 'Yes. You. White man'; and the spectators 'witness' the postmodern attempt to distinguish between appearance and reality, theatre and world. But something peculiar happens here to the tradition of stage phenomenology with its gap between reality and theatre. While Gallimard confesses to Song, 'I know what you are....A – a man' (87), and Song insists, 'Wait. I'm not "just a man"' (84), Gallimard sends him away: 'You showed me your true self. When all I loved was the lie....Get away from me! Tonight, I've finally learned to tell fantasy from reality. And, knowing the difference, I choose fantasy' (89–90). The postmodern ambiguity of multifaceted identities prevails throughout the scene, but Gallimard's choice is more complicated than he thinks.

In the postmodern world, with simulation found not only in theatre but permeating all cultural forms, distinguishing fantasy from reality, theatre from world, is like distinguishing constructed identity from concept of self. There is no difference between them insofar as both are equally imaginary. Likewise, the Orientalism of the world and as re-presented in M. Butterfly is also equally imaginary. As Guillermo Gómez-Peña puts it in his performance piece The New World Border, 'Is this re-a-li-ty or performance? Can anyone answer?!' (Gómez-Peña 1994, 127); 'I want everyone to repeat after me: "This is art (pause); this is not reality (pause). Reality is no longer real"' (131). As Hwang's theatre suggests, in spite of the illusory gap between world and simulation, any hope of attaining reality in theatre depends on whether the audience merely shuffles mental content and its constructed identities, or enters the interstices of pure consciousness. For theatre to close off its re-presentation in reference to an all pervasive simulacrum, the audience must know the self as consciousness by being it, not by observing it.

After donning the kimono, Gallimard says, 'Death with honor is better than life...life with dishonor. . . It is 19__. And I have found her at last. In a prison on the outskirts of Paris. My name is Rene Gallimard—also known as Madame Butterfly' (92–93). As Lye notes,

> If what Hwang objects to...is that the West 'wins,' then it is not surprising that the response should present a scenario in which the East 'wins' instead. This structure of winning and losing expresses itself...in problematically conventional ways, through gender and sexual signification. The feminizing effect of Song's gender disclosure upon Gallimard follows from M. Butterfly's proposal that Orientalism functions to secure Western masculinity....The problem, however, is that M. Butterfly attempts not just to dramatize the effects of Orientalist desire, but to naturalize its origins. Orientalist fantasy, in M. Butterfly serves to secure Western masculinity because the West is shown as 'actually' 'emasculated'. (Lye 1995, 274–75)

If the underlying hierarchy is preserved rather than subverted in act 3, it is because the mind, although intermittently transcended during the play, will continue to identify with limiting conceptual constructs until fully liberated. Theatre can aesthetically point the way by providing a taste of pure consciousness (rasa). Gallimard directs us beyond rhetorical constructs, but then reverts to a binary either/or logic, as represented by the familiar world of all-pervading simulated conceptual boundaries, however repugnant. This action shifts the burden of dis-identification back to the spectator, who must learn to act on the level of witness as well as thought. Gallimard's suicide reveals the danger of mental constructs, the illusion not only of unitary conceptual identity but also of the pseudo-freedom of choice. Angela Pao has faulted critics for their inadequate 'reading and viewing competencies' that have led them to 'ignore' the postmodern impulses of Hwang's formal techniques (Pao 1992, 4–5). But simply choosing among shifting postmodern identities does not engender freedom from simulacra, which calls for renouncing all identifies on the groundless ground of self beyond attributes, as opposed to self as essentialist concept.

(vii) *Theatre and Metanarrative*
As we have seen, Kondo (1990) and Lye (1995) (among others) argue that the identities of self (West/masculine) and Other (East/feminine) must not be dealt with as ahistorical, as grand narratives, but instead as micro narratives based on particular historical circumstances. When Lyotard says, 'Simplifying in the extreme, I define *postmodern* as incredulity toward metanarratives' (1986, xxiv), he delegitimates not only the narrative function, but also the 'concept of self' – which in narrative as argued here serves as a (false) representation of consciousness. Lyotard's notorious vagueness about the material causes of the decline of metanarratives has led to considerable speculation. One possible cause not mentioned before, as far as I know, centres on the complementarity between mind/history/narrative on the one hand and consciousness/non-history/non-narrative on the other. Grand narratives often deal with experiences on the margins of thought, beyond ordinary conceptual knowledge, like the nature of Enlightenment, the prospect of emancipation from bondage, the development of a more self-conscious human being or an evolved 'Spirit' (Lyotard 1986, xxiii, 23). These phenomena stretch the thinking mind's capacity to know. To talk about the rational subject becoming Spirit or 'enlightened' is pointless if we limit this process to a function of mind, when it entails the transcending of thought. Narrative representations of trans-rational, trans-verbal experience, as in theatre, are in a sense mis-re-presentations insofar that they point beyond narrative form altogether, to an hors-texte. The question is not whether theatre as simulation can bridge the gap with reality – for, as Hwang dramatizes, everyday reality is simulated to begin with – but whether theatre can reveal the reality of self responsible for all simulation, both in stage drama and social drama.

The crisis of metanarratives can thus be traced to the fact that narratives are challenged to re-present that which lies beyond symbol and interpretation, beyond *gestus* – like the gaps in Gallimard's constructed identities. While narrative can render phenomenal content, it can only intimate consciousness through the aesthetic power of suggestion (*rasa*), as M. *Butterfly* so effectively demonstrates. Moreover, as third-person representation, it is not unreasonable to assume that while the delegitimizing effect of narrative can apply to the known, it cannot apply to the first-person knower, which is self-shining and knowable not through observation but only '*by being it*' (Deikman 1996, 355).

Incredulity toward metanarratives, then, clearly reflects the postmodern lack of appreciation for transcendental consciousness. We see this in the plethora of anti-essentialist criticism of M. *Butterfly*, and in the postmodern disregard for changelessness, which like the gaps in Gallimard's constructed identities so easily escapes notice. On the one hand, narratives have traditionally served to reflect phenomenal experience (Lodge 2002), and sometimes, whether intentionally or not, consciousness itself (Malekin and Yarrow 1997). The postmodern over-valorization of mental computation and materialism at the expense of a concrete experience of more abstract levels of self seems to have undermined the suggestive power of narrative, whether grand or micro. On the other hand, however, postmodern incredulity has had the ironic effect of subverting faith in just about everything that forms the content of consciousness, leading the *cogito* to disidentify with its personal attributes. Thus, by its very negativity, Hwang's post-structuralist play underscores the existence of a transpersonal, immaterial knower, without whom incredulity would not have a witnessing agent. The debate over the ending of *M. Butterfly*, whether or not it transforms the spectator, stems in part from 'the simultaneous inscribing and subverting of the conventions of narrative' (Hutcheon 1989, 49) – the simultaneity here revealing the inteconnectedness of all levels of self. You can demystify Gallimard as a social construct, but his self-referral awareness as available to the spectator and sometimes to himself transcends, while simultaneously complementing, his iconic symbolism in the staging of a theatrical presence.

Chapter 5

IONESCO

5.1 RHINOCEROS

William S. Haney II

(i) *Riding on the Back of Rhinos*

The notion of suggestion (*dhvani*) in Sanskrit poetics operates in connection with aesthetic rapture (*rasa*). The theory of *rasa* is comparable to the notion of defamiliarization in Russian formalism and to the alienation effect in Bertolt Brecht, which Tony Bennett describes as a way 'to dislocate our habitual perception of the real world so as to make it the object of renewed attentiveness' (Bennett 1979, 20). By remaining detached from any specific emotion through aesthetic rapture, a theatre audience will appreciate the whole range of possible responses to a play without being overshadowed by any one in particular. As such, the taste of *rasa* involves an idealized flavour and not a specific transitory state of mind. It invokes the emotional states latent within the mind through direct intuition and thus provides an experience of the subtler, more unified levels of the mind itself. In terms of the connection between consciousness and language, *rasa* moves awareness from the temporal to the unified levels of language, from *vaikhari* and *madhyama* toward *pashyanti* and *para*. As aesthetic experience, *rasa* culminates in a spiritual joy (*santa*) described by K. Krishnamoorthy as 'wild tranquility' or 'passionless passion' (Krishnamoorthy 1968, 26). *Rasa* allows consciousness to experience the unbounded bliss inherent within itself, those levels of awareness associated with *pashyanti* and *para*. As S. K. De says, 'an ordinary emotion (*bhava*) may be pleasurable or painful; but a poetic sentiment (*rasa*), transcending the limitations of the personal attitude, is lifted above such pain and pleasure into pure joy, the essence of which is its relish itself' (De 1963, 13). As described in Indian literary theory, this experience is the nearest realization through theatre and the other arts of the Absolute or *moksa* (liberation). As Daniel Meyer-Dinkgräfe notes, 'The spiritual aspect of the meaning of *rasa* is emphasized in Shankara's commentary of the Upanishadic use of the term: "*Rasa* is here used to mean such bliss as is innate in oneself and manifests itself [. . .] even in the absence of external aids to happiness"' (Meyer-Dinkgräfe 2005, 95; Rhagavan 1988). In *Rhinoceros*, Bérenger moves the audience from specific thoughts and emotions associated with conformity to a collective psychosis toward a release from specific emotional attachments in the self-referral experience of *rasa*. We see this happening in his arguments with Jean, Dudard and Daisy as he tries to prevent them from changing into rhinos under the false pretext of enhancing their power and beauty.

Aesthetic rapture as argued here can be induced in a manner unrelated to the notion of the sublime understood as a quality of conscious content. Ultimately *rasa* emerges from the qualityless gap between thoughts as the awareness transcends mental content. For instance, after the second rhino kills the Housewife's cat in act one, Jean and Bérenger argue over whether it had one horn or two, with other characters interjecting their own observations between their insults. Jean claims that the first one was an Asiatic rhino with two horns while the second was an African rhino with only one horn. Bérenger replies, 'You're talking nonsense...How could you possibly tell about the horns? The animal flashed past at such speed, we hardly even saw it . . .' (36). Bérenger later regrets his enraged verbal assault, which he suspects may have pushed Jean over into becoming a rhino himself. For spectators, however, his quarrel has the opposite effect of directing them toward the essential nature of humanity through *rasa* as a taste of the void of conceptions.

> Jean: I don't have to grope my way through a fog. I can calculate quickly, my mind is clear! [. . .]
> Bérenger: But it had its head down. [. . .]
> Jean: Precisely, one could see all the better. [. . .]
> Bérenger: Utter nonsense. [. . .]
> Jean: What me? You dare to accuse me of talking nonsense? [. . .]
> Bérenger: Yes, absolute, blithering nonsense! [. . .]
> Jean: I've never talked nonsense in my life! [. . .]
> Bérenger: You're just a pretentious show-off—(*Raising his voice.*) a pedant! [. . .]. (37–38)

As they continue arguing, Jean says that if anyone has two horns it's Bérenger, who he calls an 'Asiatic Mongol!' Bérenger replies: 'I've got no horns. And never will have,' to which Jean retorts, 'Oh yes, you have!' (38). What this dispute foreshadows and confirms in retrospect is that Jean is indeed full of nonsense and that Bérenger is the only one who will remain hornless. In addition, this argument like all the arguments of the play serves to shift the spectator's awareness from the level of thought toward the void of conceptions in the manner of a Zen koan. As Bérenger and Jean argue about whether a rhino has one horn or two, the audience would no doubt finds this question absurd in light of the more critical issue of where the rhinos came from in the first place, what causes them to multiply in a small provincial French town, and how many more of them might appear to the risk of not only pet cats but the entire population. Spectators may feel superior to the characters who engage in such an absurd argument, but they would also be hard-pressed to answer these questions for themselves. The difficulty of solving an absurd paradox, one that becomes even more absurd as the characters begin changing into rhinos, would preclude not only a logical solution but also the possibility of the audience piecing together a meaningful life based on the intellect absorbed in the finite material values of daily life as opposed to the nonlocal experience of pure awareness. Boyer says that 'Brain and mind are no longer just in the head, because brains, minds, and all material objects are no longer just localized physical matter, but rather are also more abstract but real nonlocal processes in a subtler underlying field of existence' (Boyer 2006, 4). Ionesco's play through the device of rasa allows the audience to swing from the thinking (apprehending and comparing) level of mind to a more subtle underlying field of existence where conventional logic no longer obtains. In other words, the audience experiences aesthetic rapture (rasa) not through the sublime as a qualitative conscious content of the mind, but rather through a process that transports them beyond the mind toward a void in thought. This void constitutes the source of Bérenger's intuition of the moral superiority of retaining his humanity in the face of pressure to conform to a collective psychosis. Rhinoceros, by dramatizing the plight of an individual caught between conformity and defiance, also takes the spectator toward a sacred experience.

In act two we first learn that humans are metamorphosing into rhinos when the wife of one of Bérenger's colleagues, Mrs. Boeuf, arrives at the office to announce that her husband is ill. She tells her husband's office mates, including Bérenger, that she was chased all the way to the office by a rhinoceros. Suddenly she recognizes the rhino as her husband: 'It's my husband. Oh Boeuf, my poor Boeuf, what's happened to you?' When questioned by Daisy, Mrs. Boeuf says, 'I recognize him, I recognize him!' (61). She exclaims that 'He's calling me', and instead of abandoning him she jumps from the window landing to join him and by implication becomes a rhino herself. Ionesco combines absurdity with humour when he has Papillon, their boss, say, 'Well! That's the last straw. This time he's fired for good!' (ibid.). Later in act two, scene two, Bérenger visits Jean, who is ill at home with a headache, and apologizes for their quarrel, explaining that 'in our different ways we were both right' (71). To his amazement, Bérenger finds Jean undergoing a distinct transformation, with his breathing becoming boorishly heavy, a bump growing on his forehead and his skin turning green. Obviously turning into a rhino, Jean accuses Bérenger of 'scrutinizing me as if I were some strange animal', and then begins to distance himself from his friend psychologically; 'There's no such thing as friendship. I don't believe in your friendship' (74–75). When Bérenger comments on Jean's 'misanthropic mood', Jean displays a change of attitude that indicates a transformation on the level of body that reflects a pre-existing state of mind: 'It's not that I hate people. I'm just indifferent to them – or rather, they disgust me; and they'd better keep out of my way, or I'll run them down' (75–76). The play suggests that no matter how morally weak and disgusting the human race, how boring and empty the life of the bourgeois working world, and how susceptible the human race is to conforming to collective psychosis, when humans transform into rhinos they will take all these negative attributes and situations with them.

In defending Boeuf's transformation into a rhino against Bérenger's feeling that it won't improve his life or enhance his pleasure, Jean says, 'You always see the black side of everything. [. . .] I tell you it's not as bad as all that. After all, rhinoceroses are living creatures the same as us; they've got as much right to life as we have!' (78–79). Bérenger goes back to the innate sense that 'we have our own moral standards which I consider incompatible with the standards of these animals' (79). Although in one sense Jean is right in wanting to replace morality with nature, his interpretation of nature, which does not extend beyond the ordinary levels of language and conceptuality, consists of no more than extending morality from mental to physical laws, which an we have seen belong to the same category. As Bérenger puts it, Jean goes for 'the law of the jungle' (ibid.). Bérenger observes that unlike animals, human civilization has evolved a philosophy of life, but Jean rejects the value of this idea: 'Humanism is all washed up! You're a ridiculous old sentimentalist' (80). Again, on a purely conceptual level Jean has a point, but the alternative provided by a new philosophy based on a different set of laws associated with rhinoceritis proves ineffectual in lifting humanity out of the jungle, whether of the natural or concrete variety.

In terms of aesthetic response to this dramatic turn of events, the audience will find itself in a dilemma. Ionesco suggests that any material change in life, which applies to both aspects of the formula 'existence precedes essence', would only leave humans in the same benighted condition. Changing existence on a physical level does not differ from changing essence on a psychological level in the sense that both mind and body constitute a physical element as opposed to consciousness, which comprises the only non-physical, non-local underlying dimension of the human condition. Through *rasa*, Ionesco's play alters the level of consciousness of the audience through the change undergone by Bérenger, the only character who transcends the physical mind/body component of life through a transformation based on knowledge-by-identity. As mentioned earlier, Samkhya-Yoga (the third system of Indian philosophy) states, 'there are two irreducible, innate, and independent realities in our universe of experience: 1. consciousness itself (*purusha*); 2. primordial materiality (*prakrti*)', which includes the thinking mind (Pflueger 48). Advaita Vedanta and Samkhya-Yoga elaborate on this distinction between mind and consciousness, with the mind including the intellect, emotions and all the qualities (qualia) of phenomenal experience: perceptions, memories, sensations, moods, etc. In contrast, consciousness (*purusha*) is distinct from primordial materiality (*prakrti*) with its 23 components, including mind (*manas*), intellect (*buddhi, mahat*) and ego (*ahamkara*) (Pflueger 1998, 48). Intellect, mind and ego along with thought, feeling and perception like those adhered to by the rhino/rationalists comprise different forms of nonconscious matter, all of which make up the *content* of witnessing consciousness (*purusha*). This tradition underlies the model for theatrical experience presented in *The Natyasastra*. The mind/consciousness distinction, in which both mind and body are unequivocally material, differs as mentioned earlier from the garden variety of mind/body dualism in western thought (Pflueger 1998, 49). The material content of experience related to the intellect, mind and ego comprises only part of experience, which is made whole by the element of consciousness itself. Ionesco's theatrical devices – the absurdity, humour, dis-identification, and unpredicatability – serve to heighten the sense of a distinction between mind and consciousness, if only subliminally. Spectators are encouraged to leap-frog into a trans-conceptual space after language has run its course, to witness the mind reflexively as it plays with logical conundrums. We find the sacredness of Ionesco's theater, then, like that of Pinter's, in its pointing away from the agitated mind toward the joys of unbounded consciousness.

The main field of play in Ionesco's *Rhinoceros*, then, is not confined to the realm of ideas, but rather leads the audience beyond conceptuality toward a taste of the gap between socially constructed identities. These identities consist of thoughts that hold us to the world of wish fulfilment and material desires. Ionesco's *Rhinoceros* induces in the audience an aesthetic experience (*rasa*) through devices such as absurdity, the dream-like nature of reality, illogical argumentation and duplicitous wrangling between friends that swing the awareness between ordinary day-to-day psychological consciousness, and a more highly developed spiritual consciousness. On the one hand we have the rationalists who operate out of ordinary self-interested cravings, and on the other hand Bérenger who exhibits an increased ethical discernment based on a greater purity of consciousness. Through *rasa*, the audience shares in

Bérenger's unconditional love, egolessness, purity of compassion and even in the taste of an experience beyond a knowledge-by-acquaintance of socially induced identities. In *Arcadia* Tom Stoppard produces a similar effect through the juxtaposition of a series of temporal and conceptual oppositions that ultimately lead to an experience of unity.

5.2 THE CHAIRS

Peter Malekin

(i) *The Play's the Thing*

Drama only becomes drama when the score (text) is performed. In the theatre this entails all the complexities of realized interpretation, as well as the quirks, skills and limitations of actors and audiences. In the modern theatre it also tends to involve the prejudices or predeterminations of the director. Even reading a play in isolation implies a mental interpretation, which may be novelistic and flat, but even so remains an interpretation. The drama thus has three aspects. The first consists of the implied action, and the thought and words in the text. The second consists of the factors of staging, the spatial dynamics, together with the pace and varied pitch of verbal delivery that together create the rhythms and suspensions or gaps of actual performance. The gaps can be anything from total immobility and silence, or even an empty stage or performance space, to moments of silent action or tension within the dialogue. The third aspect is the audience itself in performance, or to a lesser extent the reader of a play text. The range of consciousness available to an audience at the point of performance is a governing factor (it is, of course, not identical with intellectual intelligence). It can inspire competent actors to performances of which they never dreamt they were capable. It can pull down competent actors to a level of gross performance pervaded by inertia. The resonance (the range of multiplicity of meanings and the emergence of that which makes plays of meaning possible) is broadened infinitely or contracted to a narrow band of crude and obvious signification accordingly.

A drama as a totality is an abstraction taking in text, actual and potential interpretations and actual and potential performances and audiences, just as the abstraction of a human being takes in a progress and bewildering changes through time and space, a medley of contradictory relationships and behaviours, a changing physiological make-up, a changing collection of attitudes and ideas, and a potential reach before birth and after death, as well as 'sideways' to the complex amorphous totalities of humanity in general, the eco-system and the cosmos stretching to infinity. In immediate terms the abstraction is, like everything else around us, a sort of reality. We form it in the process of grasping a particular play, but in doing so we form a mental object which is unfocused yet a potentiality for mental foci of various sorts. We have a sense of the 'movement' of the play as a kind of overall shape (thus spanning static pattern and temporal-spatial extension). We also have a sense of what we thought important or striking about it, plus a lot of our own feelings and ideas, amalgamated into a preformal potentiality, from which we can call up specific formulations (anything from mental production to extended commentary) at will. The 'play' thus becomes a complex of feelings and ideas residing in our minds, part of us, a kind of presence that may go through life with us. This 'presence' then itself changes with renewed experience of productions or reading, grows and transforms in tandem with the rest of our living, in a manner akin to the way our perceptions of others as well as ourselves changes over time.

The play is thus amorphous, inclusive and non-existent. What we call a reality. In what follows I will snatch at this reality in *The Chairs*.

(ii) *Ionesco's* Working Methods

Ionesco has written quite a lot about his motivation as a writer and the source of his work, and also about some of his plays, including *The Chairs*. In 'L'auteur et ses problèmes', reprinted in *Notes et contre-notes*, he comments that he feels that he does not entirely belong to the world (Ionesco 1964, 19). In spite of having acquired the habit of being here, he adds,

> I have, rather, the impression that I am from somewhere else. If I knew what this elsewhere was, it would be much simpler. (Ibid. 19)

The consequence is 'une nostalgie incompréhensible', an incomprehensible nostalgia, which may be for a 'here' that cannot be refound. His 'I' is difficult to define. As he wanders in the world, he experiences nostalgia and astonishment. Sometimes he appears to have orienting landmarks, then they vanish. He accepts both that he has failed to impose order on the contradictions and that we live on different levels of consciousness that are contradictory.

> From time to time, I believe I believe, I think I think, I take sides, I choose, I struggle, and when I do so I do it with vehemence and stubbornness. But within me there is always a voice which tells me that this choice, this vehemence, this affirmation have no certain, no absolute foundation, that I should renounce them. I have not wisdom enough to connect my acts to my deep uncertainty. (Ibid. 20)

It is out of this quandary that he writes.

Two consequences of the predicament are the strangeness of the world, revealed to an attentive glance in moments of respite from daily routines, and the experience of the writer in the moment of creation:

> He suddenly feels a world, expected and unexpected, revealing itself and rising up before his astonished eyes. (43)

The world is, thus, new and the work is new (its individual newness is the mark of its authenticity), and there is astonishment, and nostalgia, and recognition. Ionesco does not say, but the expectedness of the new could imply, that the work is in some measure a revelation of the elsewhere, which must then lie as a memory or a reality in the artist's mind, and since the reader or audience share the experience, in their minds too.

This shared recognition of the experienced work is a sign of its objectivity: 'In his deep subjectivity, the artist is essentially objective' (29); and it is deep rather than superficial subjectivity because the artist moves beyond ambition, profit and personal motives in creating. 'All dogmatisms are provisional' Ionesco also remarks, and he rejects 'le théâtre à thèse', a theatre of theses and dogmatic propositions (22, 42). Instead he writes out of the meaninglessness of life, which is its refusal to fit into the categories of theology, philosophy or politics. It is a 'désarroi', a disarray, a refusal of the imposed order of man.

I think I am more authentic when I express in my works astonishment and disarray. Into this astonishment plunge the roots of life. In the uttermost depths within me it is night that I find..., night, or rather a blinding light. (23, marks of suspension in original)

A blinding light is not a light you can see by. Nor is it simply darkness. It is either a half-realized potentiality for objective sight, or it is the overwhelming of the mind in a 'seeing' that passes beyond the subject-object, where sight in the ordinary sense no longer has existence or meaning. Conversely the 'meaning' that such an overwhelming of seeing is in itself cannot be rendered in terms of discursive subject-object 'meanings'. If the latter interpretation of the 'blinding light' is adopted, the result is paradox, Dionysius's 'dazzling darkness of the secret silence' or the experience pointed to by Plotinus's 'strictly we should put neither a This nor a That to it; we hover, as it were, about it, seeking the statement of an experience of our own, sometimes nearing this Reality, sometimes baffled by the enigma in which it dwells' (Plotinus 6.9.3.539).

Such experience could of course be delusion. But then so could ordinary experience of ordinary reality. We can, if we wish, simply shut the question down, ignoring all but the everyday. If we do not wish to do do this, then the best approach seems to be an open-minded probing that neither prescribes the limits of questions nor imposes answers. The refusal to prescribe questions includes a refusal to confine questioning to intellectual formulation, for we also question with our feelings, our intuition and our bodies. Such a questioning implies an alert and intelligent openness. Only we do not appropriate, for appropriation is imposition.

This seems to be what Ionesco is getting at when he says:

A work, a play, is not a questionnaire with questions and answers. The true responses of a work are given substance simply by that which replies to itself, it answers itself to itself, as a symphony answers itself to itself, as one spot of colour answers another spot of colour in the same painting. In the theatre these questions and answers are the characters in a play: that's what theatre is, playing at something; and the importance of the work will depend on the density of the interrogations become life, on their complexity, on their truth, on their authenticity, on their truth as living creatures, naturally, which is not the external truth, always open to challenge, of a demonstration. (25)

It is this alert openness that is the distinct characteristic of Ionesco's drama, that gives it its unique questing and questioning, its feel of recognition and astonishment, and it is this that enables it to catch what he called 'the atrocity and the miracle of this life' (12).

(iii) *The Chairs*
The Chairs is certainly 'interrogations become life'. Ionesco wrote various letters and notes on the play and its envisaged staging, also reprinted in *Notes et contre-notes*. He commented that the theatre of 1952 was political, social, cerebral or poetic, but a-metaphysical, and that he wished to break through the boundaries of contemporary drama. The play seems to have grown out of an image of the ending, a room of empty chairs and discarded confetti bathed in an enfeebled yellowish light: 'the party is over' (263). This echoes his accounts of his own awareness of transience, his awareness of the finishingness of things, their disappearance into

a mirage of a past that may not even have existed, his awareness of the now that does not exist. The play does not argue, does not preach, does not answer. Rather it projects 'holes in reality' (260).

Ionesco notes the 'ontological emptiness' of the play and remarks to the director that the old couple should not be allowed to speak outside the 'presence of this absence' (262, 260). Part of this demand is that there should be in production no handle for explaining away what is happening, providing psychological or other 'reasons' for what is going on, which would of course immediately bring the drama down into an everyday, discursive frame of reference. The play should exploit the potentiality of the theatre as the place where that which is 'truly nothing can happen' (265). In this series of comments Ionesco is approaching what was said of the stage itself by Peter Brook, when the empty space for acting is met by the emptiness within the actor, and thus the actor conjures up illusions that are more real than reality because they reveal what he called the 'structure' of that reality. The play should go into the moment, rather than moving along from moment to moment. There should not be a beginning, middle, end; instead, the consecutive is subsumed into the instant which is subsumed into a virtual potentiality.

The play works to unmean meaning by a double dislocation. It uses expectation to undermine expectation both of everyday 'reality' and of theatrical genre. We create meaning by predictive anticipation, and if this snaps meaning too is endangered or snaps. We then have to recreate it by a new pattern that often involves recreating the past, or we have to face the void. Reality as we know it involves mental habit, and may essentially be only mental habit. To uncondition is to attack mental habit. In this context everyday life is a 'game', a game containing games. One of the contained games is theatre. The sense of reality and meaning in theatre derives from the sense of reality and meaning in everyday life. In The Chairs the Old Woman and Old Man play out the rituals and sense of the past that we experience in ordinary life, and deconstruct them for the audience. Imprisoned in a semicircle of doors that lead to no discernible place and marooned on an island in the middle of a stinking lagoon at twilight the two moon about what might have been, about the greatness the Old Man might have achieved had he had ambition, they engage in childish ''Tis-'tisn't' exchanges, tell a rambling story about a walk they took, a story involving a fat man who falls over and a legendary Paris that faded away four hundred thousand years ago. Missed career, disappeared Paris, and a general sense of loss lead into the 'Where are you, Mummy?' routine, in which the Old Man climbs on to the Old Woman's lap, crying because he feels himself an orphan and dispossessed. He is pulled out of the past by an equally imaginary future, his 'message' to the world, that a hired Orator is going to deliver for him. As the Old Woman says, 'the whole universe is waiting just for you' (135).

The guests begin to arrive. Announced by the ringing of the bell, they remain invisible, and are created by the actions and one-sided conversation of the old couple. The Lady is followed by the Colonel, and his sexual advances to her, of which the Old Woman disapproves. The incident concludes when the Old Man accidentally upsets the Lady's chair, depositing her on the floor, as he makes for one of the doors to admit new guests. The whole is a tremendous tour de force for the actors, and the stage does begin to fill with tangible presences as guest after guest arrives, each of the earlier ones being distinguished in personality, rank and history. Miss Lovely, the Old Man's childhood sweetheart, arrives marked by the ravages of time, grey hair and an enlarged nose, while her photographer husband makes up to the Old Woman, who whores it around the stage with exposed red stockings and jutting pelvis and almost gets pushed over on the floor for sex. The Old Man and Old Woman then regale their guests with contradictory accounts of the past, the Old Woman talking about their son, who left them at the age of seven because he claimed they were killing all the birds, the Old Man regretting that they never had any children; the Old Man regretting that he left his mother to die alone in a ditch, the Old Woman claiming that he remained close to his mother, physically and mentally, to the last. Shortly after the conversation peters out in a series of meaningless uncontextualized phrases and lapses into a long silence.

The silent stillness is shattered by a ring at a door, then another and another and another. Invisible guests begin to pour in, doors are shut and opened, the Old Woman scurries in and out frantically bringing more and more chairs for the invisible onstage audience with their backs to the audience in the theatre. Squashed against the side walls and hemmed in by the great crowd the couple shout over the intervening heads to each other or give enigmatic answers to unheard questions:

> I am not myself, I am someone else. I am the one in the other....Sometimes I wake up to find absolute silence around me. That's what I mean by the sphere. It's complete in itself. However, one has to be careful. The whole shape may suddenly disappear. There are holes it escapes through. (161)

Both claim that the Old Man's system is perfect, an all-explaining whole, and the Orator will disclose it. Before that, however, the double door at the back bursts open, the lights rise to an intense brightness, and His Majesty the Emperor arrives, unseen of course. As he seats himself the Old Man struggles to glimpse him through the throng of courtiers and the onstage audience, and indulges in grovelling protestations of allegiance and appeals to the Emperor as his last hope in life. To obviate the boredom of the waiting Emperor the Old Man recounts a tale about climbing as a full-grown man on to his father's knee after dinner, and being married off on the spot by the dinner guests who wished to prove him adult. His efforts are curtailed by the announcement of the imminent arrival of the Orator in a series of 'just coming's from the Old Man and the Old Woman.

The Orator is physically visible, a striking figure dressed like an artist from a Toulouse Lautrec poster. While the Old Man is unable to deliver his own message, as he finds it too difficult to express his great finding, he nevertheless gives a parodied pompous speech of formal thanks to all those who had made the event possible, including the carpenters who fashioned the chairs, the mechanics, the electrocutioners and so on. Their lives now fulfilled, the old couple announce their departure, strew confetti on the Emperor, then leap to their deaths in the lagoon out of their widely separated windows. The bright light immediately dims to the dingy yellowish light of the opening. The Orator, when he attempts to speak, turns out to be deaf and dumb. He strikes significant attitudes, then resorts to a few provocatively meaningless words on a blackboard, then finally clusters of letters and parts of letters. After that he gives up, goes through the onstage audience to the exit, bows to the Emperor and leaves.

The stage is empty, the light dingy, the double door at the back gapes on to darkness. Human noises, 'snatches of laughter, whisperings, a "Ssh!" or two, little sarcastic coughs' rise from the onstage audience, then fade into silence. After a pause the curtain falls, slowly.

From this summary it should be clear that the play has a distinct form that is not the form of meaning. There is a rhythmical process, the end echoing the beginning, the lights rising gradually to intense brightness, then dimming once more, the stage filling with people who are not there, the end returning to emptiness. The dialogue also has a shape. Rather like Beckett's stage dialogue it swirls round, only to resettle, then begin again. It is full of repetitions and echoes, a patterning of sound different in its recurring sameness, an improvised repetition of dancing words that move to no conclusion. Unlike Beckett's dialogue, however, it can lapse into an inarticulate incoherence that is always there just beneath the surface of the words. Beckett seems to be hinting always at a meaning hidden in the wings, ideas can be attached to and detached from passages in his dialogue, whereas Ionesco's are more vortices of feeling, verbalized angst or verbalized recovery. Beckett seems to be a deconstruction of something. In Ionesco there is nothing to deconstruct.

In the detail of the dialogue there can still be some sense of beginnings, middles and ends, in the overall patterning of fragments there is not an end so much as a failed beginning, and that failure is the play's success. Just as the play, according to Ionesco, grew out of the image of the empty stage of the beginning and end, so he emphasized in his stage directions the need to leave that image in the mind of the departing audience in the theatre. During the play the image has gathered not so much a meaning, in the sense of a coherent overarching frame of reference, any final explanation, a why for the whyless, but rather a resonance that gathers in much of life. The rituals detached from their contexts (the Old Man's sitting on the knee of his mummy, his wife, his daddy), the aggressive flirtations of Colonel and Photographer, the reiterated story routines, the echoing and conflicting accounts of the past, the present absence of Paris, the intrusion of surreal detail like the killing of the birds, all give a sense of the incoherence of life. Life doesn't end, it stops. During the play the largely empty stage has become a populated fullness, which dies away in the final rustle of sound. Seen and unseens, heard and unheard, have rubbed shoulders in a stage reality. In the stage reality the theatre audience has been able to perceive an unseen audience on stage, thought-created. At the end reality subsides into emptiness. But the emptiness is not the emptiness of the opening. The play has done its work – we do not observe an empty stage, we become emptiness. The barriers dividing real/unreal, subject/object have been breached. And that breaching is in the final image. The image is a kind of concluding denial of conclusion, for the total spatial image can contain the potentiality of disposition and sequence as a sound could only do if it fell back into the mind with the immediacy of total pattern, a wholeness containing the potential of extended sequence. (The end image could be linked to Plotinus's praise of Egyptian hieroglyphs, or Pound's advocacy of Imagism and his fascination with Chinese hieroglyphs.)

The end can certainly be a reality shift for an audience. Ionesco saw the possiblity of more than a relatively superficial readjustment of awareness. In his 'Notes on The Chairs' of 1951 he said:
    Unreality of the real. Originating chaos.

The voice at the end, noise of the world, rumours, debris of world, the world goes up in smoke, in sounds and colours that go out, the last foundations crumble or rather disjoin. Or dissolve into a sort of night. Or in a brilliant blinding light. (Ionesco 1951, 263)

Chapter 6

PINTER

6.1 THE BIRTHDAY PARTY

William S. Haney II

Harold Pinter's first three plays, *The Room*, *The Birthday Party* and *The Dumb Waiter*, are collectively known as 'Comedies of Menace' because they dramatize the terrors that most individuals experience in confrontation with external forces. In commenting on *The Birthday Party*, Pinter says that the play dramatizes how the true and false, real and unreal, are not easily distinguishable: 'The thing is not necessarily either true or false; it can be both true and false' (quoted in Naismith 2000, 45). The main characters in *The Birthday Party* emerge out of a past that remains a mystery except for references to the possibility of earlier encounters between Stanley Webber and the two men, Goldberg and McCann, who have come to take him away.

As Elizabeth Sakellaridou argues, in *The Birthday Party* 'ontological and existential questions' take a concrete form; Stanley 'complains he has sleepless nights, he fears the coming of strangers, he feels trapped in his own refuge, he looks in the mirror in quest of an identity for himself' (Sakellaridou 1988, 29). The external menace in *The Birthday Party*, as Gale and Sakellaridou both observe, does not end with the early plays but extend throughout Pinter's work.

When Lulu, a friend of Meg in her early twenties, who finds Stanley attractive, asks him to go for a walk and 'get a bit of air' (26), he declines, suggesting instead they go away together. When she asks where, he replies, 'Nowhere. Still, we could go' (26). Stanley implies that if Lulu wants to go somewhere with him, she will have to surrender her attachments to conventional behavior and everyday reality. Even the question of whether or not Stanley is telling the truth about his past has the effect of emptying the mental content of the spectators and other characters. Finding him impossible to deal with or even understand, Lulu tells Stanley, 'You're a bit of a washout, aren't you?' This remark further suggests how Stanley's overall performance in the play has a decontingencing effect on characters and audience – in a sense washing out their world of familiar attributes.

In contrast to Stanley, Goldberg in a conversation with McCann narrates his own past in a way that extols conformity to established values and behaviour.

> Honour thy father and thy mother. All along the line. Follow the line, the line, McCann, and you can't go wrong. What do you think, I'm a self-made man? No! I sat where I was told to sit. I kept my eye on the ball. [. . .] And that's why I've reached my position, McCann. Because I've always been as fit as a fiddle. My motto. Work hard and play hard. Not a day's illness. (1968, 77–78)

Although Goldberg does not go into narrative detail about his past, he clearly presents an attitude of conformity to what he regards as the establishment, even though what he refers to consists more of a localized system of values. As real as this attitude may seem to Goldberg, the play suggests that it is not entirely real or unreal, true or false. Whatever its reality or truth may be, moreover, pertains primarily to the linguistic self. Indeed, even Goldberg has doubts about his own narrative self-presentation, as foreshadowed by his announcement in act three: 'I don't know why, but I feel knocked out. I feel a bit...It's uncommon for me' (1968, 76). In his narrative account of his past, whether true or false, Goldberg may be trying to counteract the effect of Stanley's voided identity, which seems to undermine Goldberg's own self-confidence.

Goldberg implies that their mission with Stanley consists of re-incorporating him back into the Judeo-Christian fold, back to social and religious orthodoxy, after he has ventured beyond the attributes of ordinary identity and computation into the trans-cultural realm of direct experience. Given that members of the most oppressed communities – the Jews and the Irish – have been assimilated into a quasi public orthodoxy and become the tormentors of those remaining beyond the pale suggests that they indeed represent the opposite extreme to the nothingness and nowhere that Stanley incorporates. By setting up an opposition between the freedom pursued by Stanley and the conformism enforced by Goldberg and McCann, Pinter sets up a framework through which spectators can move toward their own innate tendency for freedom.

The Birthday Party uses various dramatic devices to call into question socially constructed identity, attenuate the mind's conscious content, and intimate the move toward an experience of consciousness devoid of attributes. The uncertain background and identities of the characters, their multiple names indicating a diversity of masks, Stanley's ambiguous musical talent, the ulterior motives of the interrogation and the insecurity experienced by the two visitors all lead to a decontingencing of the conscious content of characters and audience. *The Birthday Party*, like the other plays discussed above, leads the audience beyond ordinary waking consciousness and the duality of thought and language toward pure consciousness. In this state of awareness we can experience how language transcends its spatial/temporal dimension in the unity of *pashyanti* and *para*. Even the most profane theatre, therefore, can induce sacred experience by allowing the audience to transcend the duality of mind and thought toward the void of conceptions that characterizes pure awareness – the groundless ground of sacred theatre.

The unsayable inner dimension *The Birthday Party* points to through its decontingencing devices (and ultimately articulates through Stanley's gasps and stutters in the last scene) centres on what Jean Baudrillard calls postmodern simulacra, the work of simulation, which is not the same as feigning or pretending. Postmodern concealment consists of blurring or eliminating the distinction between truth and falsity. As Zygmunt Bauman says in *Postmodernity and its Discontents*, postmodern simulacra make 'the issues of the "heart of the matter," of sense and of meaning senseless and meaningless. It is reality itself which now needs the "suspension of disbelief," once the preserve of art, in order to be grasped and treated and lived as reality. Reality itself is now "make believe," although [. . .] it does its best to cover up the traces' (Bauman 1997, 125–26). As Baudrillard, like Stanley, demonstrates, what we take for reality is but an illusion. Art as fantasy, by uncovering the illusion of reality, is more real than the 'real' world of conventional interests. As Pinter shows, the difference between truth and falsity derives not from the outer world but from the eyes of the beholder who can see beyond the sensory to the extra-linguistic, trans-rational dimension of human experience. Art allows us to perceive the fabrication of the external world, as Pinter and Stanley may have intuited.

To quote Bauman,

> As François Lyotard put it, if since the beginning of modernity arts sought the ways of representing the 'sublime', that which by its nature defies representation – the modern artists' search for the sublime formed a 'nostalgic aesthetics'; they posited the non-representable as an 'absent content' only. Postmodern artists, on the other hand, struggle to incorporate the non-representable into the presentation itself (1997, 104).

Bauman goes on to explain that the postmodern artist works without rules in order 'to give voice to the ineffable, and a tangible shape to the invisible' (105) – as Pinter does through Stanley.

Even within the naturalistic setting of the play, the visitors' stylized language and unspecified mission add a surreal dimension to the play that implies a menace not only to Stanley but also to the conventional organization to which the visitors belong. The bizarre and improbable nature of their questions and accusations suggest that what needs to be reconstructed more than Stanley are the social and religious establishments that attempt to impose conformity to arbitrary rules. *The Birthday Party*, as an example of sacred theatre, reveals not only how a sensitive individual can fear the demands of an outside world, but also how the public world as a collection of local communities can fear the inner dimension of nonconformists who follow their innate callings.

6.2 ASHES TO ASHES

Peter Malekin

(i) *Pinter's Working Methods*
In his Nobel speech Pinter said:

'In 1958 I wrote the following.

> There are no hard distinctions between what is real and what is unreal, nor between what is true and what is false. A thing is not necessarily either true or false; it can be both true and false.

I believe that these assertions still make sense and do still apply to the exploration of reality through art. So as a writer I stand by them but as a citizen I cannot.'

If 'reality' here were taken to mean glibly everyday reality, then the resulting art would be so trivial that it avoided all fundamental questions. If on the other hand the exploration of reality is taken to include an investigation of what is real, of what reality is, then the central quest of Pinter's drama is the central quest of spirituality. Religion too often prescribes what is real. Spirituality attempts with an open mind to seek reality out. It is this quest that distinguishes much of Pinter's dramatic work from the narrower political concerns so courageously expressed in his onslaught on the criminal policies of Britain and America.

Pinter then turns to the questions of truth in art and the way his plays arise. On the first he comments. 'Truth in drama is forever elusive....The real truth is that there never is any such thing as one truth to be found in dramatic art. There are many.' In drama as in life a search for reality produces contradictory and relative truths, truth within limits. If reality is unbounded, then it is not surprising that no formulation of truth can encompass it.

On his working methods and the origin of his dramas, Pinter comments that they often start with a word or image and then unfold themselves independently of his will. He can play a game of cat and mouse with his characters, but he seems basically to be engaged in a process of listening. The source of what is being listened to is mysterious. Psychoanalytical or indeed Marxian criticism would prescribe it in the manner of a religion, but as with truths in and of drama the source is susceptible to many and contradictory explanations.

Turning to some specific plays, Pinter records his own impression of *Ashes to Ashes*, intriguingly summarized primarily as an image:

> A drowning woman, her hand reaching up through the waves, dropping down out of sight, reaching for others, but finding nobody there, either above or under the water, finding only shadows, reflections, floating; the woman a lost figure in a drowning landscape, a woman unable to escape the doom that seemed to belong only to others.

> But as they died, she must die too.

One impression from an experience of the play is that Rebecca is already dead.

(ii) *Ashes to Ashes*

The title from the Christian burial service, associated with the hollow drumming of earth falling on a coffin, corroborates a sense of the play as a kind of funeral rite, though the allusions to the Holocaust recall unfuneraled death, outside the contexts of society, of religion, of rituals of meaning. The play is loss, lost life, loss of truth, loss of meaning, loss of the loss of meaning. No framework is given for the break-up of frameworks, merely a complex of feelings that cancel one another out, but are felt nonetheless. The luxuries of guilt and blame disintegrate. It is a cross-current of feelings, without the direction of a whirlpool, outside the systematics of religions and philosophies. The cycle of time moves inevitably towards loss, but in Pinter's play not to the loss of time itself. Nor does Pinter offer the palliative of a false identity, an identity defined through suffering. The play shows the courage evinced by his analysis of politics. Escape is not an option. The stage logistics of the play, the movement of the dialogue, the logical non sequiturs, the multiple personalities within role, the palimpsest of narratives are the process of disintegration of the comforting lies of 'normal' life. The opening conversation turns on Rebecca's account of love-making with a sadistic lover, while Devlin hovers over her and conducts a jealous interrogation. Then comes the sudden question whether she thinks he is hypnotizing her, which leads to a stalemate:

Devlin: What do you think?
Rebecca: I think you're a fuckpig.
Devlin: Me a fuckpig! You must be joking.

Rebecca smiles.

Rebecca: Me joking? You must be joking.

This is immediately followed by a total collapse of the sequence of exchange:

Devlin: Do you think my questions are illegitimate?

Pause.

Rebecca: What questions?

Pause.

Devlin: Look. It would mean a great deal to me if you could define him more clearly.

Devlin starts again from the preoccupations of the opening exchange, the identity and actions of the sadistic lover. The pauses point up the dislocation between the two interlocutors, mark the jerked progression of the conversation in a new direction and provide time for each to regroup mentally for the next run of dialogue. They also create an effect rather like the apparent randomness of bubbles rising in a marsh, as if the dialogue was arising in bursts from somewhere else, not simply from the minds of the characters. It has its own erratic course and is its own creature. It is almost symbolism with nothing to symbolize. We are in the Pinter world.

The following questions, interrupted briefly by a detour on the title 'darling', then sidle round the occupation of the lover, what he did, where, what exactly it entailed. He had a job, he worked for a travel agent, he was a guide (in what sense, a Führer perhaps?), he was high up in the organization, he ran a factory, a very damp factory, the workers idolized him, his purity, his conviction, would march over a cliff (like lemmings) if he asked them, were very musical. There is a sort of progression, but it moves like a crab scuttling sideways and defensive. There is a hiddenness. He was a guide and, mentioned almost aside,

Rebecca: He used to go to the local railway station and walk down the platform and tear all the babies from the arms of their screaming mothers.

Pause.

Devlin: Did he?

Silence.

Rebecca: By the way, I'm terribly upset.

For a modern western audience the passage is an obvious reference to the Nazi concentration camps. The shock of the disclosure seems to evoke no great surprise from Devlin and Rebecca's upset feelings, introduced casually as a side issue, turn out to have been occasioned by a police siren, unnoted in the stage directions, and not by its occurrence but by its fading away. She is disturbed by the sound of the siren fading and passing into the possession of somebody else, she wants it all to herself all the time; without it she is insecure; its sound is beautiful.

Devlin's role has assumed overtones of confessor and psychoanalyst. Rebecca has become the traumatized victim identified with her trauma and threatened by the possible loss of that identification.

This is answered by an ironic diversion in Devlin's account of the police or spy state, which is now the norm in America, Russia, China, Britain, some of the rest of Europe and much of the world:

> You'll hear it again soon. Any minute....They're very busy people, the police. There's so much for them to do. They've got so much to take care of, to keep an eye on. They keep getting signals, mostly in code. There isn't one minute of the day when they're not charging around one corner or another in the world, in their police cars, ringing their sirens. So you can take comfort from that, at least. Can't you. You'll never be lonely again. You'll never be without a police siren. I promise you.

This could register as Devlin's ironic comment on Rebecca's traumatic obsession, or a comment on the recurrence of states like the Nazi state, or on the way the whole world has begun to accept intrusive centralized power and enforcement policing since the fall of Nazism, with a concomitant loss of privacy, freedom and independence. The promise of never being lonely again acquires the sinister connotations of Orwell's place where there is no darkness (an actual condition of the wretched prisoners in the Lubianko Prison in Moscow). However it is taken, it also registers as a distancing of Devlin from Rebecca's stream of thought and association. He begins to separate out from it.

 When Devlin attempts to get back to the subject of the lover's appearance Rebecca sidetracks him

> Rebecca: It was when I was writing a note, a few notes for the laundry. Well...to put it bluntly...a laundry list. Well, I put my pen on that little coffee table and it rolled off.
> Devlin: No?

Rebecca: It rolled right off, onto the carpet. In front of my eyes.
Devlin: Good God.

The repetitions, the pauses, the ponderous reluctance to blurt out 'a laundry list' lend an air of immense importance to an occurrence of no importance whatever. The sense of indirect allusiveness to some hidden significance is compounded by the subsequent heated argument on whether the pen was innocent or not and the reference to its parents. The form of the argument meticulously follows the form of emotional arguments between man and wife, where feelings are blurted out first and the point at issue is made clear afterwards, where there are crude binary jumps (if you don't think the pen is innocent you must think it is guilty) and the assertion before last is picked up in a non-linear fashion, where the feelings outweigh the ostensible subject matter, and where violent exchanges lead into patches of silence. But the subject here is not only trivial, but...well...to put it bluntly, screwy. Innocence and guilt are not categories attributed to pens, nor, as Rebecca points out, do pens have parents. When Devlin declares he is letting the matter drop, he is in a quicksand, Rebecca replies, 'Like God', which leads into Devlin's peroration about the need to keep God:

He's the only God we have. If you let him go he won't come back. He won't even look back over his shoulder. And then what will you do?

This poignantly echoes the story of the rabbi in a concentration camp who called on God to stop the atrocities going on around him. When nothing happened he went into a gas chamber with the words, 'There is no God'.

Devlin then almost forces Rebecca to say that she has no authority to speak of having suffered an atrocity. After Rebecca's reassertion that her sadistic lover had adored her, Devlin launches into an account of his own previous life as a poverty-stricken scholar in implicit contrast to the colourful lover, ending in a peroration on not letting the best man win in a marriage, the best man being presumably the absentee lover, but instead gritting your teeth and simply drudging on with the marriage.

Devlin's outburst is completely ignored by Rebecca, who recounts having seen from the windows of the house in Dorset a lot of frozen people, escorted by guides, people laden with bags and trudging through the summer woods and down the cliffs into the sea, where they drowned. Devlin knows of no house in Dorset. Rebecca intersperses a description of mental elephantiasis, where you spill a little gravy and it expands into a sea and drowns you, and it's all your fault since you handed over the bundle. Ignoring an attempt to distract her, she returns to her memory of walking through a frozen city to the railway station where her lover tears the babies from the screaming mothers.

Devlin at last manages to distract her on to the subject of a visit she had paid earlier that day to her sister Kim and a subsequent visit to see a funny film at the cinema, through which one man in the audience had sat like a corpse. Devlin attempts to establish the normality of his and Rebecca's everyday life:

Now look, let's start again. We live here. You don't live...in Dorset...or *anywhere* else. You live here with me. This is our house. You have a very nice sister. She lives close to you. She has two lovely kids. You're their aunt. You like that....Let's start again.

Devlin's 'Let's start again' apparently refers to the efforts to affirm the normality of their life. But Rebecca refers it apparently to the relationship with the sadistic lover. They can't, she says, start again, they can only end again. The distinction between Devlin and the lover begins to blur and fade. Rebecca goes on to recall looking down on a frozen city, seeing wretched people carrying suitcases, a woman listening to her baby's breathing. Then she changes to the first person, 'I held her to me. She was breathing'. Devlin tries to replay the sadistic love scene, grasping her throat, but she sits inert. Accompanied by an offstage echo, she recounts going to the trains, wrapping her baby into a bundle, trying to save it from the guards. However, the baby cries and she is forced back to hand it over. Subsequently in 'this place' (a term she had earlier used for the factory) she meets a friend who asks where her baby is. She replies, 'What baby...I don't have a baby... I don't know of any baby...I don't know of any baby'. The stage lighting has narrowed down to two bright lamps beside the chairs at the table. After a long silence it blacks out.

Even from this cursory account it can perhaps be seen that the play is very powerful. There is no clear narrative coherence to the whole. Devlin lives in England, seems to be Rebecca's husband, seems to know nothing of the Nazi past, yet is or is confused with the sadistic lover who was also a Nazi guard at the concentration camp and possibly the father of the murdered baby. Devlin knows nothing of this lover, yet ends by imitating him. Rebecca seems increasingly withdrawn from her surroundings, moving instead into her past or her fantasy, there is finally no telling which is which, and playing over and over again a painful memory, as we do in life. In life such a memory can fade, non-attachment can follow, movement can be achieved into freedom as the binding influence of the past drops away. This gaining of freedom can also happen in the process of dying (dying is indeed one of the greatest opportunities for it, and while many may not realize this, some do). In life the reaction to traumatic experience can equally be apathy, or destroyed confidence, or denial, or an imprisoning mental and emotional pattern that repetitively binds future living, or embittered hatred and desire for revenge. In the play the memory does not fade but is ambiguous, for Rebecca's statement that she never had a baby bears witness to her having had one in fact or fantasy. The loss remains, stark, unobliterated by time. We experience it, but vicariously. Like the actor in his role we are in and outside the situation. We are free to use it and free to use the freedom it has given us. This is at least a theatrical inkling, a taste of the state of spiritual freedom described at the end of the opening section on space. Given ideal performance conditions and an ideal audience it could be considerably more.

Chapter 7

GENET

7.1 GENET'S SACRED THEATRE: PRACTICE AND POLITICS

Carl Lavery and Ralph Yarrow

(i) *Introduction*

> Theater places us right at the heart of what is religious-political: in the heart of absence, in negativity, in nihilism as Nietzsche would say, therefore in the question of power. (Jean-François Lyotard)[10]

> The sacred is a privileged moment [...], a moment of the convulsive communication of what is ordinarily stifled. (Georges Bataille)[11]

Our concern here is to offer an alternative interpretation of the politics of Jean Genet's theatre by concentrating on how that theatre actively provokes a disturbing mode of experience that is conventionally thought to have little political value. For reasons that will soon become evident, we call this experience, after George Bataille's work on sovereignty and the impossible, the sacred. The sections that follow will attempt:

(i) to describe how the sacred functions in Bataille's thinking
(ii) to show the similarities between Genet's concept of the sacred and Bataille's
(iii) to examine how the sacred informs Genet's theatre after 1955
(iv) to outline Genet's enterprise in terms of his desire to reinstate sacred experience as a necessary prerequisite to radical personal and political transformation
(v) to explore in detail aspects of dramaturgy by which this project is delivered

(ii) *Bataille and the A/theological Sacred*
Unlike religious and secular discourses which generally understand the sacred as *either* spiritual truth or socializing principle, Bataille believes it to be an ambivalent and ultimately

unclassifiable phenomenon. For Bataille, the sacred belongs to the realm of a/theology, a philosophy that deliberately sets out to suspend theological notions of totality and wholeness. Mark C. Taylor, a good interpreter of Bataille's writing, supplies a useful definition of how a/theology operates:

> The / of a/theology (which, it is important to note, can be written but not spoken) marks the *limen* that signifies *both* proximity and distance, similarity and difference, interiority and exteriority. This strangely permeable membrane forms a border where fixed boundaries disintegrate. Along this boundless boundary the traditional polarities between which Western theology has been suspended are inverted and subverted. (Taylor 1984, 12–13)

By insisting on liminality and impossibility, Bataille's a/theology aims at re-vitalizing religious experience, which, he contends, has been perverted and domesticated by theology's dependence on an anthropocentric deity figure or logos.[12] According to Bataille's more ecstatic – and ultimately more troubling – view of religion, the sacred belongs to a primitive, Godless economy rooted in eroticism:

> The whole business of eroticism is to strike to the inmost core of the living being, so that the heart stands still. The transition from the normal state to that of erotic desire presupposes a partial dissolution of the person as he exists in the realm of discontinuity. (Bataille 1987, 17)

In the erotic, Bataille argues, we embrace, willingly and absurdly, the dissolution of self. To consent to the erotic and/or the sacred is to consent to death. In both cases, individuality or discontinuity is negated by, and thus becomes part of, indivisible oneness. Bataille calls this state continuity:

> Beyond the intoxication of youth, we achieve the power to look death in the face and to perceive in death the pathway into unknowable and incomprehensible continuity – that path is the secret of eroticism and eroticism alone can reveal it. (Ibid. 24)

Where theology understands the sacred in terms of totality and fulfilment, Bataille associates it, instead, with incompleteness and loss. With everything, in other words, that disturbs the boundaries of self: sexuality, death, non-knowledge. Bataille has no interest in rediscovering some authentic, uncontaminated sense of self. For him, religious experience is a journey into loss, a recognition that the self can never return home or find a proper place. This leap into the abyss should not be seen as an endorsement of nihilism, On the contrary, the sacred, for Bataille, allows the subject to discover an impossible and paradoxical mode of communication uniting with him others, and, ultimately, with the mystery of the cosmos itself:

> Communication, through death, with our beyond – [...] not with nothingness, still less with a supernatural being, but with an indefinite reality (which I sometimes call *the impossible*, that is: what can't be grasped in any way, what we can't reach without dissolving ourselves, what's slavishly called God). (Bataille 1988, 59)

The impossible, then, is neither fullness ('the supernatural being') nor absence ('nothingness'), but rather a liminal state in which absence and presence are combined. Contradicting, flagrantly, the laws of logic, the subject experiencing the impossibility of the sacred is simultaneously, self and not-self, same and different. In this state, he confronts alterity, that which lies beyond the borders of the known and familiar: 'The sacred is really [...] something that is from the first *completely other*'. (Bataille 1998, 40)

Although the sacred occurs in and to individual bodies, it is inherently social. In fact, it forms the basis of any society. For, as Bataille reminds us, the sacred is what produces authentic communication. Which is defined, by him, as the attempt to overcome our limits and to express the anguish of existence to our fellow human beings. According to Bataille's reading, the sacred, because it dislodges the foundations of the ego, is nothing less than the source of generosity (giving) itself.

The consideration that generosity and not self-interest is at the basis of the social relations is of fundamental importance. 'Self-interest varies in relation to circumstances. [...] It is therefore necessary that in any association of interests a principle, embodied in generosity and stronger than self-interest, is needed for serious communication to take place.' (Bataille 1998, 72)

The sacred's intimate relationship with the social means that it has important ethical and political consequences, too. The ethical dimension of the sacred is bound up with what Bataille terms the 'the sovereign moment' (Bataille 1973, 173), the moment at which the ego renounces its slavish dependence on self-interest and utility and affirms lack and loss instead. This celebration of dispossession and dissolution is ethical, for Bataille, because it is based on generosity and expenditure rather than conservation and accumulation: it encourages the self to give to the Other, and by extension, to discover an alternative form of community and social solidarity.

Unlike bourgeois and communist societies, Bataille's sacred community is not grounded in Enlightenment notions of reason; and nor is it steeped in nostalgic myths of organic community as fascism is. On the contrary, its source is the experience of impossibility, the recognition that totality and harmony are unobtainable. Instead of rejecting the anguish caused by this knowledge, Bataille encourages us to accept and celebrate it. Paradoxically – and this concerns the political dimension of the sacred – the most effective way of achieving a more just, less violent, social order is to affirm the destruction of that order through ritualized acts of dissolution. To this extent, the refusal of violence, the desire to create harmony, increases our capacity for violence, rather than assuaging it. In his analysis of war in volume one of the *Accursed Share* (1949), Bataille explains why:

> If we do not have the force to destroy the surplus energy ourselves, it cannot be used, and like an unbroken animal that cannot be trained, it is this energy that destroys us; it is we who pay the price of the inevitable explosion. (Bataille 1988, 24)

(iii) *Genet and A/theology*

Initially, nothing seems to encourage a reading of Genet's theatre through Bataille. In the influential *Literature and Evil* (1957), for instance, Bataille attacked Genet's work for its selfish failure to communicate:

> I admit that Genet wanted to become Evil. [...] No vulgar motive would account for his failure, but, as in a dungeon guarded more closely than real prisons, a ghastly destiny enclosed him within himself, at the depths of his mistrust. (1973, 174)

Instead of using literature to provoke a sacred encounter between author and reader, Bataille argues that Genet's writing is limited, bourgeois, a betrayal of sovereignty:

> 'Genet's sanctity' [...] is sovereignty confiscated, the dead sovereignty of him whose solitary desire for sovereignty is the betrayal of sovereignty. (Ibid. 174–5)

Bataille's interpretation of Genet's sacred quest is accurate as it pertains to his early period (the novels and plays written between 1940 and 1955). In these texts, Genet's delight in transgression disguises, as Bataille correctly diagnoses, a conservative desire for self-preservation and identity. Problems start to arise with Bataille's reading when it is applied to Genet's work after 1955, particularly with regard to the great theatrical cycle of *The Balcony*, *The Blacks* (1958) and *The Screens* (1961). In these theatrical works, Genet abandons his obsession with theological inversion and invests in a form of theatrical communication, which ironically has much in common with Bataille's view of sacred experience.

To understand this revolution in Genet's aesthetic and ethical project, we need to explore a disturbing event he experienced aboard a train in the early 1950s. According to Genet's account of this incident in 'The Studio of Alberto Giacometti' (1957) and 'What Remained of a Rembrandt Torn up into Very Even Little Pieces and Chucked into the Crapper' (1967), his view of the world and concept of self suddenly collapsed when he inadvertently caught the eye of a stranger sitting opposite him. Incredibly, Genet tells us looking at the man disclosed what phenomenal reality conceals: the abyssal identity linking all subjects:

> Behind what was visible of this man [...] I discovered, and was shocked by the discovery, a kind of identity common to all men. (Genet 1972, 78)

Unlike the joy experienced by the religious mystic, Genet's encounter with the universal provoked, at least initially, an intense bout of depression and abjection. He felt that the world was robbed of meaning and value:

> What bothered me the most was that sadness with which I had been overwhelmed. Nothing was certain or solid. Suddenly the world was a floating world. For a long time I remained sickened and disgusted by my discovery. (Ibid. 85)

In light of Bataille's definition of the sacred, it is telling that Genet's anguish is caused by the duplicity of his experience:

> There exists and has always existed, but one single man in the world. He is completely in each of us, therefore he is we. Each man is the other and the others. [...]. With the exception that one phenomenon, whose name I do not even know, seems to divide this unique man infinitely, apparently fragments him in an accident and in form, and makes each of the fragments unfamiliar to us. (84)

In the description here, the subject is simultaneously fused with, and radically estranged from, the other. This forecloses any nostalgia that subject might have for wholeness and totality. Even in continuity, Genet tells us, something always resists closure and oneness. The wound, the metaphor Genet uses to convey this liminal state, is well chosen. As well as suggesting physical and existential *douleur*, the wound is a tear or rupture that is neither inside nor outside the body. The wound is liminal:

And your wound, where is it?

Where, I wonder, does it reside, where does it hide, this secret wound that every man is quick to take refuge in when his pride is hurt, when he's wounded? This wound – which then becomes the deep, centre of self – that's what he's going to inflate. Everybody knows how to find it, and to identify with it to the degree that they become the wound itself, a kind of secret, painful heart. (Genet 1979a, 12–13. Our translation.)

Genet's description of his experience aboard the train is strongly reminiscent of Bataille's view of the sacred. In both cases, transcendence of self does not result in redemption, the experience of wholeness. Rather transcendence obliges the subject to confront the trauma and pain of the impossible. The parallels between the Genet's vision of transcendence and Bataille's are further strengthened when we look at the signifiers associated with wound in 'The Studio of Alberto Giacometti'. Just as Bataille sees the sacred in terms of 'sovereignty' communication' so Genet identifies it with royalty and majesty, the source of a more obscure and subtle form of communication:

Each human being is revealed to me in whatever is newest, most irreplaceable about him – and it's always a wound – thanks to the solitude in which this wound locates him, this wound of which he is barely conscious and yet which is the source of his entire being. [...] Solitude, as I understand it, does not signify an unhappy state, but rather secret royalty, profound incommunicability yet a more or less obscure knowledge of an invulnerable singularity. (Genet 1993, 317)

In the same way that sovereignty is, for Bataille, the foundation of poetry, the Genettian wound is the source of creativity and self-expression. Speaking about the performer in the essay 'Le Funambule' (1958), Genet states:

It's into this wound – untreatable because it's part of the self – and into this solitude that he's going to leap, for it's there that he will discover the force, audacity and skill necessary for his art. (1979a, 13)

In the concluding lines of 'The Studio of Alberto Giacometti', Genet's view of the sacred draws astonishingly close to Bataille's on ethical grounds too. For if the wound is, according to Genet, 'une incommunicabilité profonde' ('profound incommunicability'), it is also what drives us to communicate our solitude. Such an action is ethical for Genet, as indeed it is for Bataille, because it compels the subject to relinquish the ego and reach out to the Other:

Giacometti's art, then, is not a social art that would establish a social link between objects – man and his secretions – but rather an art of superior beggars and bums, so pure that they could be united by a recognition of the solitude of every being and every object. 'I am alone', the objects seems to say, 'hence caught within a necessity against which you are powerless. If I am only what I am, I am indestructible. Being what I am, and unconditionally, my solitude knows yours.' (1993, 328–9)

The view of the sacred, then, that emerges in Genet's writing from the mid-1950s onwards not only disputes Bataille's dismissive reading of his work, it reveals, ironically, a profound similarity between them. For both writers, the sacred is an event that negates and recreates identity and discloses alternative possibilities for individual and collective existence based on the impossible abyss that separates and unites subjects.

(iv) *Genet's Theory of Sacred Theatre*

Genet's experience of the wound galvanized his work and resulted in an alternative, God-less view of sacred theatre. Where plays like *The Maids* (1948), *Death Watch* (1947), *Splendid's* (1947) conform to the conservative neo-classical format favoured by existentialist playwrights such as Sartre, Camus and Anouilh, his theatre after 1955 evinces a new interest in ritual forms and mythical themes.

> If they are able to accept the idea – assuming the idea is meaningful that the theatre cannot compete with the extraordinary means which television and cinema have at their disposal, then those who write for the theatre will discover the virtues inherent in the theatre, virtues which, perhaps, derive only from myth. (1972, 67)

The actor has a central role to play in this theatre of myth. Liberated from his Stanislavskian definition as an impersonator, a vehicle for representing a fictional character, the performer is encouraged, by Genet, to see himself as a secular priest or saint, an initiate able to transmit and communicate profound human mysteries:

> This may not be an original thought with me, but let me restate it anyway, that the patron saint of actors is Tiresias, because of his dual nature. [...] Like him, the actors are neither this nor that, and they must be aware that they are a presence constantly beset by femininity, or its opposite, but ready to play to the point of abasement that which, be it virility or its opposite, is any case predetermined. (1972, 50)

The spectator, too, is expected to participate in theatre's sacred purpose. In 'The Strange Word "Urb..."', Genet writes about the audience in a way that recalls Victor Turner's analysis of rites of passage rituals in Africa in *The Ritual Process: Structure and Anti-Structure* (1969). Just as Turner sees the ritual process as an exercise in separation and liminality for initiates, so Genet strives to distance the spectators from their everyday identities, and to place them in contact with borderline situations and experiences. Appropriately, he wants his theatre to have the same solemnity and strangeness as a cemetery at night:

> As for the audience, only those who know themselves capable of taking a nocturnal stroll through a cemetery, in order to be confronted with a mystery, will come to the theatre. (1972, 71)

As with Turner's definition of ritual performance, Genet believes that theatre can produce real effects. By distancing the audience from everyday reality, he hopes to change its way of seeing the world. He wants to reveal what society represses:

> This procedure, a refusal of a natural sham, must not be carried out haphazardly: its goal, among other things, is to reveal and make heard what *generally* passes unperceived. Its real goal, of course, is a new joy, a new festivity. (1972, 57)

The intention behind Genet's ritualistic theatre, this 'new festivity', is to liberate us from historical and theological notions of beginnings and endings:

> Among other things, the goal of theatre is to take us outside the limits of what is generally referred to as 'historical' time but which is really theological. The moment the theatrical event begins, the time which will elapse no longer belongs to any calibrated calendar. It transcends the Christian era as it does the revolutionary era. [...] It destroys the historical conventions necessitated by social life [...] not for the sake of just any disorder but neither for the sake of a liberation – the theatrical event being suspended, outside of a historical time, on its own dramatic time – it is for the sake of a vertiginous liberation. (64)

Like Bataille's notion of the impossible, Genet's festive theatre is meant to be violent and violating. Its aim is to tear us from discontinuity, to dissolve the distance separating spectators from each other. This undoubtedly accounts for one of his favourite themes: the relation he posits between theatre and death:

> The spectacle, so limited in time and space, seemingly intended for a handful of spectators, will be so serious that it will be aimed at the dead. [...] If you stage *The Screens*, you must always work with the notion of a unique spectacle in mind, and carry it as far as you can. (11)

As a way of making death closer and more palpable, Genet urges town planners to build theatres and cemeteries at the heart of the city, instead of consigning them to the outskirts and suburbs:

> Whether the strange word 'urbanism' comes from some Pope Urban or from the Latin root for the word 'city', it will probably no longer have anything to do with the dead. The living will dispose of their corpses, surreptitiously or otherwise, the same way one gets rid of some shameful thought. By dispatching them to the crematorium oven, the urbanised world will deprive itself of one important theatrical mainstay, and perhaps even the theatre itself. (63)

For Genet, society's attempt to surreptitiously deny the trauma that death and dying cause only increases the subject's anguish. In a discourse reminiscent of Artaud's theory of cruelty, Genet contends that theatre can soothe metaphysical anxiety by allowing the spectator to experience a form of symbolic death (defined here as the encounter with non-knowledge, the impossible, the wound) in and through the performance event itself. In this way, death, and by extension life, becomes lighter and more joyous:

In today's cities, the only place [...] where a theatre could be built is in the cemetery. The choice will be useful for both cemetery and theatre alike. [...] Imagine for a moment what it would be like for the audience to leave after a performance of Mozart's *Don Giovanni*, making its way amongst the dead lying in the earth, before returning to the profane world. Neither the conversations nor the dead would be the same as one generally experiences after a performance at some Parisian theatre. Death would be closer and lighter. (69)

As well as Artaud, Genet's emphasis on theatre as a vehicle for existential transformation has undoubted parallels with the work of contemporary practitioners such as Jerzy Grotowski and Peter Brook. Like them, Genet seeks a form of primal confrontation in which the 'life-mask' – to use Grotowski's phrase – 'cracks and falls away' (Grotowski 1995, 23). Nevertheless, despite similarities, we need to exert caution here. Where Grotowski and Brook seek plenitude and wholeness, Genet is interested in evoking absence and liminality:[13]

But what about the drama? If its origin is some dazzling moment in the author's experience, it is up to him to seize this lightning and, beginning with the moment of illumination which reveals the void, to arrange a verbal architecture – that is, grammatical and ceremonial – slyly suggesting that from this void some semblance is snatched which reveals the void. (1972, 68)

Genet's way of producing this troubling state, this void, is to set theatre and ritual in cannibalistic opposition so that theatre eats ritual and ritual feasts on theatre:

It seems to me that any novel, poem, painting or piece of music that does not destroy itself – I mean construct itself as a 'playful massacre', cutting off its own head – is an impostor. (Genet 1991, 216. Our translation.)

The concrete outcome of this 'playful massacre' is a performance style that is marginal, ambivalent and constantly shifting: a kind of deconstructionist *jeu*. This deconstruction is particularly effective in *The Blacks*, a play in which ritual is theatricalized and theatre ritualized to such an extent that playwright, actors and spectators are lost in a dizzying vortex of perpetually changing performance modes. Initially, *The Blacks* is structured as 'un clownerie' or Black and White minstrel show: the Black actors strive to convince the White spectators that what they are watching is a piece of light-hearted entertainment, simple fun. At the start of the play, Archibald, the master of ceremonies, says:

ARCHIBALD This evening we shall perform for you. But in order that you may remain comfortably settled in your seats in the presence of the drama that is already unfolding here, in order that you be assured that there is no danger of such drama worming its way into your precious lives, we shall even have the decency – a decency learned from you – to make communication impossible. We shall increase the distance that separates us [...] for we are actors. (Genet 1979b, 12)

As the play develops it becomes increasingly clear that this meta-theatrical reference is a survival technique, a piece of camouflage: it allows the Black actors to insult the White spectators, which they do to greatest effect in two mock rituals. In the first, Marie, a White woman, played by Diouf, a Black man, is murdered and raped by Village, her Black lover. In the second, the White court, who pass judgement on Village's action from a gallery above, are enticed down from their elevated position and symbolically murdered by the Blacks. This produces a delicious, yet threatening, reversal of theatre conventions. The more the Blacks draw attention to the artificiality of the performance, the more their activity starts to appear real and authentic. During these moments, the play takes on the guise of a ritual, a symbolic activity that is intended to produce real results for the participants involved.

However, while this move to ritual certainly occurs, Genet never lets us forget that the event we are watching is still theatre. Towards the end of the play, a Black revolutionary, Ville Saint Nazaire (or Newport News in Bernard Frechtman's original English translation), enters the stage and tells the actors to bring their performance to an end. In the process, he reminds us that the entire show was conceived as a diversion, a device for concealing the real action: the murder of a Black traitor. As a result of this formal confusion, this ludic collapse, the gap between ritual and theatre is dissolved. We no longer know if the performance is real or unreal. What is certain is that we have been powerfully affected by a drama that takes place on a border, somewhere between being and non-being and absence and presence. We are given a taste, in other words, of the ambiguous nature of the sacred.

Genet's theory of performance in the trilogy is consonant with, and evolves from, his notion of the sacred. In the Genettian sacred, as in Bataille's version, the subject is not completely dissolved in the impersonality of the sacred void: there is always something, some subtle layer of consciousness that continues to register the dissolution of identity as it takes place. His theatre is constructed to express and activate this impossibility. In doing so, it transcends – without reconciling in a higher synthesis – difference and sameness, self and other.

(v) *Sacred Politics/Sacred Theatre*

From a common sense or orthodox perspective, it seems difficult to comprehend how Genet's notion of sacred theatre could serve *any* political purpose. Not only does his vision of drama radically conflict with the utilitarian agenda of political theatre (liberation through aesthetic means), he has persistently rejected the possibility of politicized art on aesthetic grounds. In 'Strange Word "Urb..."', theatre and politics are presented as mutually exclusive activities:

It's possible that the theatrical art will disappear one day. That's a notion you have to accept. If someday man's activities were to become revolutionary, day after day, the theatre would have no place in life. (1972, 71)

If Genet were to heed his own advice, the necessity of arguing against this dualistic (and reductive) view of aesthetics, though still important, would be less pressing. While we might want to challenge his conclusions on dialectical grounds, we could simply define him, in orthodox terms, of course, as an uncommitted playwright, someone who mistakenly opposes theology to politics, symbols to practice.[14] The difficulty here is that the content of Genet's drama necessitates a more rigorous involvement with his argument. In short, it causes suspicion.

In *The Balcony*, *The Blacks* and *The Screens*, Genet deals with complex historical and political issues candidly and presciently. *The Balcony* is an allegorical work suggesting that the success of fascism and failure of socialism between the wars is tied to deeper onto-theological factors; *The Blacks* focuses on the attempts of newly emancipated nations in Africa to produce an alternative, postcolonial form of identity as decolonization was occurring in the 1950s and 1960s; and *The Screens*, perhaps his most prophetic work, analyses the depressing movement from revolt to reaction in the Algerian revolution.

How can we account for this astonishing contradiction between the theory and practice of an artist who was always sensitive to how his work would be received? Since naivety is, obviously, out of the question here, we need to adopt a different hypothesis. A valid interpretation is to argue that Genet is not opposed to politics and history *per se*; rather he is opposed to how they have been conventionally represented. His target is, thus, more the history of dramatic representation than history itself. The plausibility of this reading is underlined by his comments in the 1960 edition of *The Balcony*, a text in which he grapples with an alternative and complex theory of political theatre.[15]

The preface starts by drawing attention to a dilemma that most committed artists, working within a realist or naturalist tradition, prefer to repress: the relationship between dramatic representation and catharsis:

> The imaginary representation of an action or an experience usually relieves us of the obligation of attempting to perform or undergo them ourselves, and in reality. (Genet 1991a, xiv)

To justify his critique of political realism, Genet returns to Aristotle, the founding father of western theories of drama. In the *Poetics*, Aristotle claims that tragedy provokes fear and pity for the spectators through the mimetic representation of an action: 'The imitation is not just of a complete action, but also of events that evoke fear and pity' (Aristotle 1996, 17). According to Aristotle, mimesis manipulates and produces emotions, which, as his celebrated theory of catharsis maintains, results in purification and cleansing:

> Tragedy is an imitation of an action that is admirable, complete, and possesses magnitude; in language made pleasurable, each of its species separated in different parts; performed by actors, not through narration; effecting through pity and fear the purification of such emotions. (Ibid. 10)

Using Aristotle's theory of drama as his basis, Genet argues, like Brecht and Boal, that political dramas investing in mimesis for utilitarian ends (naturalism, socialist realism, documentary drama) are seriously flawed.[16] Instead of producing social change and transformation, their commitment to realism maintains the status quo, because, in keeping with Aristotle's aesthetics, the theatrical representation of an action is intimately related to the catharsis of anti-social emotions, the very stuff of revolutionary desire.

Genet's rejection of realism is particularly applicable to political and pedagogical plays that 'offer' ideological solutions to complex social problems:

> When the problem of a certain disorder – or evil – has been solved on stage, this shows that it has in fact been abolished, since, according to the dramatic conventions of our time, a theatrical representation can only be the representation of a fact. (1991a, xiv)

Here, he argues that because mimesis assumes a reality existing independently of and prior to representation – the object is literally re-presented – it conflicts with the intentions of the politically radical learning play, which, if taken at its word, is committed to creating a nascent revolutionary consciousness for a pre-revolutionary society. This is contradictory in Genet's opinion. For if the learning play purports to represent dramatic solutions to real problems, then does not this assume, according to the logic of re-presentation, that these problems have already been solved? ('Theatrical representation can only be the representation of a fact'.) Such conservative logic is, of course, counter-productive. Genet's conclusion is simple but brutal: realism is politically redundant and thus must be avoided:

> We can then turn our minds to something else, and allow our hearts to swell with pride, seeing that we took the side of the hero who aimed – successfully – at finding the solution. (Ibid.)

Genet's rejection of realism does not lead him to endorse a political theatre based on Brechtian principles either. For Genet, Brecht's intimate relationship with Marx's meta-discourse of liberation betrays a theological dependence, which is neither revolutionary nor subversive, but, on the contrary, a mere displacement of conventional bourgeois aspirations and desires. In an important interview with Hubert Fichte in 1975, Genet compares the 'alienated' attitude of the Brechtian cigar-smoking spectator with the behaviour of the Rothschild family discussing art after dinner:

> Personally, I don't know the Rothschild family, but I imagine that you would speak of art at the Rothschild mansion while smoking a cigarette. (Genet 1991c, 145. Our translation.)

Brechtian alienation is too rationalistic for Genet. Instead of wrenching us from the safe haven of the ego and disclosing the mysteries of the sacred, it reinforces our sense of self by underlining the capacity of consciousness to master the world. In Genet's view, this does little to disturb the traditional Judæo-Christian world-view. Otherness is still reduced to the same. Like Roger, the revolutionary commander who identifies with his rival, the fascistic Chief of Police towards the end of The Balcony, Genet believes that Brecht remains part of the world he professes to despise.

If he rejects both realism and critical formalism, what type of political theatre does Genet endorse? In the preface, he anticipates the politicization of Artaud that occurred in the 1960s and 1970s by arguing that the social impact of theatre is most keenly felt when rational solutions are avoided and evil (extreme negativity) is allowed to explode on stage:

> [No] problem that has been exposed ought to be solved in the imagination, especially when the dramatist has made every effort to show the concrete reality of a social order. On the contrary, the evil shown on stage should explode, should show us naked, and leave us distraught, if possible, and having no recourse other than ourselves. [...] The work must be an active explosion, an act to which the public reacts – as it wishes, as it can. If the 'good' is to appear in a work of art it does so through the divine aid of the powers of song, whose strength alone is enough to magnify the evil that has been exposed. (1991a, xiv)

To be effective politically, Genet argues that theatre needs to reject rational and conciliatory messages and provoke disturbing experiences and emotions that resist representation and language. In other words, it ought to target the sacred.

If Genet heralds the political theatre of avant-garde practitioners from the 1960s to the present, he also anticipates the major themes of left-wing postmodern politics. From this perspective, politics is not just about the art of statesmanship and/or ideological identification, it has a more fundamental, existential meaning, inseparable from the subject's capacity for accepting difference and the non-identical. As contemporary theorists such as Jean-Luc Nancy stress, this is ultimately related to the way we respond to lack and loss, the moment when we realize that organic notions of community rooted in identity and self-presence are metaphysical fictions. Nancy is aware of the dangers involved in such communities:

> Fascism was the grotesque or abject resurgence of an obsession with communion; it crystallised the motif of its supposed loss and the nostalgia for its images of fusion. (Nancy 1991, 17)

For Nancy et al., politics are progressive when they avoid prescribing positive or transcendent notions of community and civilization and leave us free to negotiate the anxiety created by foreignness, transformation and change. In this context, dealing with the negative, confronting the void, is ethical: it reminds us that the nostalgic dream of oneness is impossible to achieve. Julia Kristeva makes a similar claim in *Strangers to Ourselves* when she re-interprets Freud's notion of the uncanny from a political perspective:

> Delicately, analytically, Freud does not speak of foreigners: he teaches us how to detect foreignness in ourselves. That is perhaps the only way not to hound it outside of us. [...] Such a Freudian distraction or discretion concerning the 'problem of foreigners' [...] might be interpreted as an invitation (a utopic or very modern one?) not to reify the foreigner, not to petrify him as such, not to petrify *us* as such. [...] The ethics of psychoanalysis implies a politics. (Kristeva 1991, 191–2)

According to this deconstructionist viewpoint, politics are negative when they insist on filling absence and gaps with representations and strive to actualize utopia by investing in theological notions of language, race, territory. Here, as we know only too well from contemporary history, otherness is considered as a threat, which must be destroyed before it destroys you ('the pre-emptive strike'). The neo-Lacanian philospher Slavoj Žižek underlines the political dangers of metaphysical thinking in his critique of fascism's dream of/for totality:

> The dream is that since the excess was introduced from the outside, i.e., is the work of an alien intruder, its elimination would enable us to obtain again a stable social organisation whose parts form a harmonious corporate body. (Žižek 1993, 210)

Interpreted in this way, Genet's desire to invoke the sacred – what we could term, in reference to the preface of 1960 edition of *The Balcony*, 'the explosion of evil' – is, undoubtedly, politically progressive. By placing us on a/theological borderline, he uses theatre to puncture mythologies and ideologies of sameness and identity (what Žižek calls fascism's 'harmonious corporate body'). What we are left with instead is the disgusting and anguished awareness of the remainder – the paradoxical sign of incompleteness, radical otherness and difference. For Genet, this remainder is produced in performance when theatre deconstructs its own representational foundations and places us in the heart of absence, 'the one we sometimes find near the confines of death'. (1972, 15)

Genet's deconstructionist attack on theatricality, and by extension the Symbolic order outside the theatre, has a distinctly utopian quality. Particularly when read in tandem with the Giacometti essay written during the same period. His suspension of metaphysical, or theological, notions of identity is intended to produce an alternative notion of community, which, like Bataille's sacred community, is founded on difference rather than sameness. For Genet – as indeed for Bataille – this awareness of the strangeness of the other, his impossible closeness and distance, constitutes a new ethical undertaking:

> The visible world is what it is, and our action upon it cannot make it radically different. Hence our nostalgic dreams of a universe in which man, instead of acting so furiously upon visible appearance, would attempt to rid himself of it – not only to refuse any action upon it, but to strip himself bare enough to discover that secret site within ourselves that would capacitate an entirely different human adventure. More specifically, an altogether different moral enterprise. (1993, 310)

If we think, as Nancy et al. do, that the political is ethical and vice versa, then politics, for Genet, is more than an utilitarian balance sheet of ends and means: it is about living ethically, learning to respect otherness and coping with absences and gaps. According to this definition, politics is radically opposed to totalitarian ideologies and theological meta-narratives purporting to fill the abyss and offering existential plenitude. Like theatre, that 'semblance which reveals the void', politics is about learning to cope with absence and lack; that is, the sacred.

(vi) Sacred Politics in the Trilogy

In The Blacks, The Balcony and The Screens, Genet manipulates dramaturgical practice in quite specific ways in order to deconstruct metaphysical identity, and thus produce sacred experience. His reason for producing such experience, as Beckett also makes clear, is that any other basis for behaviour collapses action into ideology's obsession with endless Wiederholung. It is, quite precisely, a question of life or death.

Nowadays it is commonplace for aspirants to power to employ an image consultant. Forty years ago Genet perceived the distinction between image and function and the inherent escalation of self-regard. If the clients of Irma's eponymous brothel, le Grand Balcon, in The Balcony literally erect their image, the 'nomenclature' of the world outside (or is it 'really' 'outside'?) is also composed of those who spend time polishing theirs: their activity, in Genet's vision, is no less masturbatory and perhaps more deadly. For what they seek is the ultimate narcissistic stasis of an 'unimpeachable' image, for which they are prepared to do anything and which clearly bears no relation to their acts.

Whores and actors, on the other hand, although they may (like the pimp Arthur in The Balcony) be fatally seduced by their own images too, acknowledge their illusory and equivocal status.

They play, and they know that they play: and their playing mirrors the truth that we are only things which play, roles which flicker across the void which underlies and undermines our pretensions. The truth in *The Balcony*, as in *The Blacks* and *The Screens*, is not in the images constructed inside or outside the brothel; it is in the revelation of their falsity, of the void at the heart of the Symbolic order. As the theatricality of all our props is revealed, that sinking feeling is the guarantee of the sacred experience of theatre.

The ideological universe, on the other hand, which the Trois Figures of Bishop, Judge and General strive to symbolize, is what stakes out the territory of the known: it is a hedge of thorns. Here, it proclaims, are the signs which mark the outer limit of the world. It is a theatre of high status and static highs, where the phallic goal is 'Ritual stiffness! Final immobility' (1991, 6). The most you can hope for is to become one of those signs: to erect your image and leave it as a beacon for posterity, so that, like the Chief of Police, the subject can exclaim, 'I've arrived! My image! I belong to the nomenclature. I've got my simulacrum' (94). This theologically based value system is the epitome of 'all that is dear to us' and the form of its crystallization is the same throughout Genet's trilogy: the embalmed notation of a fixed order in which Queen, Judge, Bishop, General, Blacks and Whites, and Colonizer and Colonized play out their allotted roles. This repetition of an eternal substance is achieved by rites of origins and presence which must be performed exactly, faithfully, without hurry or disturbance in a hermetically sealed space-time. In *The Balcony*, Arthur fears that he won't be able to cope with the atmosphere outside the brothel; in *The Blacks*, the Blacks are anxious in face of life without Whites; and in *The Screens* the revolutionaries are terrified by 'a little heap of rubbish' (1963, 162). The remainder, in this case the physical weight of a gun, bullets, the touch of the air, the feel of mud and rain, a little heap of shit, is a potent threat to the purity of the Symbolic order used to veil absence and negativity and thus represent ideology's eternal truth.

For Genet, however, the sacred as transformational impetus is dependent on the transgression of Symbolic 'propriety': it is not the ideal, nor is it physical death, but it is the real as a/theological liminality: tearing apart, breaking down, bewilderment, the encounter with otherness within the self.[17] Here the sacred is spelt scared, the explosions and gunfire in *The Balcony*, like the cockerel's crow in *The Blacks*, signal not an inversion (the familiar turned upside-down) but a dissolution and an ungraspable something else, which lacerates, disfigures, decomposes, cuts into the roles we play and shreds pretensions to permanence. Here I am not that which endures, I am a vulnerability which changes and decays, committed to what Bataille calls sovereignty.

Conversely, the onto-theological 'I' that can be thought is a list of attributes and roles. But if these attributes are suddenly sucked empty, I experience myself not as a fullness, a presence; but as an emptiness, an absence. 'I', however, am still the experiencer. So I am something else, I am other. Corresponding to Genet's notion of the wounded self, if I am both myself and other, I am an ambiguity, a *fuite*, a continual making and unmaking. Actors are more accustomed to this situation, in Genet's view: they are always asked to be neither their everyday roles nor, entirely, the character they are embodying: they are always somewhere in between – and Genet, in his writing about performance, makes it clear that he wishes them to live this alterity and alternation to the full: 'The thing is to discover a narrative tone that is *always* equivocal, always shifting' (1991b, xi). The requirement to do so is of course embedded in the role-within-role and character-within-character frameworks which he sets up: virtually no character in his work is not at the same time adopting a role (revolutionaries and reactionaries in *The Balcony*, Blacks and Whites in *The Blacks*, colonizer and colonized in *The Screens*); but additionally their 'basic' identity is anonymous or problematic, or they are acting a character who is acting a further role (actor acts Roger the revolutionary leader acting the Chief of Police; actor acts Village acting stereotypical white expectation of black lover, which is itself a role intended to conceal a further role as agent of the revolution). So identification in Genet's late theatre is always double, triple, undermined by extreme uncertainty. The effect on the audience is intended to be vertiginous, pulling them towards experiencing this void at the centre of their own consciousness as it fails to locate any certainties; it is equally demanding for actors, who are asked continually to play someone who is faking and are never in possession of a set of recognisable criteria in which to ground themselves. They are thus forced to undergo a kind of continuous Stanislavskian nightmare, since there can be no recourse to 'authentic' experiences at all. Instead, they are asked to draw on a continually renewed immersion in the provisional, silent space beyond 'truth'.

In Genet's dramas, ideology, like theology, repeats; the sacred fragments. Both the attempt to cling on to the status quo (acted out in the brothel, staged as White Court judging Black crimes, present in the colonizer's attempt to harness the image of cultural superiority) and the proposal to invert it in an 'offstage' insurrection and/or anti-colonial revolution, are equally real and unreal, and equally wedded to the profane. They simply replay the same Order of dominator and dominated, colonizer and colonized, *bourreau* and *victime*. This much we can grasp, though we may have to take a step beyond the more usual reality/illusion paradigms in which theatre deals to do so. What is at issue is not whether one (apparently aesthetic) order is preferable or superior to another (apparently political) order. Much more pertinently, both are orders – Symbolic orders – firmly rooted in the domain of the thinkable (what Robbe-Grillet, frequently illuminating as a parallel to Genet, calls 'the last guardians of order'). (Robbe-Grillet 1965, 156. Our translation.)

Theatre, for Genet, moves us beyond orders and into the terror of unknowing and the realm of disordering. Where what is left, is neither this nor that. Where what we can hold in mind (and body) at this moment is precisely the ebbing away of what we know and who we are. In *The Screens*, the Cadi defines this state as a form of sleepwalking, a condition in which we are neither conscious nor unconscious, but in-between and on the way to becoming something new: 'I need to sleep, I need to wander... I'm changing into something else'. (1979c, 280)[18]

Ritual either sustains (onto-theologies or ideologies) or unleashes (the sacred). Genet theatricalizes the former in order to expose and explode it; inflated to the extremes of 'parade' by cothurni, costume and rhetoric, it suddenly crumples and implodes into the void which always threatens: the void at the centre where being should be. In order to reveal this nothingness, theatre is theatricalized and used against itself.

In Catholic practice the Mass is 'elevated' in order to function as visible and sustaining ritual. But if it is elevated too far, it starts to comment on its own artificiality: in Gombrowicz's *Pornografia* (1960), Ferdinand 'dispatches' it precisely by taking it ultra-seriously, and Witold has a sudden vision of it disappearing into the stratosphere, taking its congregation along with it and leaving them all 'suspended in the cosmos...like monkeys grimacing into space' (Gombrowicz 1991, 19). Dravidian or Yoruba rites may, as ideal repetition, confirm social hierarchy and belief systems; they also have the visceral power to engage the unformulated, to leave the participant in no-man's-land, by suddenly presenting him/her with an unrecognizable but inescapable reality: a more-than-human force incarnate, a shift into a different space-time. In Genet, ritual as social performance disintegrates to provide the spectator with an experience of the a/theological sacred, which begins in the place of non-identity. All fictions of the self dissolve, since identity itself is presented as role, as fiction; what is left is not differentiated 'identity', but the identity of sacred indifference. Here performance (the encounter with what is not as yet known, which comes into being as it is performed) passes through and reveals the void at the centre of narcissistic identity and of the socio-political structures built upon it. This apparently mystical revelation is, however, both achieved by physical (actorly) means and imbued with material (political) consequence.

In Genet's theatre, the stitching is undone, the gap left open. What we are presented with is not a character who conforms to a realistic subject; but a theatricalized character, a false identity. In *The Balcony*, for instance, any talk about the dramatic reality of the Bishop is superfluous. The most that can be said is that a character whose identity is never revealed is playing the role of a Bishop. Since we, the spectators, have nothing positive to identify with, the reality of the character remains a mystery, an ambiguous sign, ushering in a massive sensation of anxiety and uncanniness for the audience. This liminal ambivalence is exploited to greatest effect in *The Blacks*. In this vertiginous play, Genet confuses denotation (what is there) with connotation (what is being represented) to disturb the standard, transparent mode of theatrical communication. We are unable, even as we leave the auditorium, to tell if the Black actors are really acting or using the cover of theatre as an alibi to express real hatred for us, the White audience.

The aura of doubt and uncertainty frames sound effects too: just as some of the bells which punctuate scenes in the *The Balcony* are explicitly 'fake' (operated by Irma herself or rigged up as part of the scenario), so we may wonder about the status of the bursts of machine-gun fire or the explosions. The Envoy laconically and confusingly attributes the second explosion to the Royal Palace, after having already done so for the first: he explains that the essence of such a building is to go on being blown up. This ironic witticism hardly helps to sort out any 'facts', which exasperates the Chief of Police to the point of apoplexy. In short, it is increasingly difficult for anyone on- or offstage to orientate themselves according to expected channels of information. A similar effect is produced in *The Blacks*, when, towards the end of the play, an offstage detonation is heard, which may or may not be the 'execution' of a Black traitor, whose trial the play is constructed to conceal.

The aim of this dramatic deconstruction is to produce a state of ontological anxiety, allowing the spectator to experience the liminality of sacred experience. At the end of *The Balcony*, for instance, the actress playing Irma steps out of character (or does she?) and reminds the audience that: 'You must go home now, – and you can be quite sure that nothing there will be any more real than it is now.' (96) 'Home' here is both the comfort of familiar domesticity and the desire for ontological security.

Through this collapse of the borders separating theatre from reality, Genet attempts to use performance to found a different mode of action upon a different sense of the self. He suggests an initial 'turn' of focus or mental energy away from the realm of external action towards an internal situation of 'nakedness'. This nakedness implies a recognition of the insubstantiality of visible appearance: the known self is 'undone', 'stripped naked'. The traditional active, egoic western subject is suspended in favour of a hollowness, an unknowability, whose absence (of the previously known configuration of self and world) is a dynamic nexus for potential political and ethical reorientation.

(vii) *Conclusion*

Reading Genet's theatre through Bataille's notion of the sacred radically alters the conventional approach to Genet's drama. Almost unanimously, critics working within this field have tended to see his search for the sacred as something intensely apolitical and asocial. What we have hoped to show, by contrast, is that, the political significance of Genet's theatre does not lie in the solutions it offers or the representations it gives; it is found in how it suspends ideas of totality and presence. Appropriately, this celebration of impossibility and incompleteness leads to the following paradoxical conclusion: namely, that the most politically committed theatre is the one which is the most radically disengaged, that is, the most sacred.

7.2 DECONSTRUCTIVE ACTING: GENET, BECKETT, THE ABSURD

Ralph Yarrow

(i) *Genet*

In *The Maids*, always, to us, the performers play a doubled and tripled playing (maids playing themselves, playing their mistress; men perhaps playing women; actors playing all of these). For the maids it only enmeshes them further in the cycle of violence: death only confirms the relative positions in the hierarchy; but the play itself incarnates a mode of continual ambiguity, of transition between roles, genders, frames and possible outcomes. Genet's underlying intuition, rendered more fully in his subsequent trilogy, is that the ambiguity he so deliberately cultivated himself is the only possible strategy of resistance in a world in which fettered minds are revealed in the binaries of oppositional moral posturing.

Even more so in *The Balcony*, the aim seems to be to unsettle actors and audience, to make things difficult, to disallow any equation (except ironical) of actor and character. To generate this discomfort, actors have to experience it directly and physically themselves; whereas 'Claire' and 'Solange' are relatively coherent entities to migrate between, character in *The Balcony* is much more an *ad hoc* composition, as here each player is either quite consciously adopting a false persona or engaged in assisting others to do so, whilst at the same time both revealing and concealing their motives for so doing; the actors thereby signal a radical confrontation with any claims for 'truth'.

The Balcony is a real *bal des cons* in at least two senses; ideological and idealized pretensions are caricatured in a kind of Bakhtinian revelry; but here, as in *The Blacks*, any lasting 'revolution' is unlikely as the new order seems likely to replicate the old, though Irma's final admonition that things 'at home' will be no different enjoins the audience at least to be aware of the prevalence of such a situation. *The Screens*, on the other hand, offers an alternative scenario, and thus requires an encounter with further levels of deconstructive acting.

The experience generated in and by the different spaces in *The Screens* – Arab village, colonialists' lands and houses, battlegrounds at night, the afterworld – is mediated *vocally and physically* through a series of levels and tones: that of the oppressors; that of the oppressed; that of transition, miscegenation, hiatus and hesitation. Its complexity is further manifested by the reality of 'real' objects (although they are on stage); the reality of the illusions (drawings on screens, 'false' objects); and by the theatre of the colonialists and the theatre of the brothel.

The interaction of all these factors institutes a process of continual juxtaposition, relativization and shifting focus; everything is always *provisional*, never defined or set.

The cast list has 98 characters. So performing, as well as receiving, is a process of continual transposition, transformation and transubstantiation. Each actor has to be many bodies, voices and potentialities. Identity for performers is plural; there is no single or even easily reducible trajectory or thematic solution.

Taken together with the procedures of the earlier plays, what this seems to suggest is something we could call *interstitial acting* (where 'acting' also implies a way of thinking and thus of being, and thus is at least potentially applicable to audience as well as performers). Interstitial acting requires, is produced from and produces interstitial being. 'I' am most freely and fully when I am in the gaps of 'myself' (as defined socially, politically, existentially or metaphysically). From here, perhaps, I may speak before that which speaks for me.

Actors from Copeau to Lecoq have been learning to access this; and not, I think, simply for technical or narcissistic reasons: we are talking about an ethical necessity in a world in which not to accommodate the other in oneself is to participate in ethnic cleansing. Genet understands it this way.

The blanket Leïla takes to prison is mostly holes; she and Saïd, in their anti-picaresque journey away from all the parameters of property and propriety, learn more and more how not to be, how to be the opposite of what everyone might want or expect, how to inhabit the holes in any pattern of role or image.

Such an incorporation of otherness involves a passage through an emptiness: an abandonment of the known or normal self which owns or has a place; or a location of the contours of the material in the not quite manifest realm of the imaginary. Bodies abandon their everyday modes, transfigure themselves (Leïla, Saïd and the Mother become strange amalgams of human and object – a suitcase, a clock); Leïla at other times crawls, emits strange sounds, squats; Kadidja and Warda 'watch' their own death; the Dead incorporate it, wryly and with amazement ('that's it!') (1963, 143, 147, 158, 160), or enact its grotesqueness (the Sergeant shot as he shits). They pass through themselves, as it were, to become another.

Saïd, Leïla and the Mother journey through nowhere spaces towards a non-place or condition (a *u-topia*); they constantly pull each other up for any lapse back towards more familiar or comfortable zones. (Leïla: 'I want you to lead me without flinching to the land of shadow and of the monster...I want you to choose evil and always evil') (108–9).

In *The Screens*, actors have to approach a kind of not-acting, but a very specific and physical kind, a difficult and unfamiliar condition with which they have to learn to operate, very close to the need to 'repartir de zéro' inherent in neutral mask or Lecoqian work. In particular, Genet offers Leïla no help from scenery, props or stage directions in the strange monologue of her death, which she has to realize from this absence of resources as an entry into further and further degrees of strangeness. Like much of the work described above it is a production from, or across (*à travers*), nothing, and what is produced cannot quite recognizably be called 'self' any longer.

(ii) *Beckett*

Interrogating Performers

Following a production of some Beckett shorts at the University of East Anglia in March 2000, I asked actors and directors what they had experienced and how they evaluated it. I asked them to consider particularly.

- The nature of the 'pause'.
- What happens to 'I' during it?
- What happens to language and thought during it?
- What happens after it?
- The nature of this 'passage': is it thinking, feeling, and, if so, in what senses; is it a 'loss' and/or a 'gain'?
- How does this kind of moment/process affect your relationship with: the whole piece; the audience; yourself; your fellow performers (if any)?
- How do you feel 'after Beckett': as a performer; as a person?

The questions tend towards the abstract or metaphysical. Their responses, which are more immediate and physical, included the following:

Actorial:
- *Physical difficulties* arise from stage directions about positions, gestures etc., e.g. hand on jaw, in a dustbin, in an urn, in a sack;
- *Vocal and intentional problems* from instructions *not* to point, emphasize, give any intonation etc.;
- *Character/narrator confusion* from shifting or unclear/oblique narrative position ('I' or 'he/she', 1st or 3rd?); am 'I' subject or object, teller or told? Who is telling which story for whom?
- *Motivation and pace/delivery* are rendered difficult by 'external' 'control' from prompter, goad, listener, knocker, invisible force etc.
- *Lack of punctuation* and indications often make it difficult to get the words out, heightened by bizarre and cramping posture requirements which affect breath.

A summary of responses produces something like this:

- ■ Physical *restrictions* (body position, breath, movement, voice distorted, distended, hampered, encased or muffled by set/costume) are intensified by
- ■ *incitements* (promptings, goadings).
- ■ Resulting in an oppositional or paradoxical energy: 'I can't go on'/'I must go on'

The *subject position* is problematic:

- ❖ Who am I?
- ❖ What do I do?
- ❖ How do I say this?
- ❖ What does it mean?
- ❖ Why am I saying it?

The *actor's process* becomes:

- ✚ Not acting;
- ✚ Removing intonation and 'pointing';
- ✚ Breaking all units down as far as possible;
- ✚ Getting left in a *vide/bide* (Lecoq's term for the moment when all 'props' are taken away but you have to go on...);
- ✚ Starting again from there.

All of these features seem to reduce the scope of the performer, to *make it difficult or impossible to 'act'*. Actors ask what they are supposed to do in this situation: what 'function' do they have? How do they operate from where they don't know who/what they are and what resources they should deploy? (Yarrow 2001, 77–8)

'Stuttering', or how to say and not to say simultaneously

In Beckett, says Gilles Deleuze, 'language stutters' (Deleuze 1994, 23–29), because it is aware that it can't say but that it must go on (hence, the pauses, promptings and goadings which proliferate the texts and stage-directions). It is the locus of our inadequacy, it expresses the void which it appears to cover. The 'I' expressed in language is thus always recognised as *not the 'I'* which expresses, because whereas the expressed is (relatively and ambiguously) defined and finished ['défini/fini': *Molloy*, 59], the expressive is unconditioned, in production, potent. Language always limits the 'I', places it in time and space, and has, thus, constantly to be refuted even though it is the only available method of expression. No, that's 'not I', because 'I' is a performative dynamic, not a circumscribed entity. The equally powerful compulsion to 'mean', however, always reinscribes the I in the linguistic ontology, immediately subject to (= object of) the expressive (Symbolic) order, i.e. the inevitability of repetitive gestures and moves, physical and/or verbal, which thereby confirm their inadequacy (e.g. *Act Without Words 1* and 2). Stuttering is this continual vacillation in Beckett; a kind of repeated hiatus of language, which attempts both to suspend itself and to say fully what it intends, whilst being unable to do either completely. (Ibid., 82–3)

In terms of performance practice, we are also operating here at the junction of 'voice and 'text'. 'Voice' is what is capable of expression, of resonating, of taking form as rhythm and timbre; but is not necessarily as yet clogged or freighted with the context or significance of 'text', which carries the development of form and content into more fully materialized dimensions.

To retire beyond or before even this initiatory enunciation is the *desire* of Mouth in *Not I* (or of the Unnameable), the goal of Molloy's *desiderata* or Murphy's modulation into a body rhythm, the most fragile thread of breath and being (as in the title *Breath*, which itself may locate what in India would be called *prana* and in China *Qi*, the liveliness of the fully alert but not-yet-engaged performer) (ibid., 84).

I is not I

Language then is performance-text, and as such it is a phenomenological articulation of what is not yet 'I' or identity. *Not I*, in performance a text which exemplifies the stuttering described above and which continually returns to the point of negating any defined identity for the speaker, when examined as written structure reveals further manifestations of the same tendency. The first page includes four questions and nine negatives, plus many instances of ellipsis; any forward drive or possible teleology is broken up, blocked; the body of the text is fragmented, narrative energy and the exhalation of the actor is constantly halted, pushed back to the beginning. 'I' is only this starting; 'she' is what is articulated and then denied as inauthentic and stultified.

Mouth vehemently refutes the label 'I' being attached to the miscreant, devious, alien identities which emerge as her unstoppable flow of 'buzzing' words. 'She' (which *others* as it defines) is her insistent attribution for these personae, in a move to allow 'I' to escape unwanted Symbolic fixity. This quest for an ideal freedom is not only psychoexistential but also rhythmic, structural and vocal: each denial of 'I' figures in the stream of sound as an excavated absence into which voice and text dive and from which they re-emerge ('what? who? no! she!'). Each question mark requires an inhalation in which the dynamic of the text is suspended. Then it stutters into fragmented sound, before violently expelling as other all that has gone before. The performer is nailed down to practising the reduction of language to sonic quanta, which both reject any coherent naming of world and self in narrative flow, and insist that she and her listener(s) attend to the moment of birthing over and over again. The voice re-emerges in the exclamations just cited as all the long vowels (rather like a voice exercise: oo-a-o-ee); and these are, in fact, the open, initiatory, exhalatory ground of language, although in terms of the sense of Mouth's exclamations they represent the apparent opposite, denial and restriction. *Not I*, like *Krapp's Last Tape*, keeps starting up as a new flow of sound and struggling with some difficulty towards comprehensibility; but only temporarily, since it keeps returning to the point of origin, the stopping and starting of tape and vocalization. Performance here requires physical swallowing and regurgitating; the performer stops the flow, swallows air, spits out sound. Language emerges from her mouth to enact what is not and can never be: 'I' I is not entity, but quantum energy (ibid., 84–5).

Notes to Part 2

1. I follow the definition of consciousness in the Vedic tradition, specifically Shankara's Advaita (nondual) Vedanta, and its derivative in perennial psychology as expounded by Jonathan Shear (1990), Robert Forman (1998), Arthur Deikman (1996) and others. The Vedic model of the mind posits higher states in the development of consciousness. Vedic psychology, as Charles Alexander notes, proposes 'an architecture of increasingly abstract, functionally integrated faculties or levels of mind (1990, 290). The term 'mind' as I use it here derives from the latter of its two uses in Vedic psychology: 'It [mind] refers to the overall multilevel functioning of consciousness as well as to the specific level of thinking (apprehending and comparing) within that overall structure' (Alexander 1986, 291). The levels of the overall functioning of mind in Vedic psychology extend from the senses, desire, mind, intellect, feelings and ego, to pure consciousness. As used here in the analysis of sacred theatre, self as internal observer or void in thought refers to pure consciousness (turiya or the fourth state), which is physiologically distinct from the three ordinary states of waking, sleeping and dreaming and which underlies and is transcendental to individual ego and thinking mind.

2. Vedic psychology also proposes higher stages of the development of consciousness. The permanent experience of pure consciousness (turiya chetana or the fourth) along with any of the other three states (waking, sleeping and dream) is called cosmic consciousness (turiyatit chetana or the fifth). This becomes refined cosmic consciousness (Bhagavat chetana or the sixth) through the refinement of sensory perception. Finally, in unity consciousness (Brahmi chetana or the seventh), one is able to perceive everything in terms of one's own transcendental self (Alexander 1990, 290).

3. In Sanskrit poetics, rasa is an aesthetic experience through which awareness, 'transcending the limitations of the personal attitude, is lifted...above pain and pleasure into pure joy, the essence of which is its relish [rasa] itself' (De 13). It 'consists in blissful enjoyment of the self by the self' (Chakrabarti 144–45), with self here referring to pure consciousness or turiya.

4. No theory of consciousness has yet been generally accepted by the scientific community. Cognitive scientists like Daniel Dennett (1993) and Francis Crick (1994) define consciousness in material terms as a 'virtual machine' and 'a pack of neurons', respectively, while others like David Chalmers (1996), Joseph Levine (1983) and Colin McGinn (1991) point to the failure of purely materialistic theories to explain consciousness or the nature of subjective experience. Science has yet to resolve the 'explanatory gap' (Levine) between materialism and qualia – the phenomenal properties of our experience such as colours, smells and tastes. Western theories of consciousness include materialism (Dennett, Crick and Michael Tye 1995), dualism (Chalmers) and mysterianism (McGinn, who believes we lack the right concepts for understanding consciousness, which therefore remains a mystery). Relying on third-person observation, western theories of consciousness are still in the developmental phase, while eastern theories, based on first-hand experience and the record of sacred texts, have long reached their full maturity.

5. In a footnote Throop distinguishes between his use of pre- and trans-conceptual awareness and Ken Wilber's notion of the 'pre/trans fallacy' used in the defense of a non-regressive transpersonal experience. In Wilber's usage, pre-conceptual is viewed as regressive and 'pre-egoic', and trans-conceptual is viewed as progressive and 'trans-egoic' (see Wilber 1997, 182-85; 1996, 59-65). Throop, on the other hand, views pre-conceptual awareness in

opposition to post-conceptual awareness, the stages of 'consciousness or perception that have already been shaped and mediated by conceptual constructs and models'; and trans-conceptual awareness in opposition to sub-conceptual awareness, 'which is precisely the level of consciousness that corresponds to the developmental state of an infant's consciousness early in ontogenesis' (note 22, 48). Thus, Wilber's pre-conceptual corresponds to Throop's sub-conceptual, while their definitions of trans-conceptual awareness seem to be largely the same and are shared by Forman, Shear and Deikman.

6. The term 'self-referral' as used here means the process of the self knowing itself as pure consciousness, a process of growing self-awareness. In the Advaitan tradition it also means that pure consciousness (Atman) is fully awake to itself, undifferentiated and self-shining, beyond space and time, 'aware only of the Oneness of being' (Deutsch 48).

7. Phenomenological critics like Poulet describe the audience as the passive recipients of the content of the author's consciousness, while in the experience of M. *Butterfly*, as suggested here, the audience actively transcends content into pure consciousness.

8. For an analysis of the relation between levels of language and consciousness in the Vedic tradition, see Haney 2002, 67–88.

9. In the context of Vedic aesthetics, the incipient experience of pure consciousness together with qualia, the qualities of the ordinary waking mind, carries a flavour of the higher state of cosmic consciousness (see note 2 above).

10. Jean-Francois Lyotard, 'The Tooth, the Palm', trans. Anne Knab and Michel Benamou, in *Mimesis, Masochism, and Mime: The Politics of Theatricality in Contemporary French Thought*, ed. Timothy Murray (Ann Arbor: The University of Michigan Press, 2000), 282–88 (282).

> We have used, for the most part, established translations. When translations were not available, we translated the citations ourselves. These are marked in the text and refer back to the French originals.

11. George Bataille, 'The Sacred', trans. Allan Stoekl with Carl P. Lovitt and Donald M. Leslie, Jnr, in *Visions of Excess: Selected Writings 1977–1939*, ed. Allan Stoekl (Ann Arbor: The University of Michigan Press, 1985), 240–45 (242).

12. For a further discussion of this idea, see Rudolf Otto, *The Idea of the Holy: An Enquiry into the Non-Rational Factor in the Idea of the Divine and its Relation to the Rational*, trans. John W. Harvey, 2nd edn (Oxford: Oxford University Press, 1973).

13. Monique Borie highlights the distinction between Genet's theatre of absence and the more affirmative theatres of Brook and Grotowski in *Mythe et théâtre aujourd'hui: une quête impossible? (Beckett-Genet-Grotowski-Le Living Theatre)* (Paris: Nizet, 1981):

> The loss of confidence in the foundations of the old world is also expressed in 'theatre about theatricality' whose greatest exponent is Jean Genet. In his work, the old Order is identified with a sterile, patently artificial Imaginary, which is now devoid of any constitutional power. The most it can achieve is to construct a game of reflections, the simulacrum of a ceremony, that has no impact on society or history. (9) Our translation.

14. The Marxist critic, Fredric Jameson offers a plausible alternative to Genet's argument in *The Political Unconscious: Narrative as a Socially Symbolic Act* (Ithaca: Cornell University Press, 1981):

'The convenient working distinction between cultural texts that are social and political and those that are not becomes something worse than an error: namely, a symptom and a reinforcement of the reification and privatisation of contemporary life.' (20)

15. The only critic to discuss the importance of this text is David H. Walker, 'Revolution and Revisions in Genet's *The Balcony*', *Modern Language Review*, 79: 4 (1984), 817–30.
16. See Bertolt Brecht, *Brecht on Theatre*, trans. John Willet (London: Eyre Methuen, 1964); Augusto Boal, *Theater of the Oppressed*, trans. Charles A. and Maria-Odilia Leal McBride (New York: Urizen Books, 1979).
17. In post-structuralist philosophy, propriety, or, to use its original, French, spelling, *propriété*, signifies both possession and cleanliness. These are metaphors for totality, plenitude, self-presence.
15. Our translation. This important line is absent from Frechtman's translation of the play.

PART 3: PROCESSES AND DIRECTIONS

Chapter 8

PROCESSES

Ralph Yarrow

(i) *Transitional Moments*

What is it in ritual that is useful in exploring our model of the sacred? In Chapter 2 we discussed the structural features and the functions of ritual in terms of the 'confrontation of temporal, spatial and ontological limits'. Ritual, and the operation of mask and trance, seems to offer a situation in which to investigate transitional moments and processes, changes from one state, one kind of being, one form of knowing, to another. (Though they don't by any means only occur in ritual: George asks 'whether performance in general and Noh specifically can provide...such realizations [or] "hana" moments' George, 150). So in this chapter we will look again at what is involved in these transitions, which can occur between actor and character, one character and another character, performer and audience, event and participants, space or location and the bodies in it, self and other, self and other kinds of self; we will aim to see whether what occurs in these Janus-moments (which may in some or all cases be a kind of non-occurrence, a suspension, a pointing nowhere as a trigger for moving in either direction) can signal important criteria for the construction of our psychological, social, ethical and political spheres.

The chapter also indicates how theatre practice resonates with these features across various historical periods and cultural contexts (for example, ancient Indian, Balinese and Japanese performance forms and twentieth-century European directing and actor-training practice – in which Copeau's and Lecoq's identification of a condition of psychophysiological neutrality is central to the kinds of transformation actors need to develop). In talking about process and discussing these reflections and inflections across cultures, we may run the risk of editing out cultural specifics and committing a form of interculturalist neocolonialism similar to that with which Rustom Bharucha charges Barba and Brook. It is true that in adopting for some of the discussion a 'psychobiological' stance, we are in part suggesting that human bodies and their perceptual and sensory mechanisms work similarly wherever they are found: we would claim that, if it is no more or less entirely verifiable, this is at least no more or less plausible an assumption than the opposite, namely that there are *no* connections or parallels between humans born into different cultural matrices. Moreover, the transitional phase which we suggest is key to instances of realignment is itself precisely 'beyond, behind, before' any discourse or form of in- or ac-culturation, occurring as 'moments of insight in which things are apprehended by an empty, enlightened consciousness "just as they are"' – in which there are 'no ideas in consciousness, only direct realizations' (George, 148).

Chapter 4 of *Consciousness, Literature and Theatre: Theory and Beyond* investigates a number of forms which suspension may take; these include balance, breath control and 'neutrality' and the condition of 'not-not-I' (for performers), death or absence of stable ego (for characters), defamiliarization or amazement (for the audience) and gaps or 'impossible' events (in the performance-text) (Malekin and Yarrow 1997, 132). George reminds us that 'the times of action in Noh exist for the sake of the times of stillness' and 'the music carves time into cells of ever more intense silence' (George, 194). It's important to note that all these markers of 'pause' or hiatus are situated at the junction of the 'dramatic' (or we could also say 'performative'), in other words at the point at which one thing or state or configuration turns into or gives access to something else.

Margaret Coldiron's *Trance and Transformation of the Actor in Japanese Noh and Balinese Masked Dance-Drama* (Coldiron 2004) looks at the use of masks and masked drama in Bali and in Noh. Underlying both kinds of practice is a strong cultural matrix which supports the need for performers to inhabit or become the masked 'other', which is not however perceived as radically separate from the everyday world but rather contiguous with it. Among key features of trance and transformation are:

- dissociation
- 'to don a mask is...to lose one's self'
- 'a kind of metaphorical death...to bring the mask to life'
- practice is 'neither somnambulistic nor...frenzy...rather...a state in which the actor both is and is not himself'
- being able to operate both subjectively and objectively (Coldiron, 19–20)

These then are all occasions or conditions in which there is a passage from one state to another, or to a condition of in-between-ness. Some of the ways in which this may occur are: as receptivity to mysterious powers or gods (*taksu*) in Topeng (43); as 'divine inspiration...radiating from within – beyond mundane capacities' (92); as *hana*: the feeling that transcends cognition, in Noh (163–5), which Kyoshi Tsuchiya identifies as the 'meeting point between the two worlds' (Tsuchiya 2001, 102). Noh also has important terms like *mushin*: creative emptiness that allows for transformation; the source of phenomenal change, emerging from silence, from the void; also rendered as 'no-mind' (Chinese *wu-hsin*, cognate with Sanskrit *samadhi*) (Coldiron, 43); and *kokoro* – a condition of 'selfless concentration' on which depends the animating force required to bring the character to life. *Kokoro* also serves to 'bind together the moments before and after that instant when "nothing happens"' (Rimer and Yamakazi, 97). In addition, *yûgen* (subtle and dark form) indicates a minimalism producing a semiotic richness; and according to George, the aim of Noh is to produce for performer and audience a moment of *hana*, equivalent to the *satori* of Zen, 'the moment of breakthrough' (George 199). There is a plethora of terms here which circle around similar conditions and are concerned to pinpoint the phase of transformation, which involves a slipping out of one form and a passage across silence, emptiness, void, no-cognition, before re-forming occurs. Coldiron suggests that the 'dual consciousness' generated by having to perceive both subjectively and objectively when working in a mask is cognate with *satori* and may also tend to reduce egoic investment in self-image (279–283). The crucial factor in all these situations is the foregrounding of the generative condition which performers can assist the audience to enter and share.

In the case of Indian theatre, both ends of the 'classical/folk' spectrum – though such terms need caution – quite consciously engage with strategies to extend 'self' via aesthetic and visceral experience. Classical *rasa* theory, derived from the *Natyasastra*, locates the goal of theatrical experience in a synaesthetic intuition of the mechanics of production, which suggests a form of perception and reception 'outside' time, located rather as a direct apprehension of the originary mechanics of symbiosis; whilst rural ritual forms engage with kinds of otherness (see Chapter 2, section iii above re. Patayani) through bodily enactment. Traditional Keralan forms like Kudiyattam appear to incorporate understandings from esoteric lore and martial art practice in order to produce what Eugenio Barba would refer to as a 'decided' body, signalled in terms of the flow and operation of breath in conventional and subtle modes. In all these manifestations, body acquires or engages 'extra-daily' capacities of sensibility and productivity: the body-in-performance exemplifies this capacity, but 'performance' here does not merely mean an everyday kind of doing.

[Some] major characteristics and outcomes of Indian forms...could be framed as follows:

i) liminality
ii) plurality
iii) physicality
iv) transcendence.

[...] Taken together, they compose a model of theatre as a site of change, as a locus of negotiation on and across the borders of the familiar and the known, as a launching-pad for extended configurations of self and world. (Yarrow 2001, 8)

Among examples of this, the south Indian ritual form Theyyam produces a 'visceral effect' for performer and spectator-participants, through the 'achievement by the performer of liminal status, paralleled by the liminal performance space and time' (ibid., 72). As a result of this, the performer who incorporates the 'god' becomes a 'moving icon', in between several different versions of status, significance and effect (Varadpande 1992, 145). In much traditional performance, the oil lamp placed in the performance space may be read as a sign of Agni, 'the phoenix-flame of transformability,...the point at which forms arise' (Yarrow 2001, 52); and the kind of 'knowing' that is in question here is one which involves a passage 'through the dark' (traditionally for Kathakali and other forms, from sunset through until dawn). We are in Murphy's 'third zone' here, where there is only a continual 'generation and passing away of line' (Beckett 1977, 65); and getting there involves what de Nicolás identifies as the operative force of 'sacrifice': readiness to give up recognized structures and systems of thought; opening out to the unknown. Grotowski's concept of 'disarmament' has similar implications; for him, 'a state of sacred theatre' is one in which 'spontaneity and discipline co-exist' (quoted in Meyer-Dinkgräfe 2001, 4).

All the situations referred to above seem to include two key phases: i) a phase of 'no-cognition'; and ii) a phase of wider cognition and/or integrated functioning: of the receiver, in the sense of being more alert, sensitive, tuned-in; of the performer, in terms of a sense of integration with 'other' bodily, spiritual or linguistic modes, of some kind of connection with the trans-individual etc.; of the event, in that it serves as a channel to kinds of 'cosmic' or 'collective' consciousness. Quite often there is only partial recall, or no recall, of the actions and thoughts occurring during this passage, although there is awareness that functioning has been of an exceptionally smooth and 'flowing' quality and that the resultant activity – which may be that of apperception as well as production – has probably been very effective. ('Flow' is an 'optimal state...in which there is order in consciousness', according to Csikszentmihalyi in *Flow: The Psychology of Optimal Experience*: quoted in Schechner 2002, 98). (In non-ritual occurrence, such was sometimes my awareness following examinations.) So the consciousness in extra-daily mode seems often separated by a 'gap' from that of everyday; this gap (the phase of 'no-cognition') remains as a palimpsest or hallmark of the passage between.

Coldiron quotes Kanze Hisao's remark that 'the Noh actor is something like a soul, always drifting between this world and the other world'. The training for Noh enables physical and verbal elements of performance to 'exist at a level of subconscious automaticity' where the *body* remembers and performance is without 'self-expression' (157). George says there is 'no loss of 'self' in 'character' for the performer in Noh, but talks about the effect of the performance as manifesting ways of 'breaking the bubble of self' (George, 191–2). Kiyoshi Tsuchiya reminds us of Yeats' indication that the 'originality' of performance is located in 'those thoughts which have been conceived not in the brain but in the whole body' (Fenellosa and Pound 1916, xviii), which recalls Lecoq's explicit claim that 'man thinks with his body' (Lecoq 1987, 17); and my discussion of origins in Indian performance as 'events, processes or modes of operation in consciousness' (Yarrow 2001, 17), leading to the ability to conduct operations '*at the point of origin* of form, language, meaning and physical action' (ibid., 20).

In her account of a production of *Tôru*, Coldiron signals the complete transformation achieved by the Noh performer from a fragile old peasant to a virile and youthful aristocrat (275); Topeng Pajegan requires the portrayal of a number of different characters by the same actor (188). Both these would seem to link with what Keralan forms call *pakarnattom* (multiple transformational acting) or Lecoq would characterize as *disponibilité*.

Coldiron's examples from Noh and Balinese forms, the Indian ones mentioned above and in Part 1, Malekin's focus on Greek Mysteries, and Chamberlain's consideration of Núñez's work with Tibetan and Mexican forms, all belong to categories which have been conventionally (i.e. in terms of the cultures within which they operate) defined as sacred. We have however emphasized in this book that we are not necessarily accepting such definitions, not least because they may be freighted with all kinds of inculturation and its political and social baggage; what is crucial is whether or not the kinds of experience and process which may occur serve to open out or close off the scope of being, and whether they offer the possibility for the kinds of transition we have identified. There would appear to be instances within western sacred ceremonial which illustrate this too, for example, the signalling of the 'transubstantiation' of communion bread and wine by the ringing of a bell, whose sudden tonal i(nte)rruption may jolt the participant into another dimension. Paul Claudel's Christian drama attempts to create such moments, as in *L'Annonce Faite à Marie*, where the moment of the child's birth to Mara is also that of the sacrificial death of her sister Violaine, and this ambivalent passage is intended to give the audience sudden access to the mystery of Christ's mortal incarnation. From a kind of Zen perspective, or that which might be appropriate to the reading of English Metaphysical Poetry, there is an incitement here to think two opposing concepts at once – a kind of juxtaposition or rapid shuttling which may lead to a moment of void or suspension of sense. Since Claudel's drama is intended to be enacted, it also more directly and simultaneously offers two contrasting emotional states: loss and gain, sorrow and joy. The effect of this impossible conjunction may be a viscerally impelled psychophysiological shock: not 'knowing' whether to laugh or cry, the sentient body finds itself in a kind of gasp or hiatus, perhaps the only kind of state in which the *conjunctum oppositorum* may be registered.

Many of the writers at different places on the 'creative' and 'theoretical/critical' spectrum whom we have been invoking, explicitly or implicitly (e.g. Beckett, Derrida, Wilber, Stoppard, Zeami, Zarrilli, Plotinus) make frequent use of juxtaposition and paradox, in their quest to find a discourse which may suggest dimensions which require another kind, level or quality of thinking to engage them. Maybe, too, this is not so far from the effect of what, with reference particularly to the Forum practice of Augusto Boal, has been called 'difficultat[ing]': like the actual moment of *Verfremdung* for Brecht or *ostranienye* for Russian Formalists, it signals a situation in which the subject 'knows that I don't know', a shift out of the comfort zone which opens up the possibility of new seeing and acting.

(ii) *Absurd Leaps*
In Part 2, Haney, Malekin, Lavery and Yarrow have indicated some ways in which the absurd works in performance, both as text to confront all texts and as theatre to go beyond conventional definitions of theatre, confronting its performers and receivers with impossible demands (to become a rhinoceros, be dead and alive simultaneously, think/experience the nature of otherness or absence) and extraordinary sequels (to articulate the pomposity of rhetorical claims of status and significance, conflate the artifice of theatre and life, recognize the void at the heart of both, enter a condition of reservation from all their blandishments). I will look now at some other examples of how performers and receivers of 'the absurd' are shifted physically and mentally across borders and out of known dimensions of their being in the world, through a variety of work from different countries.

Surd is what adds up. Absurd subtracts, takes away. The absurd comes into play in and as suspension: of language, rationality, good form, categories of organization and discourse, conditions of being and knowing.

This voiding ('ab') of sense challenges understandings and configurations of identity, social organization and belief. Its chief modality is surprise or astonishment, a sucking-in of breath or sudden floating off the ground, a hovering hiatus between words, bodies and things: 'how could I have thought things were like that?'

Across this void, communication, meaning, maintenance of dignity, propriety or status, narratives of role or purpose, fracture and fragment; (self-) importance teeters despairingly on the edge of collapse. Whatsoever 'I' might be in their terms is put on hold, left in abeyance. And this amazement (Ionesco calls it 'stupéfaction') can engender – for receivers – shock and hilarity, awe and horror, paradoxical extreme physical reactions to the sudden recognition of the sensation of being adrift. Performers have to learn to accept as matter-of-fact the experience that their character's pretensions to significance are decorated with a permanent red nose, mounted on a non-detachable banana skin (rather as Indian elephant-god Ganesh rides his precarious and risky 'vehicle', a mouse); and that, Basil Fawlty-like, their body's uncontrollable limbs and the desperate psychic need to assert dignity will produce a collision of manic activity and ironically framed pathos. They have to learn, physically, to work from here in order to sculpt the exact images of outraged frailty which we, as audience, recognize as mirrors of our own efforts.

Maybe this is a key to the distinction of the moment of suspense for performers/players and receivers/replayers. We 'get it' because they 'produce' it: but the two parties inhabit it differently. Lecoq trained performers to work with the red nose, the 'smallest mask', to inhabit the clown's crisis of being expected to be funny (see Frost & Yarrow 1997, 67–70, 118–119); so that they could familiarize themselves with the business of producing themselves over and over again from le bide, the moment of 'failure', the knowledge that my learned resources are of no use here and now and that the only possibility is to connect from this vulnerability with the audience. Lear comes to this too (see below). So it isn't just a practical tip for actors. It's about the business of human interaction and political authenticity. An audience may 'see': individuals in that audience may encounter a profound moment of realization. Actors cannot afford the luxury of profound realizations. They have to make the next move, say the next line. But if they haven't lived through the experience of loss, panic, total blankness, utter incompetence, they won't be able fully to recognize its parameters, trace out its 'score' in the ways it affects their voice, their body, their rhythm. We laugh because they have accommodated themselves to the moment and condition of supreme insecurity and engraved in their physiological memory its traces and patterns; and because they offer us the chance to share that most human vulnerability. Moment of panic and loss; moment of recognition of communion. It happens in the pause, in the momentary hesitation, the shy smile, the unvoiced appeal. For the watchers and acknowledgers it is the moment of their stutter, their almost or not quite, which triggers our engagement, tips us into the sense we too have known and now know again what it's like to be Piglet falling into the heffalump trap or Pooh on the end of a balloon string just below the bees' nest.

The forms of the absurd are linked to the violation of perspective of the grotesque, the clown's amazement at small things, the out-of-bounds explosiveness of the bouffon, the status inversions of commedia, the childish destructiveness of Dada; they pick up on the refractive and transgressive energies which burst from moments of personal and cultural crisis, from the sense that it can't and mustn't go on like this. They all operate a reorientation and they all require a letting go of whatever constituted good form.

Some of the modalities by which the absurd manifests are as follows: inversion; reversion; deflection; escalation; deflation; explosion; impossibility; bypassing limits; juxtaposition; opposition; paradox; disjunction; dissociation; derailment. They result in: laughing until you burst; crying yourself to sleep; not knowing who/where you are; thinking you are everything/nothing; not getting it; losing it; getting out of your head; not making sense of it; shitting yourself; splitting your sides; getting on the wrong track; going down the tubes.

'They told me I was everything', says Lear as he begins to comprehend the ephemerality of status. 'Edgar I nothing am', is the crucial recognition which marks Edgar's passage to 'Poor Tom'. *King Lear* is a play with at least three Fools (The Fool, Edgar as Poor Tom, Kent as Fool) and two others (Gloucester, Lear) who begin to intuit the folly of their previous apparent self-assurance. All of them spend time on the heath, in a hovel, in the stocks; collectively they abandon or are robbed of privilege, position, clothing, protection, eyesight and the 'sanity' of the world-order in which those things count. They only find themselves in the recognition of their own nothingness, in a no-place of exile, reduced to something like Agamben's 'bare life' which Lavery has discussed above (pp. 62–69). If it is bare and sacred here, it is because it is the touchstone of 'unaccomodated' being, the only modality in which being is not covered by the illusions (*maya*) of value/dignity/egoic inviolability. It is the business of the Fools (and of theatre) to disclose this condition, for better and for worse; this return beyond the origins of thought and feeling (Lear has one further step to take, into the zone between life and death, as he emerges with the corpse of Cordelia, whom he engendered and in effect condemned to death, in his arms). 'Folly' is this technique, and though the humour is always on the borders of life and death, it never abdicates its equivocation. The comic becomes a mode of engagement and negotiation, a form of Janus-vision.

So too for many playwrights and performance-makers in twentieth-century Poland, or for those who elsewhere in Europe lived through one or more of the scarifying experiences of war, invasion, break-up. Here too, in another form of response, the dis-articulation of the absurd becomes the only viable reaction to annihilation. For Daniel Gerould in *Iconographic Images in the Theatre of Tadeusz Kantor* (Gerould 1989, 39–49), theatre involves a transition between worlds – here between the living and the dead. Gerould claims that, for Kantor, 'Art is a religion, theatre a spiritual voyage – a journey into the past undertaken by making contact with the dead' (Gerould, 41). And Kantor asks: 'Isn't profanation the best and perhaps the only way of making ritual live?' In this context, 'the dead' are both the thousands who have been exterminated and, rather as in Noh, the death of childhood, of lost dreams – in Kantor's *Dead Class*, attached as 'extra' bodies or 'bio-objects' to those who still live, which they cannot forget and which shape their current existence, quite literally. 'The grotesque', says Gerould, 'helps the artist penetrate through the outer layer to reach the sacred essence' (ibid.).

'I am empty like a cathedral at night', and 'there is a colossal clapping in me', says the 'Hero' in Ròzewicz's *The Card Index* (Ròzewicz 1969, 49). The words also reverberate in an emptiness, addressed to an 'uncle' whom grammar struggles to reach ('to uncle,...of uncle,...with uncle,...Oh uncle!...in uncle': ibid., 47) by a protagonist whose name is equally elusive (Franek, Stefan, Romek, Piotrysh and Henryk, just in this scene); and who spends the play unheroically passive in bed as a series of relatives, colleagues, friends and authorities file through, alternately pleading, demanding and reprimanding, under the petulant tutelage of a choric gaggle of 'Elders'. The clapping may be the echo of vast nocturnal rallies (Uncle's rejoinder to the Hero's guilt is 'everybody clapped'), another emblem of acquiescence in the abjection and violation of the frequently renamed and reappropriated territory sometimes known as Poland throughout the twentieth century (and before); it reverberates in an emptiness from which all masks of identity and value have been erased. So this void of being (of play and hero) etches the shadow-play of violator and victim, and the sound of silence is haunted by the scream of shame. The scene and the dialogue are 'absurd': that is, the words and images enact a visceral sensation rather than offering abstract description or analysis. But central to the process is the location of the play as and in emptiness.

This works for performers, for the audience, for the performance-text and for the space of performance – the frame-categories or matrices of theatre. In order to play a role like that of Ròzewicz's Hero, or the ambiguously silent Ivona in Gombrowicz's *Princess Ivona*, the performer must engage a kind of repeated decontingencing of self like that discussed by Haney, Lavery and Yarrow in Part 2 with reference to Stoppard and Genet. You have to establish a role, with precise psychophysiological criteria, in order to be able to mark the transition from it to another, or to signal what it is to lose it. The matrix of the play as text in performance is frequently punctuated or suspended, by such shifts of role or recognizable identity, by gaps in logic or sequence, breaks or absences of plot or structure, disruptions of time-frame; there is frequent confusion of the where, when, what and the who of what is occurring and why. The playing space is de-theatricalized, as in Pirandello's *Six Characters in Search of an Author* and in much of Brecht; it has lost any specificity, it floats in unrecognizability like the vacant or unmarked locations of Beckett. In so doing it tends to undermine the audience's sense of its place in what is occurring, to confuse them as to their role; and in addition, in order to receive or 'read' such a de- and re-constructed nexus of parameters of meaning, they have to jump back and forth across a series of crevasses. There is more than one sense here in which such performance 'stages loss' as Peggy Phelan puts it (Phelan 1993, 60).

(iii) *Actor-training*
It would appear that the sorts of process which operate in ritual, for example, via trance and masking, and in the absurd via disjunction and elevation, or as aesthetic experience as in the Indian concept of semiotic transfer and heightened receptivity, *rasa*, are also to be found in actor-training. The preceding section has outlined some of their physical parameters. Why do people get interested in training performers or exploring what they can do in the kinds of context we have discussed? Probably (i) because it looks as though performers can access some kind of 'heightened' condition of sensitivity, mental and physical functioning and being-in-the-moment (Stanislavsky, Michael Chekhov, Barba, Meisner, Lecoq); and/or (ii) because performers trained in this way may act as a means to deliver a similar kind of access to spectator-participants (*Natyasastra*, Zeami, Grotowski). So the performer may tend to become (i) a virtuoso and (ii) a shaman: s/he operates as a fulcrum state or passage between the daily and the extra-daily.

Now I tend to think that Zarrilli is right about what he (or is it someone writing to him) calls the 'tempering work of psychophysiological discipline': in other words, you need some form of training or development in order to be able to function continuously from the condition of what we are thinking of as sacredness, which in performative terms may mean something like revelatory origination, being able to amaze by the quality and degree of innovation. Performance training – especially of the relatively lengthy and consistent kind found in some traditional forms – seems a useful channel to deliver this. The *Natyasastra* clearly also intends audiences to have trained themselves – perhaps through repeated immersion in the aesthetic, learning gradually to become one with its multiple meanings delivered through physical, metaphorical, rhythmic, visual and intellectual modes and fused into a kind of unitary perception and comprehension. These kinds of requirements have not generally been in vogue in theatre work in the north and west, though certainly the sequence of actor-trainers and theatre-makers from Stanislavsky to Mnouchkine (or better, Meisner) have targeted, and not infrequently compiled, methods which approach this.

However, these processes all instigate shifts in the operation of fundamental parameters like mind, body, self, other, world, discourse and frame, and intersect with those suggested by terms like play, act, perform, produce and present. We have indicated some of the psychophysiological processes which occur and are stimulated by the combination of the sensory and the intellectual, both at the beginning of this chapter and in Chapter 2 sections iii and iv; we discuss some others below; and the intervening chapters have also attempted to suggest ways in which text in performance may affect modes of cognition and orientation of self. With specific reference to relatively recent actor-training in the west, Copeau states:

> An actor must know how to be silent, to listen, to respond, to stay still, to begin an action, to develop it, and to return to silence and immobility.

> This is the first expression of the central concept of *neutrality*... work on neutrality included what Bing called 'pre-formation of the expressive idea', a phrase which suggests strong parallels with the later work of Eugenio Barba on 'pre-expressivity'. (Frost & Yarrow 2007, forthcoming)

To explore this a little further with reference to Copeau's successor Jacques Lecoq:

> Neutral work opens to that sensitivity towards the least perceptible impulse or sensation, it is the most basic level of Lecoq's work of 'preparation'... Lecoq uses the *masque neutre* as the first and fundamental stage in the development of this condition; through it he aims at a physical condition ('état neutre'; 'état de disponibilité silencieuse'; 'masque du calme') which is at the basis of dynamic extension in space (*l'espace*), time (*vitesse, rhythmes moteurs*) and matter (*animaux, éléments, matières, couleurs, lumières*).

> Anthropologically and anatomically, movement precedes language, and Lecoq seeks to return students to that situation where they discover emotion and meaning through gesture: the *mime de fond* is also the *mime du début* – of the beginnings of all knowing and all articulation. (Ibid.)

This is one route to the shifting of gear we have often encountered. It may be paralleled by breath modulation and control of direction in Kudiyattam and Keralan martial arts or tantric practice, which seems to 'enliven' the face and body in a 'decided' manner (Sreenath Nair 2007). Central to this is a practice and condition Nair describes as the 'restoration of breath', a mode of internalized breathing in which no external flow of air can be traced at the nostrils.

Another route, which is more similar to the kind of experience recalled by Chamberlain in Chapter 1 or to the situations Coldiron discusses with reference to Balinese forms, can occur in the midst of activity, rather than as a temporary cessation of it. The following discussion of ergotropic and trophotropic functioning likewise suggests that the crossover can occur as the result of more intense or less intense physiological activity; but it is also important to place this in the context of all the other investigations we have collected together here, and to be aware that many different factors may be involved and that a single strand of explanation does not suffice. Actor-trainers can legitimately call on a whole range of processes whose essential aim is to move performers into an 'extra-daily' condition. As discussed below, this will involve either a reduction or a heightening of mental and physical activity; and it may draw on meditative or contemplative practices of focusing attention, on kinds of internal imaginative engagement, or on work with particular kinds of body movement, vocal work, rhythm and so on. There is no single recipe. But what is essential is that the trainer has an understanding of the process and the outcomes, and that it is undertaken in a focused and engaged way. (See also what Chamberlain says on 'craft and technique' in A brief note on ethics in Chapter 9.)

(iv) Physiologies

The ergotropic/trophotropic analysis used by Schechner (from Fischer) and Coldiron mainly considers what happens to performers, although with some suggestion that similar processes may be operative for audience-participants, particularly in ritual-like events. The terms refer to specific modes of psychophysiology as measured through brain activity. The ergotropic system stimulates muscles and reduces activity in internal organs; the trophotropic relaxes muscles and stimulates internal organs. Active ritual behaviour (dancing, chanting) tends to excite the former, whilst meditative practice moves towards the latter. Whereas Noh in performance and in training methodology favours the latter and Balinese dance the former, elements of both combine in both these forms and may engender modes of functioning 'other' than the everyday (Coldiron, 301). Certain features of the use of masks in performance also seem likely to contribute, for example, in affecting breathing patterns, reducing the field of vision, and producing a sensation of disjunction or dissociation between the performer and the entity signalled by the mask. Markers of these modes could also be indicated as:

overbreathing	}
enhanced synaptic flow	}
multiple or plural processing	} ergotropic
'overdrive' or 'flow' experience	}
'buzz'	}

reduction or suspension of breath	}
abeyance of 'information'	}
reduction or cessation of 'doing' in favour of 'being'	} trophotropic
'unity' experience – everything is one	}
'simplest state of awareness'	}

There is a tendency for the outcome of each path to begin to resemble the other, and this somewhat odd juxtaposition may be significant in other kinds of training, performance and reception. However, it is important to note that for our purposes we are not so much interested in whether, or how far, these phenomena explain what is happening, as in whether they seem to support the claim that moments or sequences of altered perception and action occur in performance.

Both modes lead 'outside' daily functioning and may result in a kind of 'super' state – superheated or supercooled could be appropriate metaphors, as could quantum superfluidity. Taken in conjunction with many of the training-related criteria discussed above, with the explicit aims of Indian and Japanese aesthetic theory, and with the effects of plays in performance outlined in Part 2, what is important is that theatre and performance foreground and further these kinds of possibility. Reduction or overload of sensory stimulus may both lead to the same point.

In Beckett's *Not I*, the unbroken text which Mouth needs to get out (be rid of) requires almost continuous exhalation, producing overbreathing and the feeling that you are about to faint (lose consciousness). It can only be managed by intermittent gulps of air along with which the words 'What? No! She!' are *inhaled*, insisting that the self or entity which is being articulated ('she') by the unremitting text of another is not the same self as the articulator. The claim that language constructs a coherent self is thus refuted, pushed out of language. As the 'I' floats free of language, presence is located in/as absence; the in-breath claims that what can be (has been) articulated as out-breath is not me, so 'I' am that what is not (or as John Donne puts it, 'I am of nothing the elixir made').

(v) *Desiring the Other*

So theatre – perhaps here I mean 'serious' theatre of almost all kinds – is left with the task of trying to wake up its audience at the very least. If it wants to wake it up to the possibility that sacred experience may be available to it (leaving it up to individuals to find ways of further accessing and developing it), that requires – as Artaud's frustration seems to indicate – some kind of shock or revelatory effect, probably momentary. (It is another matter as to whether repeated exposure to such moments might begin to alter the receiver's psychophysiology in such a way as to culture it towards the possibility of more permanent access.) Malekin, George and Zarrilli share with Goethe the sense that the synchronicity of the moment enfolds the dynamism of all history and change; or, as psychologist Elizabeth Wright puts it, the effect of the 'theatrical' is to produce 'a recognition of the risk that is at the heart of all play' (1996, 178).

What seems to be essential as far as the nature of the shift of perception, understanding and being are concerned is that it involves form and frame, rather than content.

Performance is event: it is largely diachronic. Theatricality is a degree of functioning: largely synchronic. Suspend the diachronic, you can amend the conditions of operation; suspend the synchronic, you can recalibrate the order of operations.

To be jerked or ferried across the borders of the aesthetic, imaginative or conceptual world you currently inhabit, requires a shift of interpretative mode, that is to say a different way of feeling, thinking and knowing. This is also the only kind of shift which will effect structural reorientation of the individual, social and political tectonic plates.

To get to this means passing through the phase of 'I don't understand', however briefly.

It only needs a moment. 'Now, now, very now' hammers Iago at Brabantio, splitting apart his comfortable status with the image of a black ram at his daughter's white thighs. Sometimes it's a word, sometimes an action. The blinding of Gloucester in *King Lear* is so well known that everyone is rightly afraid of cliché, but it too offers that sudden experience of the unimaginable. One problem of our age is that contemporary dramatists like Sarah Kane remind us that the unthinkable has become routine, and we have become skilled at protecting ourselves from it. Here the shock intends to make us reflect on our reflexes, and it is an example of the fact that shock serves a number of different, quite legitimate, purposes. Here it invites us to look at our habitual defence mechanisms, our ways of protecting what we think of as 'ourselves'. Shock as we are considering it with reference to the sacred is the sudden discovery that we are no longer ourselves: so Kane could be giving us access to that also. The two things are not disconnected, because the channels of sensitivity are what enable us to experience both; but they work in different dimensions. Rather as in the case of Ionesco, the first phase of looking at ourselves indicates that things are not what they might be in what we call 'reality', and that there is a kind of nostalgic sense that they might be different. But the second level of discovery is that difference, taken to the extreme, means totally different to the point of being beyond the kinds of knowing we operate with in normal life.

In Kafka's *Metamorphosis*, Gregor Samsa wakes to discover that he is a beetle, and one thing that Steven Berkoff's theatrical version opens up is the awareness that one can play a man as a beetle, inhabit this otherness. Gregor, in whatever manifestation, has to learn how to function anew. There are plenty of examples of characters doing this; it's one of the key structures of drama. Sometimes it's devastatingly painful (Oedipus, Gloucester, Lear), sometimes extraordinarily ludicrous (Bottom as a beloved ass), sometimes amazing or wonderful (Miranda's brave new world). So presumably this represents both an experience and a desire, something like a memory trace that there are other possibilities of being.

If performance may be said to have an 'intention', or in a more Bataillesque or Lacanian sense, to be a 'desiring machine', perhaps the desire to form or to play (Schiller) has at its core the quest for its own source. Writers, performers, actor-trainers, psychotherapists – maybe even entrepreneurs – may seek to engage the most subtle mode of volition, that which lies closest to the origin of intentionality, which drives the 'desiring machine' of the egoic self but may not quite be it. The moment of sacred experience may be where the engine and the energy of desire are kick-started.

This chapter has aimed to further extend a sense of the spectrum of ways in which sacred experience is cunningly approached or involuntarily stumbled into, and to suggest how it is handled and evaluated. The next will open the debate to some other areas of our environment.

Chapter 9

PLACES, SPACES AND GENERATIVE DIRECTIONS: A SYMPOSIUM

As part of its interrogation of the modes and forms of sacred experience in and as performance, this book starts the exploration of a number of tracks: sacred ecology, sacred and place/space, politics of the sacred, performance phenomenology and sacred experience, sacred as bare existence. It aims to suggest and open up the sacred as a site (within and through the body?) of reorientation of modes of living in the contemporary aesthetic and political context, and to indicate that theatreing is an efficient method of stimulating this. Here we attempt, in a multivocal debate, to push some of the lines of argument further in order to see to what extent and in what ways they might give rise to profitable reflection on the processes of practice. The plurality and intersection of voices is in itself an attempt to weave a (non-'academic') form of writing in order to approach a subject which resists language; where a kind of sensing may occur in the interstices or collisions of discourse.

Franc Chamberlain now reflects further on experiences and processes in workshop situations in which space and the sense of self in and as performance perform a dialogue.

(i) *Liminal or Liminoid? Turner and Grotowski*

Franc Chamberlain
Victor Turner distinguished between the liminal and what he called the liminoid, the latter having the shape of the former but without its obligatory nature. He considered that the 'essence' of liminality was the 'ludic recombination' of cultural factors in 'any and every possible pattern' (Turner 1982, 28). Any attempt to limit the combinations to certain 'conventional patterns' he saw as an intrusion of social normativity which inhibited the playful experimentation and thus narrowed the field of liminal possibilities. A theatre that was attempting to return to ritual, to restoring the liminal would be regressive, moving back towards the 'communal/anonymous' pole which Turner also saw as being an aspect of communist societies. In terms of the views of the sacred presented in this book, it would appear that Turner's conception of the liminoid is closer to what is intended than the liminal, and Malekin and Yarrow's notion that the liminal

can 'extend to pure transcendence' (1997, 158) can be applied to the liminoid, which would appear to indicate a greater sense of fluidity and potentiality than the liminal in Turner's view. Similarly, whilst the work of Ionesco, Beckett, Arrabal and (perhaps) Genet might be considered 'liminal', Turner explicitly points to them as 'liminoid' (1982, 112). [Haney and Lavery also use 'liminal' in this sense.]

The distinction between the liminal and the liminoid and the valorization of the latter over the former, goes some way to explaining Turner's reaction to Grotowski's move away from theatre:

> [I]t seems to me that Grotowski, who is very much persona grata with the Polish Communist party, has abandoned the theatrical tradition in order to create new forms of ritual initiation which inscribe desirable personae on human prima material, that is form men and women in a humanistic image which is to replace older forms, especially those carried in the great religious traditions. (1982, 117)

Turner's distinction between the liminal and the liminoid, his opposition to totalitarianism, and his evaluation of Grotowski's work raises questions of authority and power. For example, he writes of descriptions of Grotowski's *Night Vigil*:

> One is uneasily reminded of not only of circumcision rites in Central Africa but also of Triumph of the Will. The role-stripped self is to be remoulded by what Grotowski calls 'the guides' into...what? (1982, 118)

The 'into...what?' is at the core of Turner's concern and he points out that an initiand is 'usually being initiated into something' (1982, 120) and this 'something' is usually another social role and the elders (or guides) have the task of making 'indelible marks' on the body and psyche of the individual in order to inscribe them firmly within this new social role. Following Burridge, Turner distinguishes between individual and person (social persona) and individual and 'individuality' as the ability to move at will between the two. He does, however, see the positive possibility in Grotowski's work, the creation of a 'liminal space-time "pod" or pilgrimage centre where human beings may be disciplined and discipline themselves to strip off the false personae stifling the individual within' (120).

The trick then, for Turner, is to facilitate the development of individuality by generating a fluid sense of the relationship between persona and individual (or self) without this being re-inscribed by an external authority. As Malekin and Yarrow point out: 'authoritarian discourse restricts significance (and hence the scope of action)' (1997, 7). They suggest that spirituality is something which challenges conventional frameworks, and the limits to understanding imposed by them; it is this playful interrogation of boundaries that links the spiritual, the sacred and the liminoid. Given that each of these has a processual meaning here, perhaps it will make sense to say, after Deleuze, 'becoming-sacred' and 'becoming-spiritual', to open out the sense of unfinished and open-ended process; the zen monk still meditates after 'enlightenment'. The liminoid could then be seen as the emptied out potentiality that escapes the content and frame of liminality, an emptiness that 'makes the possibilities for play limitless' (Olson 2000, 35). As Turner put it: 'One works at the liminal, one plays with the liminoid' (1982, 55). [But see Zarrilli's comments about 'work' above.]

Turner's concerns about Grotowski's work, and he considers it 'work' rather than 'play', although mostly rebutted by Wolford (1996), remain something to bear in mind in the following pages as issues of authority and control return. In what follows I make extensive use of my notes from workshops with teachers associated with Grotowski. I don't do this in order to claim a special authority for my experience, but to use the personal as a way of destabilizing the authority of the theoretical text. Theory is intertwined with experience and one without the other leads inevitably to an unbalanced perspective. Turner, for example, favourably contrasts the work of Schechner with that of Grotowski, but he had an intimate practical experience of the work of the former and only a second-hand articulation of the latter's work. Like Turner, I never participated in a workshop run by Grotowski although I have participated in events with Rena Mirecka, Wlodek Staniewski, Jairo Cuesta, Jim Slowiak and Nicolás Núñez. I listened to Grotowski speak, but I wasn't particularly engaged by what I heard. I will draw on Grotowski's writings and make connections to the work of others who were more familiar with his work, but I would warn the reader that my view is necessarily unbalanced. A further problem is that my notes are spread out over twenty years and the questions I asked then are not necessarily the questions I would ask now, but it seems to me to be important to use these texts, however inadequate they may be, as a way of avoiding giving the impression of a simply bookish learning. Grotowski was of the view that 'only through doing can the thing be researched' (Grotowski 1998, 102) yet, at the same time, he was quite happy to discuss things he only knew from books.

My first encounter with the work of Grotowski was, as for many others, through *Towards A Poor Theatre*. I was twenty-six years old and had conducted some practical research into contemporary spiritual traditions over the previous nine years, including some academic study in comparative religion. I had, for some time, been interested in the relationship between contemporary approaches to the sacred and the theatre. Unlike Wolford (1996, xvii), I wouldn't describe myself as being 'unimaginably naïve' or 'looking for something I vaguely defined as "spiritual work"', though I had (and still have) much to learn. In common with Wolford, *Towards a Poor Theatre* didn't particularly inspire me, there were some good ideas and exercises but it didn't move me. Wolford writes of a 'shock of recognition' when she encountered Grotowski's 'Holiday' and his words on 'the quest for what is most essential in life' (1973). I didn't read this text or any of Grotowski's writings apart from *Towards a Poor Theatre* until after my first experiences with Rena Mirecka.

(ii) *With Rena Mirecka (1)*
In March 1984, whilst I was a mature undergraduate student at the University of East Anglia (UEA) in Norwich, England, I had opportunity to participate in a workshop with Rena Mirecka from the Teatr Laboritorium.

When I was preparing for the workshop with Mirecka I was warned by one of my tutors that I should be careful not to laugh as freely as I was wont to because this was serious work and I wouldn't be allowed to participate if I didn't take it seriously. One of the first things I remember Mirecka saying to me after I started the workshop was: 'You don't laugh enough'. Immediately, then there was a clash between the perceived seriousness of this kind of practice by an outsider and the playfulness inside, yet the playfulness was a responsible one that respected the process, rather than a transgressive one. Also, in this moment, there's the possibility that the two people were viewing my laughter in different ways, one seeing it as an expression of my social persona, the other of my individuality.

> [...] We started in a circle, swaying and chanting [...] lots of yoga; dynamic meditation [...] a water ritual, free improvisation with a scarf – Rena playing a recorder, we clapping and dancing. Afterwards Rena said there is no need to discuss, analyse the work – it is the process, the experience that is important. [...] Spoke to Tony Frost today [...] We talked a little about Rena's sensitivity [...] she gives the impression of listening with her whole body. (Journal entry, Wednesday, 21st March 1984)

The impression that Tony Frost and I had of Mirecka 'listening with her whole body' hints at a quality I sensed in her, and a few days further into the workshop I wrote: 'Standing next to her was to be in the presence of a holy person – darshan if you like – very strong and I left [...], blissed out.' One way of putting it is that I experienced her as having another dimension to her being and, for me, the glimpse of that something beyond the ordinary was linked to a sense of the sacred. There was experience in the workshop in particular that had moved me:

> I banged my head yesterday and later Rena is giving us a talk on not pushing the energy – on how the energy's infinite – you've access to more energy than you've ever dreamed [...] and she says we must take risks and I turn inwards and I think: 'I did take risks and my head hurts' and felt her eyes on my head, no, that's a cliché, I felt her attention focused on me and I looked up and met her dark eyes. (Journal entry: Friday 23rd March 1984)

This was a very powerful moment and there was an inability to find the words to fit the experience: 'her attention focused on me' is hardly better, if at all, than '[I] felt her eyes on my head'. It was a moment where time seemed to slow down and, at the end of the day I stayed behind in the studio after everyone left and played "Who is in my Temple?" on my recorder whilst Rena and Mariusz listened. This was the tune to a song I'd learned whilst participating in *Dances of Universal Peace* in Leamington Spa around 1979. The dances were taught by Vivienne Sarida Brown, a student of the Sufi teacher Pir Vilayat Inayat Khan, and more recently, editor of Caduceus. The song was, and still is, important to me because it brings an intensity of spaciousness, peacefulness and warmth accompanied by an image of golden light and soft shadows which seems to be a quality that belongs to the melody itself. The spaciousness connects to the sense of time slowing down and indicates that I was feeling enough at ease to share a song which I regarded as being an intimate expression of sacredness.

I had an unusual level of trust in Rena as a teacher and felt that she was able to guide me in the process. I did not feel at any time that I was supposed to surrender my individuality, nor that I was going to be 'imprinted' with a particular social role. If anything I was being invited to engage more deeply with my individuality by putting aside everyday habits of relating and performing. People were free to leave at any time and only ten out of the twenty people who had started stayed the course. I did, however, make a reference to the possibility that Artaud and Grotowski's work could be used as a means of social control; I don't believe that I'd read Turner's essay by that point but it was obviously something which also concerned me. My solution was what I referred to as 'double consciousness' in my journal entry; the importance of what I've referred to earlier as a 'metacommunicator' (see also Brook 1998, 34) or 'witness'.

The training process required a willingness to go through tiredness, to go past the moment when you felt that you couldn't go on. There was a mixture of discipline and spontaneity that served to create a temporary communitas and a creative freedom that was aligned with something more than the individual, a sense of connection with others and the whole field. This was something more than a feel-good factor from a successful improvisation workshop and had more in common with the dynamic meditations of Rajneesh (Osho) or Roth's ecstatic dance than conventional theatre workshops. Yet it was clear to me how this process was useful for the actor and for the theatre and a short time later I saw Helen Chadwick's *A Gift for Burning* (1985), a piece that drew on her experiences with Molik, not in a narrative sense but in terms of performance qualities.

The exercises were to help us get beyond habits and into a creative flow and in this process:

> ordinary things: a bowl of water, a drop of rain, a flower, a headscarf all become imbued with cosmic significance... A headscarf had a picture of a woman in a headscarf feeding some birds...Santa Sofia it seems to me... (Journal entry, Friday 23rd March 1984)

This sense of things being more than they seemed to be before can be understood as the uncovering or the adding of another dimension, one of apparently greater meaning. The experience is a result of the stripping away of habit and the cleansing of what Blake and Huxley called the 'doors of perception'. It's not that we see through to another world that is separate from the one we normally live in but that we perceive this world in a different way, as fresh, new and meaningful; as a pattern of interlinked and radiant intensities. Hall and Ames have argued that:

> The defining purpose of the Daodejing is bringing into focus and sustaining a productive disposition that allows for the fullest appreciation of those things and events that constitute one's field of experience. (Ames and Hall 2003, 11)

This allowance for the 'fullest appreciation' also involves an awareness of the multidimensional creativity that is the dao, so creativity, flow, connection, appreciation, value and meaning come together in a multidimensional experiencing which is something of what I understand by the sacred or, in the terms I'm suggesting here, something of the sense of a 'becoming-sacred'.

Although Mirecka's sessions all took place in a black-box studio, there was always a sense of the space beyond the walls, of the walls of the studio being a permeable membrane. The studio had to be kept clean and tidy, and we were asked to avoid alcohol and other intoxicants for the duration of the process; our internal and external spaces were to be kept as clear as possible to assist with the journey.

(iii) *Meeting Gardzienice*
Five years after the experience with Mirecka, in April 1989, I witnessed a performance of *Avvakum* by the Gardzienice Theatre Association in the Great Hall at Dartington in Devon as part of the Centre for Performance Research's second Points of Contact symposium: 'Performance, Nature, Culture'. I was thoroughly engaged by the intensity of a performance which was:

Non-stop, mostly sung, an alive, vibrant carnivalesque Brueghel version of the passion it seemed. A parody, very funny at times, skilful, impressive, full of joy/fun. Not many people laughed. [...] Pictures [in the programme] don't capture the humour, the parody. Rhythms of movement undercut ritual seriousness, repetition becomes humorous (stomping feet). (Journal entry, April 1989)

The set was made of wood, the colour and texture of which was very much part of the performance. There were a large number of candles in the space, giving a golden light to everything. This indoor dimension of the formal performance, however, could not meaningfully be separated from the outdoor prelude:

[...] A clear sky, half moon, and sharp stars. We stand, talk, and look...Three Poles amidst us, whispering... Then, opposite the moon, which is silver in the branches of a cedar, along the path, two torches appear between the trees, accompanied by the sound of bells, or finger cymbals. The red-orange flame of the torches contrasts with the moon as the newcomers move along one side of the rectangle [...] The sound of their boots on the steps is a good percussive accompaniment to their arrival. We move to mark a vague semi-circle to accommodate them...They sing, bodies expressive, contorting but not with excess tension, making shapes with body and sound...they sing in a group, a moving sculpture of bodies. They have blankets wrapped around them, one or two carry censers; the smell is of Frankincense/Myrrh...the feeling for me is like Christmas or bonfire night; a special, communal, festive occasion. (Chamberlain, 2006, 41–46)

Wlodek Staniewski made an explicit comment on the connection between inner and outer landscape at the conference and in a subsequent workshop we were encouraged to attune our inner music to the outer music, our inner rhythm to the outer rhythm, and our inner environment to the outer environment. These were some aspects of Staniewski's search for an ecology of theatre.

My experience of the workshop was, however, very different from my earlier experience with Mirecka. My journal entries indicate a more detailed concern with the documentation of techniques and exercises rather than the experience of doing the exercises. There is also much less of a sense of the exercises functioning to strip away old habits, somewhere, perhaps, I had become stuck. I was quite resistant to what I perceived at the time as a formulaic injunction to be aware. At the same time, however, one of my journal notes states: 'I walked on my own, upstream, felt good, am tired but very alive...' (20th April 1989).

I was very impressed by the company's training methods but uncomfortable with some of the attitudes. At one level this was because in some areas my craft was poor and I received due criticism, although I did at one point feel that Staniewski greatly over-reacted to one of my errors. I didn't trust Staniewski in anything like the same way that I trusted Mirecka. Walking back after one evening's training on the beach, Staniewski was sitting wrapped in a blanket on the side of the path watching us go by. I felt very critical of him, that he was someone posing as a shaman, whereas Mirecka was a 'true' shaman. The following morning we each had whispered in our ears: 'Would you like a meeting with Wlodek, later?' I remember having the sense that this was supposed to be a special invitation – as if being invited into the presence of a special 'teacher', but I didn't buy into that at all, so I was rebellious and said: 'I'll know later' which, in the context, was the equivalent to saying: 'No'. The contrast between Mirecka and Staniewski, in my perception, was that my respect for Mirecka emerged out of the practice rather than through any role I perceived her as playing. The meetings she had with each person, for example, felt very personal and intimate, organically emerging from the process, whereas the invitation to meet with Staniewski felt contrived. Grotowski said:

> There is a point [...] at which one discovers that it is possible to reduce oneself to the man as he is; not to his mask, nor to the role he plays, not to his game, not to his evasions, not to his image of himself, not to his clothing – only to himself. This reduction to essential man is possible only in relation to an existence other than himself. (Grotowski quoted in Blonski 1979, 68–9; also quoted in Kumiega 1985, 162)

This didn't seem to me to be the kind of meeting that was being proposed by Staniewski, and so there was an absence of trust between us, even if that absence was on my side, which prevented us meeting outside of our masks and roles. We could only meet, if at all, as social personae and not as individuals

I mentioned above that I felt that Staniewski over-reacted to a mistake I made in the training. The intensity of the reaction was framed in terms of protecting a member of the company from my clumsiness in an exercise, but its intensity seemed out of proportion to the danger and this may have contributed to the lack of trust I felt in Staniewski. Mirecka, for example, was strong in her criticisms during the 1984 training, but I felt much more confidence in her assessment of situations. Of course, the 'I' who attended the work with Mirecka, and the 'I' who attended the training with Staniewski weren't identical, and the later persona in the earlier situation might have experienced things very differently.

Paul Allain, who had much more opportunity to observe Staniewski's approach, wrote that he was 'provocative, forcing the performer to plunge emotional depths and attempting to cut through psychological and physical resistance' (Allain 1997, 75). Provocation can take may forms, and gentle provocations can bring about extreme reactions, but Allain quotes the director Katie Mitchell:

> He [Staniewski] had used a very aggressive attacking energy to open Helen, knowing that the only way to prize someone open is to break them – take them past the tear barrier. (Mitchell in Allain, 1997, 74)

In this view of actor-training it is the teacher's task to 'prize open' and 'break' the resistant or non-compliant person. Aggression from teacher to student, director to actor is not only accepted it is regarded as 'the only way'. This isn't a view that is unique to Staniewski or Mitchell and is one that I have shared in the past and have, on occasion, been convinced that the person would be more in touch with themselves and the world as a result, that the 'breaking open' would be a sacred wound. I consider this to be a dangerous delusion that can encourage us to rationalize abusive behaviour and carries with it an implicit view that the ends justify the means. Rather than encouraging an opening or unfolding of an individual vision it appears to assume that the teacher already knows the 'right way' of seeing. It also brings to mind the parable of the young boy who wanted to help the chickens hatch and so he smashes all of the eggs...

Staniewski's 'ecology of the theatre' involves making one's home of creativity and spirit, and this involves both discipline and compassion and an avoidance of extremism. In one intervention he made at the Dartington symposium in 1989, Staniewski claimed that 'each and every extremism, whether political or artistic, has something against life and something against art' (journal entry, April 1989). There is a question as to where the boundary between craft discipline and extremism lies but Mitchell's comments, and Staniewski's actions in this instance seem extreme.

Dziewulska (1989) pointed out the significance of walking to Gardzienice's ecology, considering that in contemporary culture there was a loss of the rhythm of walking. The recovery of walking as a 'spiritual exercise' and 'measure of eternity' adds another dimension to our relationship to the cosmos, walking itself then provokes a 'metaphysical solution'. Macherek (1989) echoed the significance of walking and spoke of the discovery of 'the inner landscape in the outer landscape' and a process of coming home to an experiencing of the whole cosmos within the body. But in order to make this journey we have to leave the 'fallen mechanical world' of Ulro which is identified with the big cities. Grotowski saw the average person in a big city as being 'wrapped up in a film' and separated from organic reality lacking 'any direct contact with the world or with any other human beings' and viewed his work in the Theatre of Sources (1976–82) 'as a path towards making a hole in the wall and hence making contact with reality.' (Grotowski quoted in Núñez 1996, 57.)

Night-running is perhaps a more significant practice in the Gardzienice work than walking, although the two are intimately connected. Staniewski has described night-running as 'the first word', 'a basic state of human nature' and 'initiatory purification before work' (Allain 1997, 64).

Night running is one of Gardzienice's key strategies for 'making contact with reality' and can lead to a transformed awareness where we can sense the 'pulse of the earth and shooting stars' (Golaj in Allain, 1997, 65). Its conception possibly comes from Staniewski's visit to the Tarahumara in the Sierra Madre Occidental region of Mexico in 1987 following not only the path of Artaud (Allain 1997, 64) but also that of Grotowski and Nicolás Núñez.

(iv) *Nicolás Núñez and the Taller Investigación Teatral (1)*
Núñez and his colleagues have striven to re-introduce the sacred dimension into theatre (Octavio Paz epigraph to Núñez 1996, xx).

I first encountered the work of Nicolás Núñez at the Centre for Performance Research's fourth Points of Contact symposium: 'Performance Ritual and Shamanism', in January 1993. For some reason my notes of this workshop and a subsequent one on Theatre as Personal Rite in Huddersfield (1996) are very sparse and I am left with fragments of memory unsupported by contemporary documentary evidence.

In the first workshop Núñez had us performing the contemplative trot (trote contemplativo), one of the key tools in his training process, in search of an animal ally. This exercise was done in a studio but just as easily have been undertaken outdoors. Indoors, however, the trote contemplativo doesn't enable our organisms to become more attuned to nature in the manner of Gardzienice's night running, but it does assist in attuning us to the space we are in, to others in the space and to our own internal environment. On this particular occasion we would drop into a squat from the trot, freezing with the backs of our thumbs against our foreheads, waiting for an image of animal to emerge. We were to consider whichever animal emerged to be our ally and to develop a dance from the qualities we associated with it. The animal that appeared to me was one that was very meaningful, condensing a number of personality traits, both attractive and unattractive, in a single image. I still (in 2007) refer back to this image and the associated meanings and I can still recall the simple dance that I developed.

The similarities between the night running of Gardzienice and the trote contemplativo of Núñez and his colleagues of the Taller Investigación Teatral are not coincidental being related both to the work of Grotowski and the practices of the Tarahumara. Núñez describes the aim as to:

> trot floating through the area, relaxing at every step, avoiding the tension in the arms which one gets in a running race, and do not try to advance, since there is nowhere to reach and no-one to beat. We keep our look open, i.e, without focusing, and the same goes for our active internal chant; we must feel we are hanging by a thread which comes from the crown of our head and is tied to the stars, and flow at our own pace in a constant here and now. (Núñez 1996, 88)

The trote contemplativo was a development out of Núñez's work with Grotowski on the Theatre of Sources in 1980 as 'a form of meditation in motion: a means of focusing and quieting the mind, and at the same time centering consciousness on somatic experience' (Middleton 2001, 51). Grotowski developed a practice called Watching which has, at least in part, similar aims. Watching can be divided into ten sections, the third of which is running, Slowiak and Cuesta describe this section as follows:

> The running is counterclockwise. It is running, not jogging. The arms are not chugging – they are relaxed. The group is like a herd of wild horses running together. Look for the complicity of wild horses. No noise. No stomping. No calling. No heavy breathing. Sometimes you may be the locomotive for your partners; sometimes you may be alone and yet in coordination with the others. Let your body run. Don't make it run. Run with a purpose. Run towards something or away from something important to you. You can pass the others, but do it on the outside. Otherwise, just run. (Slowiak and Cuesta 2007)

This recalls Dziewulska's remark about the loss of the rhythm of walking in contemporary culture and Golaj's sense of night running 'naturalizing' the performer. This isn't in the interests of removing the performer's individuality but of making more intimate contact with that individuality on the understanding that this brings the individual into a more intimate relationship with self, others and the wider environment. The initiation isn't into a new social role, as Turner feared, but into community with the cosmos. This isn't a fixed process that results in everyone being the 'same', on the contrary, as Núñez asserts in his articulation of the principles of Anthropocosmic Theatre, what's offered is an opportunity for the individual to work out his or her 'personal path'. The aim of this path is to make contact with the individual's 'entire body and its cosmic resonances' (Núñez 1996, 40). Whilst there is a search for practices which can be used by different people to develop their own path, the results of the practices are individual even if they carry very close family resemblances. The recognition of the interplay between all aspects of the individual and the cosmos, which is one aim of Núñez's teatro antropocósmico, can be viewed as the 'new existential dimension' that Eliade thought could defend us from from 'nihilism and historic relativism without removing [us] from history on account of this' (quoted in Núñez 1996, 38).

The individual's recognition of his or her connection to the cosmos, because it is directly lived experience, cannot be transmitted to another any more than one person's experience of tasting of an apple can be shared in such a way that another person has an identical experience: each person has to have their own direct experience which has similarities but is not identical to that of others. On the other hand, opportunities can be provided for others to connect with this dimension of their experience. Mirecka, Staniewski, Grotowski and Núñez, amongst others, aim to provide these opportunities through researching actions that can be shown to be effective with different groups of people and thus are, in Grotowski's terms, 'objective'.

In between my first encounter with Núñez in 1993 and the second in 1996 I re-connected with Rena Mirecka. I had left the first meeting with Núñez thinking that I would like to make contact again with Mirecka and, within a few weeks of the conference, I received a letter from Mirecka, the first contact for nine years, inviting me to attend her Now It's the Flight event in Southern Sardinia in September 1993. I went.

(v) *With Rena Mirecka (2): Sardinia*

> Up 0545, still dark – tea (herb) then outside, stood under tree. Instructions: we're going to walk in single file. In-breath [for] four paces, out-breath [for] four paces. Keep eyes on horizon. Rena introduces [it] as [a] zen meditation. We walk, sometimes stumbling up the mountain – a labyrinthine walk. I know we are walking to see the sun but must not look for it.
>
> GUNSHOTS.
>
> Standing on a rock. Rena chants praise. Sun like a bubble blown from the mouth of the mountain. And then like an eagle's eye. (Journal entry, Sunday, 19th September, 1993)

This journal entry was written on my first morning at Mirecka's base, Casa Blanca, near Castiadas in Sardinia. One thing that stands out in my handwriting is 'GUNSHOTS', there's no further explanation and it's clearly something that I knew I would remember. As we walked up the mountain, there were a number of people out hunting with guns and dogs, it was, I understood, the first day of the hunting season. I'm not comfortable around guns and this was quite frightening; I was partly afraid that we would be shot for being odd. Part of the instruction for the walk which is missing from this first entry but present in a later one is that we shouldn't look to the right or left, or at the ground but straight ahead, something which I noted at the time was quite difficult on rough ground. Not being able to look to the right or the left meant that I had to resist the impulse to look at what the hunters were doing.

Calling the action a 'zen walk' clearly draws attention to it as a spiritual practice, and links back to the importance of walking for Gardzienice. The zen walk was repeated on several occasions with variations and more than once I was brought face to face with my fears. I remember one moment in the middle of a walk when I became momentarily afraid that I was participating in some bizarre suicide cult but the fear is absent from my account:

Received a note at 2.58[pm]

For 5h
Change Clothes
& also underware

Before my shower I washed my black trousers – they were still wet at five, but I wore them anyway. We met under the carob tree and sang another hymn to Shiva – and then we were off, single file, Rena in front, me second, with a piece of cotton with freely moving beads, we each had a bead and held it, thus we could adjust our distances etc. When the link pulled tight it could be sensed differently from a sharp jerk. We walked along the road, leaving Lidia behind to watch the fire.

We [...] suddenly turned off into scrub and rocks and eventually came to a small waterfall and deep pool.

Suddenly Rena started to strip off. Gianni looked at me and said: "I don't have any slip on" and I said: "I don't think it matters", and there we all were holding hands and squatting in the water, naked, and chanting OM – I really enjoyed the sound I was making.

Then we lit candles and Angelo brought out a bow-saw which he unwrapped from a tablecloth, and washed and swam with (he works with trees).

Then out [of the water]. Stick our candles on the cliff, and lie on a rock. Pick up the thread and off again – then came my favourite bit, Rena started running and then twisting and got a knot in the thread and we stood in a group completely focused on the problem (actually, not everyone was) until it was solved – it was a real problem – that was part of it – then over the hills back to the house. (Journal entry, Monday 20th September 1993)

The moment of fear was when we were squatting naked in the water and the bowsaw was unwrapped. It was a moment that quickly passed, but was connected to an uncertainty I was feeling and perhaps indicative of the fact that I didn't feel as trusting as I had nine years earlier. One thing that annoyed me was the arbitrary changes that Mirecka made to the cooking and cleaning rota that participants had mutually agreed. The changes seemed to be simply an exercise in authority. One of the other participants felt that Mirecka spoke too much at times and said that she sounded like a priest, which he felt detracted from the work. I think that both of us wanted to just do the actions and see what happened rather than listen to a discourse on the 'love that made the stars'. The problem for me at that time was that such discourses got in the way of my experiencing because they elicited a critical resistance; I could follow instructions and explore what happened in the manner of an investigation, but I wanted to resist any imposed meaning.

My experience of Mirecka's work in Sardinia was very positive on the whole. I was quite happy to accept most of the discipline that we were required to follow and only questioned it where it seemed capricious, which was only on one or two occasions.

There was a very strong ritual dimension to the work, much stronger than there had been in 1984 and more overt than in my experiences with Gardzienice or Núñez. The rituals seemed to be a formalization of the sort of spontaneous actions that had occurred during the work in Norwich. Below are my notes of one of these ritual events which I hope will give a flavour of the work. There were eleven participants in the ritual, including Mirecka who was conducting it. The first few lines indicate the instructions I was given in preparation for the ritual.

5ish Rena/Ewa will show me where the glasses are for the oil, and I'm to fill them and put them in place by six o'clock.

At 6.30 move the drums into a circle with Franco.

In ritual – when Gianni dries the rock with a white cloth – I'm to pour a little oil into Rena's hands and then into everyone else's including my own

[...]

Earlier in the circle under the tree, we stood (men to Rena's left, women to her right) she sat and Lidia produced crowns of myrtle bound with coloured ribbon (small pieces) and crowned us all.

Then right step forward, left together, right forward, left together [...] in single file behind Rena.

Into the work circle, lighting of incense, prayer to the four corners, singing Jai Ram and she told us we were going to do the sun dance, basically we bounce up and down and shake, it's our horse. Rena said that whatever we wanted from the dance, if we asked for it with sincerity, we would receive it.

Entrance to the work circle is in the East, the place of the eagle.

Men and women separated. Men to the left. Women to the right. All drummed together (1-2-3-4-5) fifth beat full. When a good rhythm was set up the men moved into the space facing east and 'danced', chanting and shouting came from the drummers and we joined in; I allowed some sounds to come out without worrying whether they fitted in to anything. As each man felt ready they returned to their drum and as the women were ready – once the men had been reabsorbed into the drumming they went out.

After the dance we paraded to the fire lodge.

We had lit candles around the altar and, looking from the fire lodge, the drums looked huge, like giant spirits.

[...]

Huddled together around the central stone, candles in hand, the structure open to the sky [like a skeletal tepee]. Elena sets her hair on fire. It's snuffed out.

Gianni takes a jug, silver and copper coloured, takes its cover off – a white cloth tied with a turquoise cotton (thick) – he pours water into his right hand and places the water on a large stone in the centre (a stone which I saw Rena and Franco choosing earlier, and which was smoke-blackened and was scrubbed clean by Albert. Gianni washed the stone as we sang Om Namaha Shivaya, gradually pouring more water on. He washed it carefully and lovingly, and then dried it off with the white cloth, which he folded carefully. The washing went on for a 'long time'. The Gianni kissed the stone and lay prostrate over it for a time, we touched him and there was a chant...

Then I reached behind me and grasped my covered cup of oil (white cloth, turquoise binding) [...] I poured olive oil into Rena's hand and then anti-clockwise (my choice, seemed simplest) round the circle pouring for each persona and finally myself, and Rena led us in pouring oil over the stone, chanting OM and giving it a good oiling.

Next came Elena with flowers, then [?] with a bundle of grass, Franco with sticks and we set it all alight, Giusi produce rice for us to pour in the fire. I forgot someone. I think Franco poured milk on the pile before we ignited it.

> At one moment during the ritual, Rena began to chant: an old medicine woman – I was impressed by the technique – [...], and had a sense of watching some of Apocalypsis. At such moments I ask myself questions about active/passive culture; are we only active here insofar as we slot into pre-ordained roles?
>
> (Journal notes, 19th Sunday September 1993)

Grotowski said of ritual that 'the elements of the Action are instruments to work on the body, the heart and the head of the "doers"' (Grotowski 1995, 122). When I read though my account of the ritual it seems an empty shell. I think that it is important to have some sense of what was done, but the living essence has gone. I notice reading this in 2007 how little reference there is to an affective dimension. When I returned home after the project, however, I felt much more in tune with the creative process and with myself.

One of the questions I asked Mirecka when I was with her in Sardinia was why she'd written to me after nine years. She said that she'd no idea why but promised that we'd find out by the end of the event; I didn't.

(vi) Nicolás Núñez and the Taller Investigación Teatral (2): Cura de Espantos

In 1999 I funded a number of students who were working with me on an extra-curricular project to attend Núñez's Theatre and Transformation workshop in Huddersfield, and then we all travelled a month later for *Cura de Espantos*, one of the Taller de Investigación Teatral's participatory performances at the University of Huddersfield, on Thursday, 13th May 1999.

Staithes Hall is a University Residence about 10 miles from Huddersfield – steep drive – everything wet – barrier, gatehouse – I have a joke with the woman at the gate and she points left and says: 'On the right...' [...] The sky is heavy, grey. The ground wet. The area is wonderfully wooded. I buy the tickets – we're given sheets of coloured paper, brightly coloured tissue and told to take them along. [...] The voyagers from UCN excited by the journey. We stand in the rain, there's a stillness but we're joking and laughing, [...],

We play under the trees, try to improvise a structure together but it falls apart. Eventually, the time for the performance arrives. There is an audience of about thirty gathered. The rain has slowed. We begin to walk on a tarmac path. There's a floodlit, all-weather, football pitch. There is a field with two five-a-side goals strewn carelessly, the pitch, if it is one, is waterlogged. We walk between trees, lots of bluebells on either side. People are chatting, Steph [Hall] says: 'Wouldn't it be nice if people walked in silence?' I say: 'We can' And we walk in silence...I wonder if our silence will affect others...walking in silence on this wooden path makes me think of Odin, ISTA, Gardzienice. We arrive at a clearing – there's a pavilion and a sign: 'RESTRICTED ACCESS' which we go beyond. White painted concrete steps...Looking across and slightly down into a field we saw four or five wet-looking people – one in a bright Kagool – they're performers, although we don't know it yet, they'll create the boat...We walk down the steps to the grass, performers standing to the side of the steps. We turn and face the steps, a chorus before the gods...the rain has stopped.

Nicolás welcomes us...we're going to be involved in a piece of participatory theatre – it might rain – we are free to leave if we don't like the rain: 'You know the way back, I suppose'. We're going to go on a journey to the underworld in a boat...we're going to re-vitalise our bones...Some of us may get something...others not. 'You are standing at the threshold'. At the end of this welcome, the conch shell is sounded and an answer comes from the bush behind us.

[The use of the conch is a significant aspect of Núñez's practice: 'We use vibration to induce states of deep consciousness. We use the conch...' (Núñez 1996, 14)]

The boat emerges to the sound of drum and whistle. A ritual boat, a folk-theatre boat. One figure in the prow, a piece of cloth stretched around his trunk, two slightly behind [...], straps – ribs of the boat – link the prow to the stern. The boat moved slowly...the bare bones of a boat appropriate for our descent.

We begin the descent, it's literal, it's steep. We're able to descend without falling head over heels; our ship safely navigated (piloted?).

A wet branch strokes my paper mask – later a blue mark is observed on my forehead, how did it get there? When asked I don't know.

We arrive in our underworld. The drum slows. We're invited to remove our masks and to look around. We're to keep our paper – our bones – to hand as we begin. We're guided into the wood in the falling night and meet the denizens trapped by grief or loss (?), jealousy, lust, and wrath, one after the other. They are all female. All dressed in white with chains.

Each character is lit by a hand-held lantern with different coloured gels (red, blue, green, yellow)...Each is spoken to by our guide – summoned as a spirit and commanded to tell their story (they're hungry ghosts?) The guide speaks to us in English – then to the spirit in Spanish. The spirit [answers] in Spanish.

[I describe the entrapments as I perceived them in the performance but Middleton (2001) lists them as self-doubt, lust, jealousy, and anger. Because of her long-term involvement with Núñez, she is a more likely to be correct. Middleton also suggests that the chains are there 'as a reminder of the extent to which our unresolved human passions can imprison us' (2001, 57).]

The first looks lost [self-doubt?]. She appeals to us, strokes the hair of one member of the audience, he's got long hair. I get a sense of greyness from this figure and as everyone moves off, I stay awhile and watch her walk off amidst the trees, a shade in Hades.

Jealousy lay with her head on logs. I wondered about insects crawling into her hair. She talks in Spanish and English about her lover and the jealousy she felt...

Lust, intensely lustful sitting on a wall, the sense of extreme pleasure and pain mixed – as if one couldn't stop coming, stop desiring, no matter how painful, how extreme.

Wrath [anger] was chained to a tree and at first she looked like a wrathful Tibetan deity or an angry woman mask from the noh. She was chained to a tree and tried to reach the audience – she was sullen when questioned: 'Why should I tell my story?', 'Because it is ordained.'

We walk on, I wonder about compassion, about leaving these figures behind as if they were exhibits in a museum.

We walk on and we come to a place where we are invited to look into ourselves for the spark and to notice which of these vices relates to us. We are to 'pay attention to the fire' [at some point a fire is lit – I don't remember if we come to a place of fire or if we see it lit – my notes are unclear and there is an indication that I was still writing the event up a week afterwards.]

After a few personal moments we turn to join the fire...we dance around holding hands. We run, inner circles, outer circles, some stumbling over the same tree stump.

We're invited to find a partner, the person nearest to us. The young man I do this with [...], late 20s perhaps, face softened in the dark and the glow of the fire, his eyes shaded. In my memory now [one week later] they are dark and possibly empty sockets (looking into the absent eyes of death). We place our left hand over our partner's heart; they do the same to us. We draw out the badness and throw it into the fire; we forgive them. Then we do the action to ourselves; we forgive ourselves. The literal tearing out of the heart in human sacrifice becomes a symbolic action. Some people try to get closer to the fire; I throw mine from a distance.

Then we dance again – or maybe this is the first time; I think we just ran before. The guides always running outrider. We stop. I notice that the ghosts have come into the circle. They are welcomed. I had been wondering about leaving them where they were...we had looked to the stars and then the ghosts entered.

We touched the earth; some lay down. I just felt contact. I notice Steph lying face down.

The conch shells sound. The boat reappears. Before we board the boat Nicolás said: 'For some a door opens. For others, a dead end'. This time we travel with our eyes open, led by a woman holding a large candle. We see the steepness of the incline as we climb. We descended at the edge of daylight, we return in night, across the dale the lights of a town, perhaps Huddersfield itself, decorate the hill like stars, seemingly connectd by more than just pattern, something more substantial than mere pattern...

We gather where we began in front of the steps. The ghosts stand before us. Nicolás tells us we are to come up two by two. The candle is on the steps. We are to set alight to our bones, our papers and put them into a bowl on either side at the foot of the steps. Our bones turn to ash and are purified. (When people burn their bones the fire reaches up some arms. I have no idea if anyone was burned.) We then walk back to our first starting place. People are much quieter. I walk alongside Debbie [Middleton] for most of the way. We don't speak. The lights from the all-weather pitch are blinding. They create interesting patterns in the trees...I remember the bluebells from earlier.

None of the events discussed above occurred in a space previously marked as sacred, although each of the practitioners mentioned has created work in such places. Nor did any of the events take place in a theatre space. The event that was closest to a conventional piece of theatre was Gardzienice's *Avvakum*, which also took place in a space regularly used for arts events. Whilst the subject matter of *Avvakum* was connected to questions of the sacred and religion, it was in the prologue in the open air, and in the subsequent workshop, where a more intense sense of becoming sacred was generated in a tuning of individual and environment. Gardzienice, however, were also involved in a process of transforming the spaces they were working in whether for public performance or workshop, and this involves an approach that brings out the sacred dimension of the space, something which they have in common with Grotowski, Mirecka and Núñez. This 'bringing out' of sacredness is simultaneously a 'making sacred', an interaction between individual and environment which intensifies the relationship. It is this intensification of relationship and the ongoing process of maintaining it that is a becoming-sacred.

This awareness of the process of becoming-sacred, of tuning in to the pulse of the earth and the vibrations of the stars, of moving beyond our personae to meet as individuals, as participants and witnesses, marks a difference between this kind of theatre, if it is appropriate to call it that, and a theatre that has no sense of becoming-sacred. To return to my earlier remarks, it seems inappropriate to lump these all together as 'liminoid' because we lose the difference, and simply calling them liminal begins to close the gap between the obligatory and the voluntary, the religious and the sacred that is being held open here. Whilst there is clearly a ludic combination of cultural motifs in the work discussed, it makes little sense to reduce becoming-sacred to such a play of surfaces when the aim is to add another dimension to our experiencing of the world. The problem is always how to find a language to discuss such becomings that pays attention to the added dimension without falling into clichés and generalizations. This is where the individual voice is important where we can struggle to speak and hear each other with a resonance that disturbs habits, even, or especially those of thinking about becoming-sacred. Throughout my testimony I can hear moments where there is strong resonance and moments where it is lost.

A brief note on ethics.

I noted above that I had an unusual level of trust in the first workshop with Mirecka and have suggested that this wasn't the case with the other teachers in this tradition that I had worked with, or even with Mirecka herself on the second occasion. Attempting to explain something of the trust I placed in Mirecka I would say that if she had told me I would be all right leaping through a high window, then I would have believed her. Yet, at the same time, there was also a feeling that this would never be asked of me. If she had asked me to do something that I felt was an abuse of that trust, I am sure I would have refused and the projection would have been broken. The claims about Mirecka's 'specialness' are mine, not hers and this idealization is something which can easily be abused.

Turner's concern about the potentially abusive nature of Grotowski's paratheatrical work summons the images not only of totalitarian social systems but also the authoritarianism of religious cults such as Jim Jones' People's Temple. Whilst I have indicated above that sometimes abusive behaviours can occur and are defended on the grounds that the actor 'needs' to be 'broken', this is not the norm in either the theory or practice of the work stemming from Grotowski.

Wellwood (2000) was involved in a study of authority in New Religious Movements (NRMs) and indicated several characteristics of pathological spiritual groups which are quite useful in differentiating the work of Grotowski and his successors from the authoritarian cults that disturbed Turner.

The first pathological characteristic is that the leader takes the power to 'validate or negate the self-worth of the devotees' (Welwood 2000, 268) and makes extensive use of this power. Whilst there may be idealisation of the leader or teacher, witness my idealisation of Mirecka and the reverence in which Grotowski was held by inter alia Richards, Wolford and Slowiak, there is no evidence that this idealization has been abusively manipulated.

Each pathological group has a mission or an ideology that is not open to question and may be justified by the leader claiming a privileged access to divine knowledge (270). Again this doesn't apply to any of the teachers under discussion here. Nor does the manipulation of hope and fear or the maintenance of rigid boundaries between the group and the world outside. Welwood's fifth pathological characteristic is that the dangerous cult leaders usually lack training within a spiritual tradition.

Whilst the work of Grotowski, Mirecka, Núñez and Staniewski has a spiritual or sacred dimension, the emphasis is on craft and technique rather than on a specific spiritual content. In fact Grotowski claimed that all 'spiritual discourse' was avoided in the meetings with groups who had come to witness the Art as Vehicle work because it was something which: 'very easily degenerates'. Instead the focus was on the 'technical elements of the craft' (Grotowski 1998, 80). Each of the teachers discussed here can be regarded as masters of their craft, operating in a lineage of transmission which gives their teaching authority.

This lineage of transmission involves an interweaving of theatre and the sacred which goes back at least as far as the beginnings of the twentieth century and the work of Stanislavsky, Craig, Copeau, Osterwa and Michael Chekhov. Grotowski inherits this interweaving through his training. When speaking of the relationship between his work and that of Gurdjieff, Grotowski said that he didn't come across Gurdjieff's work until after he'd written *Towards a Poor Theatre*, but that he was struck by the similarities in the terms they each used (Grotowski 1998, 87). The similarities probably emerge from the intense relationship that had existed between the theatre and the new spiritual movements, including Gurdjieff's.

Gurdjieff had a reputation as a difficult teacher and Grotowski believed that he could detect an 'extraordinary change in attitude' in Gurdjieff in his later years. According to Grotowski, Gurdjieff became far more tolerant and, in a certain way, more direct as he developed 'physical koans' (96). It's not altogether clear but there appears to be a sense in which Grotowski was reflecting on the changes in his own attitude, continuing the parallels he had already discovered in their concepts.

One concept that links Grotowski, Gurdjieff and Welwood is that of 'awakening' which can be articulated as:

> The process of (a) waking up from unconscious tendencies, beliefs, reactions, and self-concepts that function automatically and keep us imprisoned in a narrow view of who we are and what life is about; and (b) waking up to our true nature as the free and spontaneous, transparent presence of being. (Welwood 2000, 299)

When we are dealing with such powerful processes often guiding participants into dimensions of experience beyond 'consensus consciousness' (Tart 1998) or 'consensus reality' (Mindell 2001) it is important that, as leaders, we have some mastery of the techniques we're attempting to teach, and also that we have some understanding of the difficulties we can encounter. Welwood indicates that part of the process of waking up is to become aware of our 'basic vulnerability' (2000, 148), and this brings with it an awareness of the basic vulnerability of others. If we keep this awareness in mind, and bring it together with an understanding of the pathologies that can afflict leaders, can we ever justify attempting to 'break' another?

(vii) *The Dog's Moments*

Ralph Yarrow

At one stage in the development of this book, Carl Lavery proposed that 'the sacred is a site of radical ambivalence where subjectivity encounters destitution and abandon'; he later suggested a link with Rilke's opening phrase in the *Second Elegy*, 'every angel is terrible' (Jeder Engel ist schrecklich). That's no doubt sometimes what it feels like: but isn't it also what it feels like more probably for a (western post-Enlightenment) subject who, however much s/he proclaims a postmodernist and deconstructionist understanding of the fictionality of essentialism, nevertheless in practice clings onto that old Lawrentian 'stable ego of personality'? But hang on a minute: how many Buddhists or Hindus do you know who actually live all the time as ephemeral configurations of illusory coherence? Perhaps, in spite of the plausible charge that giving up on stable ego was particularly painful at the beginning of the twentieth century for a dilettante aristocrat in Austro-Hungary, Rilke's 'Jeder' isn't altogether wide of the mark. This kind of angelic intervention does herald a little death: no more or less significant perhaps than any other of its kind, but at least one which can register for many of us. Maybe the pain of loss is necessary just because it is what registers, what prises us open (see also our discussion of the 'wound' for Genet, in Part 2 and below); but also at the same time ('radical ambivalence') the moment is one in which the loss of one envelope of being is the glimpse of something beyond. 'Her moments. The dog's moments', says Krapp (in *Krapp's Last Tape*) of his recollection of throwing a ball for a dog whilst gazing at the window where his mother had just died. The moments are a triangulation and a reconfiguring of self, other and world; loss and recognition and encounter with what is beyond, both in and as the present and future Krapp, and as his awareness of death: his mother's death just past, his own death to come, death as a passing over and out, all refracted in the expectation of the dog. Both Rilke's and Beckett's words are potently ambivalent here, because they pinpoint not so much an event as an eventing, a passage between; a performance not a narrative.

> Ein Mal
> Jedes, nur ein Mal. Einmal und nicht mehr. Und wir auch
> ein Mal. Nie wieder. Aber dieses
> ein Mal gewesen zu sein, wenn auch nur ein Mal;
> irdisch gewesen zu sein.
> (Rilke, *5th Duino Elegy*)

> [Once
> Everything, only once. Once and no more. And we too
> once. Never again. But this
> once to have been, if only once;
> to have been earthly.]
> (Trans. Yarrow)

Forced Entertainment's *The World in Pictures* is an example of a performance built on the suspending of narrative. A single actor wearing everyday clothes is abandoned by his colleagues to 'start the show', after being given all kinds of unhelpful advice. He invites the audience on an imaginary journey in an unfamiliar city; the hesitant, apparently unstructured attempt is itself abandoned as the subject is about to crash to the ground after jumping from a building. These unpromising and arrested beginnings are, however, followed by a show which enacts, in frenzied, comic and cartoon-like style, the history of civilization – increasingly revealed as a series of false starts, empty postulations of grandeur and entropic transience. The (highly organized but apparently random) performance produces this repeated falling apart, a demonstration of the postmodern voiding of grand narrative. The inadequacy of narrative is present throughout as an onstage narrator frequently admits to omissions or excessive telescoping, and has to be prompted more and more often. From the situation of suspension, 'on an empty stage, with an impossible story to tell and inadequate tools for the job' (Tim Etchells, programme note to *The World in Pictures*, 2006), emerges performance – although performance which itself is continually undermined, interrupted, deflated, criticized – as a way of 'reinventing'; and its continual insertion of moments when action or words don't work (a performer who is offering banal labels for a series of projected images looks at one and says 'Don't know') replays the situation of not really being anything/anywhere/anyhow for the audience and allows them to experience its strangeness. The production deliberately and riskily stimulates this sense of the unheimlich, the unsettling: as in another of Rilke's *Elegies*, unease is a touchstone of our condition in a world which we reinscribe in inadequate signs ('wir sind nicht zu verlässlich zu Hause / in der gedeuteten Welt'), and the audience is similarly reminded, both obliquely and, at the end, in another unsettling address, directly, of its mortality. As Lavery notes below in his discussion of space, the uncanny is a powerful mode of producing transition (back?) across this kind of frontier.

Perhaps, however, sometimes there is no sense of fear or loss, or even of strangeness: once, walking by a stream, my sense of identity migrated and I was no different from the wind in the grasses and the ripples on the water; they were in me and I was in them. It was just so. There was no anxiety at the passage between. Maybe a recognition that there was some mode of I-ness or am-ness which was just as much at home in other things as in the anxious desire to secure my ego. Sometimes too the 'shock' is so sudden that only the change of state registers, not the transition to it: marked perhaps as an 'Oh', an inhalation, a recognition that I/this is something different. Leontes' 'Oh, she's warm' when he kisses the woman he thought was only a statue in *The Winter's Tale*, which also astonishingly acknowledges that there is an imaginative domain in which his heinous sexual, political and ethical injustice can be suspended; my sudden access to Arielness, described in Part 1, Chapter 1 is less complex but equally reformative: I was, I saw, as and from a different kind of being. Perhaps there is something here too of the Romantics' 'sublime', and the attempt to eff the ineffable as 'numinous awe' – correctly so in that the moment of passage is a gap in consciousness and being, a hiatus. But although the moment of passage may not register in such cases, there is nevertheless a process and a crossing: it has to occur phenomenologically and psychophysiologically. That something is what we are tracing as the per-form-ance of the sacred.

Emigh's 'sudden and playful resonance between previously disparate informational fields' (Emigh 1996, 277) gives a further clue. He parallels the zone in which this resonance arises – that, as Koestler indicates, of jokes, poems and scientific discoveries – with the relationship of the actor to the mask she contemplates before putting on, in which there is 'an area of congruence between two circles representing the life of the self and the life of the other' (ibid.). The moment of dislocation and relocation is perhaps, like this, 'akin to Winnicott's notion of a "potential space" created by a gap in the seeming continuity of events' (Emigh 278), offering a 'locus for creative work in the mode of play...characterized by Turner's subjunctive "liminality"'. It's a kind of creative stumble, or a stutter (as Deleuze suggested of Beckett's language) – which also could be interestingly linked to James Thompson's current work on what isn't articulated in post-crisis rehabilitation drama or story-telling therapy. Dislocation can be painful; Thompson, drawing on Scarry (1985, 1999), wants to value that which is too painful to speak, but is also conscious that the same kind of moment is the genesis of 'beauty'. Here too there is a move across or as paradox: pain says: 'I can't go there, my "I" is negated by this'. Silence may be the appropriate signal to this cessation of identity; but it may also be what allows the 'beauty', if by beauty you mean the incredible awareness that it is possible to 'start all over again', the sense that something new is taking shape, that there is a new configuration to me and world.

(viii) *Performance and Sacred Space: A Polemic*

Carl Lavery [rejoinders by Ralph Yarrow and Franc Chamberlain]
In this section, I take issue with the importance attached to the largely static idea of theatre advanced in this book up to now

> [RY: actually, this is not at all the case: see the opening section re. George and performance, the sections on ritual, and the contributions Franc makes about sacred ecology. Plus, of course, your own sections on categories of the sacred in Durkheim et al. None of this evinces a view of theatre and/or the sacred as necessarily linked to fixed spaces; nor does my discussion of aspects of eastern performance. I think you are tilting at someone else's windmills here.]

and argue instead for a more dynamic mode of sacred performance that refuses traditional notions of theatrical space. The intention is to create dialogue and debate, and to that extent the tone of this section is largely rhetorical and polemical. In my view, this is a conversation that we need to have. I have used the term space-based performance rather than the more usual phrase site-specific performance because it expresses a sense of mobility and movement, and is not confined, as site-specificity often is, to a given place or locale.

> [RY: My view would be that, just as Peter Malekin says the sacred of theatre lies not in the what but the how, so the sacred of space is not a question of what the place – I think you mean place rather than space here – is, but of how people function in it.]

In general, when critics write about the relationship between the sacred and space, they conventionally talk about static sites, that is, specially designated areas that have been set apart from everyday life and consecrated, what Henri Lefebvre, in his brilliant, but highly complex text *The Production of Space*, calls 'absolute spaces':

> The cradle of absolute space – its origin, if we are to use that term – is a fragment of agro-pastoral space, a set of places named and exploited by peasants, or by nomadic or semi-nomadic pastoralists. A moment comes when, through the actions of masters and conquerors, a part of this space is assigned a new role, and henceforward appears as transcendent, as sacred (i.e. inhabited by divine forces), as magical and cosmic. (Lefebvre 2004, 234)

For Lefebvre, absolute or sacred space is paradoxical, for, while, on the one hand, it is supposedly saturated with cosmic or religious significance, it is, on the other hand, produced by political or profane power structures:

> The paradox here, however, is that it [absolute space] continues to be perceived as part of nature. Much more than that, its mystery and its sacred (or cursed) character are attributed

to the forces of nature, even though it is the exercise of political power therein which has in fact wrenched the area from its natural context, and even though its new meaning is entirely predicated on that action. (Ibid. 234)

Lefebvre's notion of absolute space as a site where religious and political power come together in a unified whole is reminiscent of theatre, another arena in which, as Jean- Francois Lyotard points out (Lyotard 2000, 282), the sacred and the political are combined. The temptation to see theatrical space as a form of absolute space is further increased by Lefebvre's description of the phenomenology of absolute space:

> Here and there, in every society, absolute space assumes meanings addressed not to the intellect, but to the body, meanings conveyed by threats, by sanctions, by a continual putting-to-the-test of the emotions. This space is 'lived' rather than conveyed...Considered in itself – 'absolutely' – absolute space is located nowhere. It has no place because it embodies all places, and has a strictly symbolic existence. (Ibid. 235–6)

Strangely, in spite of the theatrical analogies he uses (according to him, absolute space is lived, symbolic and body-based), Lefebvre does not mention theatre in the examples he gives of absolute space, preferring instead to list churches, graveyards and monuments. Nevertheless, there is little doubt, as David Wiles has convincingly demonstrated, that Lefebvre's theory offers a useful model for exploring how theatre sacralizes space (Wiles 2003, 23–62).[1]

> [RY: Note that Lavery's version of 'absolute' space is different from Malekin's: Malekin is talking about the experience of space-without-qualities, whereas although Lavery acknowledges this (only) as a virtual state ('located nowhere') he seems to be using the term mainly to indicate space which has been designated as having 'absolute' status by some interest group. That is very different. Of course any space can be so designated, theatres included; but it is also the job of architects, theatre/interior designers, directors, performers/participants etc. to perceive and use the 'absolute' capacity of any locus to afford them an exit from the deterministic. That in my view would be one of the principle functions of 'theatre', or 'theatreing', – i.e. the re-making of space, time and event – which can occur anywhere: but may in some cases be assisted by design factors, which support precise attention to subtle phenomena of words, harmonies, visual stimuli, and help to produce a psychophysiological state in which new possibilities of 'significance' become available.
>
> I think this illuminates a key distinction, in that Lavery/Lefebvre appear here to be validating a sense of 'sacred' as Durkheimian taboo (societal reservation, preserve of the powerful), whereas I think that all of us, including CL elsewehere, are proposing the sacred throughout this book as precisely the opposite: the moment at which you break out of such restrictions.]

In A Short History of Western Performance Space, Wiles shows how theatre has long fulfilled a sacred or absolute function in western society by communicating types of radical knowledge that bypass the intellect and impact on the body. For Wiles, and he is drawing here on the work of countless theatre historians and anthropologists, theatre has historically been a place where the rules governing everyday life can be questioned (and if need be suspended) in a relatively safe and circumscribed space. In Wiles' reading, the theatrical site, be that an altar, temple or theatre building, has a special role to play in this process, since, amongst other things, it prevents potentially dangerous energies aroused during the performance from seeping into the society at large. The site, then, acts as both house and haven: it localizes and contains sacred experience.[2] *[RY: So it reinserts autocratic power in exactly the way I discuss above in relation to ritual (Chapter 2 section iii): I would therefore say it utterly prevents sacred experience.]* In his discussion of Terence's play *Eunuch*, Wiles notes:

> The young men in Terence's comedy defy all the social rules that governed the behaviour of Roman youth. Whilst the audience appeared in Roman dress, the actors wore Greek costume to mark their otherness. Terence's plays were Greek rites which played out, in a normally forbidden environment, sexually incontinent, anti-patriarchal and non-militaristic behaviour antithetical to all official Roman values. The dangerous Greekness of the event was defined and circumscribed... (Wiles 2003, 33–4).

> *[FC: I was intrigued by the material from Wiles on Terence – because I thought that the plays were performed at a festival sacred to Cybele – and so The Eunuch has a specific reference to the self-castration of her followers in its title. The comedy creates a distance that, it seems to me, makes it difficult to hold a simple anti-patriarchal reading – indeed it seems to me that to offer one would surely be to reinforce the link between violence and the sacred. There are multiple frames of reference operating – the play exists within the festival that exists within a wider cultural context – missing out the festival simplifies the situation and makes an easy set of binaries. RY: Yes, the grotesque/bouffon mode destabilizes as much, if not more, than it protects; in addition to the festive 'transgressive' implications, the ambivalent 'Greek' sexuality functions as both parody and satire.]*

While he is concerned to trace theatre's historical relationship with the sacred, Wiles is also committed to showing how theatre's sacred function – its role in the production of absolute space – has diminished as society itself has become increasingly disenchanted and rationalized. To that degree, Wiles' history of performance space reflects Lefebvre's history of western space in general. Although there are still remnants of absolute space existing in today's society, Lefebvre suggests that since the triumph of the capitalist mode of production (which he traces roughly to the start of the sixteenth century), a new spatial paradigm has come into being: abstract space – space which is based on the commodifying logic of exchange value, and which increasingly eradicates difference: 'Abstract space is not homogeneous; it simply has homogeneity as its goal, its orientation, its "lens". And indeed, it renders homogeneous' (2004, 287). For Lefebvre, abstract space is space without a sacred or enchanted value, the space that we live today, the space of the shopping mall, the entertainment park, the house. *[RY: So one restrictive mode is simply replaced by another. Neither opens to sacred experience.]*

Like literature and art, but more so, theatre, because it deals with bodies in the present, has always appeared to hold out the possibility of resisting the alienation produced through the colonization of abstract space. And throughout the twentieth century, experimental theatre practitioners – one thinks here of Jacques Copeau, Antonin Artaud, Peter Brook and Jerzy Grotowski – have all struggled to produce what the team of authors writing in this book have called sacred theatre, that is, a type of theatre or performance bringing its audience into contact with different forms of experience and knowledge. Does such a project remain tenable today?

Personally, I think not.[3] In fact, I would suggest that it has never been tenable, primarily because the type of the absolute or sacred experience such a theatre sought to provoke was at odds with the prevailing ideas of the twentieth century. The sacred theatres of Copeau, Artaud, Grotowski and Brook all based their notion of the sacred on a form of communal experience that was opposed to the individualistic and fragmented nature of everyday life in developed western societies.[4] Hence, the importance that Copeau and Brook, for instance, place on the theatre building, which is meant to exist as a special receptacle (les tréteaux nus) or 'empty space' for the performance event – which, in its turn, is the very thing that will, according to them, create a form of redemptive togetherness uniting scène and salle, performers and audience. The problem with this view of the sacred is that it relies on the existence of shared, transcendent values in a society characterized by pluralism, rationalism and privatization. To return to Lefebvre's terminology, Copeau, Artaud and Brook have confused absolute experience with absolute space. Although the remnants of sacred space certainly exist today (churches, theatres, ancient burial sites), the value-system of the societies that produced these spaces has long disappeared. Subsequently, theatre is no longer, as it once was, organically linked to the world that surrounds it. On the contrary, it has lost its sacred function, a development that is all too apparent in the fact that audiences today have to pay to go to the theatre – even sacred theatre. The commodification of theatre makes a mockery of any attempt to create a sacred theatre in the terms envisaged by Brook or Artaud, particularly since, as we have argued throughout this book, the sacred is that which resists exchange value.

> [RY: I agree with much of this, but I think it overstates the case. This argument would suggest that individual experience is totally impossible in a theatre building (or concert hall etc.), which seems unlikely, although there have, of course, been many attempts, both architectural and performative, to overcome the restrictions you describe – much of the history of the improvisatory would fit in here for one thing. 'Audience' is, of course, a difficult term, and in using it there is a tendency – too readily accepted perhaps by the people you mention, plus, e.g. Brecht – to assume that it means everyone. Grotowski is rather different in that he explicitly restricted his events to a small selection of individuals. And, seductive as it is from an anti-capitalist position, I don't think that whether you pay or not makes much difference to whether or not you can experience the sacred. I still get a buzz from walking up a mountain even if I have to pay to park the car at the bottom.]

While these criticisms of twentieth-century, western notions of sacred theatre are, I think, valid, I do not want, in any way, to dispense with the idea of sacred performance. Rather, I want to make it more relevant to today's audiences. This can only be done, I believe, by shifting the focus of attention from building-based theatre to space-based theatre. For me, the problem with the types of sacred theatre discussed above

> [RY: as I say, actually not – depending perhaps though on where this comes in the book; if it's after the textual analyses of Part 2, then perhaps – though again the arguments throughout this section often have to do with how the performance-texts operate some form of 'de-matrixing'.]

resides in their attempts to separate the sacred from everyday life. As I have pointed out, for Artaud, Copeau and Brook, theatre is a heightened event that takes place in a site cordoned off from reality. From this perspective, the theatre building performs the same function as a church – it is a site where the community comes together, and where the sacred is experienced as a communal event. This model of sacred theatre is inherently problematic, since it assumes that sacred experience needs to be localized and controlled. In doing so, it ignores the essentially anarchic nature of the sacred: its ability to occur at any time, and in any place

[RY: yes, but almost certainly not through any psychophysiological condition].

As I see it, the fact that the sacred is not reducible to everydayness does not mean that it is divorced from everyday life. On the contrary, I believe that the sacred haunts everyday life and is experienced, most intensely, when the parameters of the everyday are dislocated. For me, transcendence is immanent; it occurs in the world. Moreover, while the sacred is at the basis of all community (inasmuch as it opens the subject to the Other), it is not, for all that, a communal experience. As I see it, the sacred is always singular – it explodes in and on individual consciousness, before expanding out into the world and cosmos. *[RY: Agreed – see above.]* This open-ended, non-static view of the sacred has, I think, important benefits and consequences for contemporary performance practice.

The principal benefit is that theatre does not have to refer back to older, and now largely irrelevant, forms of theatrical practice (rites, rituals, ceremonies performed in demarcated areas) in order to establish its sacred credentials. For if the sacred is, as I claim, essentially timeless, placeless, and defined by dislocation, then trying to restore it to the present on the basis of what was used in the past is largely meaningless and futile. The sacred is not reducible to a fixed, historical form.

[RY: Yes, of course. That is precisely what we have said 'above': it is not the what, but the how, that is important. So if it is useful to refer to these kinds of events and practices, it is in order to interrogate their structure and analyse their processes.]

What is required for today's audiences, by contrast, is a more dynamic, space-based form of performance that locates itself squarely within the parameters of everyday life. I am thinking, in this instance, of the work of companies and practitioners such as Welfare State International and Mike Pearson who are engaged, primarily, in a process of re-sacralizing the post-industrial landscapes and places they inhabit. In his 1991 text, 'A Plea for Poetry', John Fox, the founder of Welfare State International, articulates the type of culture this new, space-based type of sacred theatre is aiming to create:

We are seeking to create a culture which may well be less materially based but where more people will actively participate and gain power to celebrate moments that are wonderful and significant in our lives. Be this building our own houses, naming our children, burying our dead, announcing partnerships, marking anniversaries, creating new sacred spaces and producing whatever drama, stories, songs, rituals, ceremonies, pageants and jokes that are relevant to new values depicted with a new iconography. (Fox 2002, 142) *[See guest contributions by Fox below.]*

Although Fox does not mention this specifically (he is too canny for that), his *plaidoyer* for a performative culture is entirely pragmatic: his intention is to find new ways of resisting the ever-increasing inroads made by the society of the spectacle into everyday life. In such a world, traditional theatre has, Fox suggests, lost its power, and become just another performance event, a banal representation without the capacity to affect us. We are not only protected from the disruptive power of the sacred here by theatre's vicariousness (its mode of representation); rather, we are also protected by its spatial logic – the fact that it takes place in a building. This, I think, permits us to deny theatre's sacred charge, to see it as spectacle, a commodity to be consumed and then forgotten, mere divertissement. On the contrary, space-based performance has the ability, as Fox points out, to produce a more radically estranging effect. Because it takes place in everyday life, space-based work refuses separation and confinement. There is nothing to remind the audience, in other words, its experience is somehow divorced from its 'real' existence.

The performance theorist Allan Kaprow is particularly good on this. According to Kaprow, space-based performance undermines the spectator's habitual response to reality in a fundamental manner. This is because, continues Kaprow, space-based work does not just distance the audience semiotically; rather, it distances the audience spatially by dissolving the ground of the real itself. For Kaprow, the dislocation caused by such estrangement provokes a profound sense of uncanniness: 'Such displacements of ordinary emphasis increase attentiveness...to the peripheral parts of ourselves and to our surroundings. Revealed in this way they are strange. Participants could feel momentarily separated from themselves' (Kaprow, quoted in Gorman 2003, 89). Kaprow's words point to an alternative reading of the Brechtian alienation effect – they show how site-based performance can estrange us from the present and thus contest our sense of reality in an immediate and concrete fashion. Interestingly, the architect Daniel Libeskind makes a similar point for architecture, which he regards as a kind of living theatre. In his formulation, there is an intimate relationship existing between how the actor and architecture intervene in space:

Acting is the breakdown of space. So to act is the breaking of space, the dissolution of space. Acting is a continual breakdown of distance, which brings spacing or acting back into architecture, since architects are increasingly realizing that their interventions are really of a negative sort. (2001, 68)

According to Libeskind, architecture has the capacity to affect a shift in the way that human beings interact in space. For him, certain buildings, like certain forms of performance, have the capacity to dislocate our sense of belonging and thus disturb our sense of identity. They dislocate subjectivity. In his celebration of Bauhaus architecture, Libeskind comments:

The Bauhaus ideal of modernity was a call for an exodus – an exodus from the mythology of space, from slavery to idols; that is, from all forms of aesthetics, of hollow rituals and banal responses. This ideal calls one to sever the root, to leave one's soil, tribe, and place in order to create an architecture that is universally naked... [and] permanently displaced. (Ibid., 21)

For Libeskind the displacement caused by Bauhaus architecture – the sense of radical estrangement it produces – has little to do with rationality and reason; rather, it reflects and communicates a sense of 'impossibility', or what he calls 'the mechanics of the spiritual':

[T]hese buildings make vivid that the whole spectrum of biological life – sleeping, eating, working, etc. – is on the way to becoming part of the mechanics of the spiritual. These rooms and their public visage offer the dweller an environment that, in its desolateness, reveals that the adult needs no figure to hide the desert of the human condition and the body ready to experience the eternal. (Ibid., 22)

Libeskind's definition of the spiritual has much in common with my definition of the sacred.[5] In both cases, what is at stake is a form of experience that dislocates the subject and renders him/her placeless. In this strange space (a space that has nothing in common with Brook's empty space, in so far as it is not housed between walls), the subject is opened to the transcendence of the Other, that is to say, to the value that transcends value. Crucially, this opening occurs in everyday life, and is not confined to theatre space.

[RY: I like this notion of dislocation; it seems to be very close to what many of us are arguing in other contexts. But isn't it true that, even though the events you refer to may be more rooted in the everyday, they are still 'crafted', precisely in order to incite this dislocation? Indeed, it seems to me that if they were not, there would be little chance of anything spiritual or sacred occurring. My argument about 'theatre' would be that it often requires this kind of precise attention, in training, in structure, in delivery, as process, to the mechanics of 'dislocation'.]

[FC: I find the stuff on space a little difficult to get – I guess because it doesn't appear to deal with the non-building based work of Copeau, Brook and Grotowski, so it lacks a specificity for me as the body of work becomes generalized into an abstraction. Whilst I can see the 'space as container' operating in say Brook's production of the Mahabharata in a quarry at Avignon, or to Orghast, even if they're not building-centred, I'm not quite sure how it relates to the work of the African adventure, for example. Grotowski's work before 1970 does appear to be building-centred, but I'm not sure that it is for the next thirty years – and the 'space as container' model would only seem to hold if it is expanded to include 'mountain-range-as-container' or 'forest-as-container'...and it seems to leave aside something of 'score-as-container' (see Cieslak) or 'event-as-container' (which might suggest a different reading of Kaprow). Grotowski, Brook, Artaud and Copeau become objects which are read through a particular philosophic lens which doesn't allow them their voice (in contrast, say, to Derrida's reading of Artaud). Lefebvre's voice – mediated through you (Carl) – silences that of the 'marked' practitioners such that their words aren't even used as evidence. Fox and Kaprow, of course, are allowed their voices – but there is an authorial voice that only allows one side of the debate. Any attempt to challenge the use of Lefebvre by using evidence from the practitioners though runs the risk of failure in a shift of registers – discourse about craft being outmanoeuvred by a philosophical discouse that has a privileged position within the academy. So I look for philosophical allies – Casey, perhaps, Merleau-Ponty? Levin? But I might choose different philosophers to ally with different practitioners (Deleuze for Artaud? Needleman (or Kearney) for Brook? Levin for Copeau (or, perhaps, Marcel or even James!)?...and, perhaps, Heidegger's 'Building Dwelling Thinking' for Grotowski?). To use 'building-centered' in a non-literal way would bring a diffferent understanding to the challenge to Grotowski and help to destabilize the term 'building' and the 'boxing in' of Grotowski, Artaud (think of the tarahumara, or his visit to Ireland) and the others.]

On the other hand, how about this?

(ix) *Theatre and the Wound*

Carl Lavery

In Jean Genet's theatre (see Chapter 7 of Part 2), the notion of the wound is central to the experience of the sacred. However, what is the wound, and why is it so relevant to theatrical experience?

Like Genet, I don't see the wound as negative, and nor am I willing to define it in Judaeo-Christian terms, despite the obvious associations with images of Christ's suffering. Rather, I see the wound as a kind of opening to what we might define as 'cosmic epiphany', a strange, unsettling moment when you realize that your hereness, your sitedness, transcends your immediate surroundings, and provokes a spiralling form of awareness: the sense that your being-in-the world is part of a being-in-the cosmos. I am reluctant to attach transcendental significance to this event, by which I mean I do not see it in terms of a Godhead. For me, it's primarily immanent to our existence in the world. The wound, then, is a form of knowledge – it stuns you into recognition. But – and here we encounter the paradox of the wound – this recognition is strange recognition. There's no object to grasp, no gestalt, no ground. There is simply awareness of a reality which transcends you, and which always remains distanced, estranged, Other. The wound then is unsettling; it punctures you and opens you up. Yet – and this is crucial – the vertigo provoked by the wound always occurs in real time and space. It takes place between *[within?]* bodies. And this is, why, I believe Genet saw theatre as the medium best suited for inflicting the wound.

Although he's not talking specifically about theatre as we conventionally know it, the sound artist Graeme Miller makes a similar point about the 'strange placefulness' of the sacred. Speaking about the processes involved in making his 1987 piece *Dungeness: The Desert in the Garden*, Miller notes:

> In 1987 I rebuilt a square mile of headland in Kent from fragments of film and audio recorded over five years of random collection. The whole work, *Dungeness: The Desert in Garden*, ICA 1987, was conceived as a re-creation of the sudden and singular moment of recognition I had experienced there the first time I had visited some years before. A moment overtook me, place-full and timeless, urgent and meaningful with meaning which seems not to refer to anything or anywhere else. In an overpowering second you are revealed exactly where you are. (Miller 2006, 104).

The key phrases here are 'recognition', 'place-full and timeless', 'not to refer to anything or anywhere else', 'and 'revealed exactly where you are'. These, I would argue, are examples of the spatialized language of the sacred, language that tries to convey – not grasp – the moment of being present and absent at the same time. This focus on presence and absence, on being there and elsewhere, is an intensely theatrical experience, and to that degree 'the ontology of performance' might well be an 'ontology of the sacred': the thing that binds actors, audiences and spaces together – the thing, that is, which wounds us.

[RY: I think this picks up George's suggestions about performance very succinctly. The moment of 'slippage' is the moment of truth, and that slippage is endemic to performance, or to what

I called 'theatreing' earlier on. What also seems crucial here is the identification of the condition of 'knowledge of...no object, no gestalt, no ground': ref. George Ch. 1, and Malekin, re. Miller's other forms of knowing which are 'place-full and timeless', or occur as a 'moment of being present and absent'.

There is a different mode of cognition in operation here, not one which works within conventional frameworks of subject and object. It's not even a phenomenology in the ordinary sense, because there is no 'movement' from intending subject to constructed object of perception; this is a knowing that neither I as knower, not the object as known, nor the process of knowing which conjoins them, nor the epistemology or ontology which might ground them, really 'is', in the sense that we might have conceptualized any of the dimensions of this process. It is a knowing of unknowing. An awareness that distinctions of this kind are not relevant here. Not that they may not be relevant before or after, or in the normal business of daily perception; but that in this moment they do not count. So this is not a knowing of, but rather a knowing as; as something that is other than a subject which frames objects; perhaps then as something which is of the same kind as both the position of subject and the position of object: the field within which they both appear and disappear. I am that something and that nothing. And in that state, I know that I am both something and nothing, and that I am in some measure that which holds the tension between them.

We can't usually know and we can't usually be here because those are precisely the dimensions which stop us knowing or being anything beyond the configuration of the familiar. But in this not knowing and not being we may have the chance to move across to being and knowing otherwise. I think that's what happens in most of the 'aha' moments in theatre (or perhaps nowadays they might be 'shit, that's it' moments).

Genet's beggar flings this in his face. You are me. You are not what you protect yourself as. You are my leaking at the edges, my seepage, my unravelling. Our being is not watertight. In this occurrence,'opening...to the other', as Lavery puts it on p. 68, is being prepared to live this absence, this unknowing.]

In the following 'guest' contributions, John Fox, Artistic Director of Welfare State International, suggests why we need secular ways to're-engage' with the sacred.

(x) *Facing Death*

John Fox

If we are to believe that theatre came inside for the first time with *Macbeth* and that we have been lumbered with the black box ever since, then there is some compensation in knowing that on the graph of theatrical evolution there is much more theatre time before than after the black box.

We can imagine aboriginal hunters 50,000 years ago resonating with animals. After the kill and the blood-feast they danced on stilts in the skins of beasts celebrating their anima with Dionysian excess. We can imagine too that when the hunter died his own cremation was accompanied by a practised procession, a beating of stretched skins, a wailing of bone flutes and the foot-lit melodrama of the fire pit.

As one of the founders and Artistic Director of Welfare State International (which I archived on April Fools' Day 2006 after 38 years), I always assumed these were the roots of theatre. When we re-invented or re -discovered carnival, giant puppet effigies, site-specific events, lantern parades, fire-shows and ceremonies for contemporary rites of passage, such 'primitive' alchemy re -emerged quite naturally. Every shaman or performer, working a congregation or audience in landscape and weather, is bound to use such elemental practical and metaphysical systems.

At least so I thought until one brain-boggling moment over a decade and a half ago when the (then) Drama Director of the Arts Council of England said: 'John, what have funerals got to do with theatre?'

As 'Engineers of the Imagination', more interested in eyes on stalks than bums on seats, we always had a problem with categories. We worked in communities with artist-performers–musicians, creating fearsome sculptural images that moved, with pyrotechnics, in a cacophony of hybrid Cumbrian Samba. So, were these seasonal festivals to be funded through the department of Drama, Art, Music, Tourism, Applied Vernacular Anthropology, Surrogate Social work or Exotic Lunacy?

But funerals? Real ones with a variety of functional coffins; wooden ones constructed from recycled pallets, stout cardboard ones painted by artists and others fashioned from woven willow. Real coffins heavy with corpses that would decompose. Such funerals were no theatrical illusion and in funding terms were evidently on the outer limits of tick box decency. However, as there was an urgent job to do we persevered.

In 1994, Sue Gill and I wrote *The Dead Good Funerals Book* (updated edition 2004) and in 1995 started running training courses for secular celebrants. This radical DIY manual of funerary practice, which connects history, religion, ceremony (and the aesthetics and methods of theatre!) together with educational gatherings has had a significant effect on the UK funeral industry.

Now thanks to these practical trials and those of other pioneering practitioners some funerals in England are less formulaic, less Victorian, more green, cheaper and, paradoxically, more life-enhancing than they were ten years ago. In our opinion in a few years secular celebrants and ecologically desirable woodland burial sites will be regularly available through standard Yellow Pages. If your local authority will not provide one ask them why not.

New intentional ceremonies for funeral rites and other crossover points, such as weddings, baby namings, divorces, retirement and other public and private occasions are crucial. Free of hidden agendas, they release people from the often addictive habits of outmoded, (if not discredited) religion, they challenge the avarice of commerce, and give people place, permission and method to re-engage on their own terms, with what we used to call the 'spiritual' or the 'sacred'.

Unfortunately, in our domain of new age romanticism, even these two words have lost meaning. However, as we all still crave beauty, understanding, belonging, mystery, an escape from the mundane, and even peace of mind, it is an appropriate field of work for artists, poets, musicians and theatre workers.

To take just one of these rites, facing up to the inevitability of our own death, and designing our own funeral ceremony, is probably the most revolutionary act we could undertake.

Our culture peddles surrogate death. This is a dangerous pursuit. Every hour through television, films, newspapers, children's comics, cartoons, war toys and video games we are exposed to thousands of chases, fights, sanitized killings and murders. Many of our lauded films contain dozens of fake and gratuitous violent deaths. So we are led to believe we have to kill to survive or fight to win any dispute with so-called 'Evil'. Programmed with propaganda images we do not challenge the bombing of thousands of civilians, ('collateral damage') and come to believe that guns, terrorism and warfare are inevitable and natural and that in a free enterprise market economy selling weapons of mass destruction is morally acceptable. De-sensitized by censored images from the theatre of war we neither experience real blood and rotting flesh nor wash and bury dead children splintered with cluster bombs made in the UK.

At the same time as we are exploited with 'death-entertainment' the majority of us rarely see an actual dead body. Most of will live longer than any tribe ever has and die in hospital. Although Aids has changed consciousness among certain groups, in the main we are conditioned to believe dying is not for us and anyway they will invent something before we get there. Our political and capitalist system controls us through fear but, except for life insurance, it is not in its interest to bring home the full reality of actual death. More life. More selling.

To contemplate one's own death is not morbid. It is liberating.
Standing freely outside our own real or imagined coffin we hold hands with our ancestors; those hunter-gatherers who re-enchanted themselves under the once roaring stars.

Strangely enough if we do become incarcerated inside that other black box, where the stars are gelled and rigged on lighting bars, if the artifice of poetry rings true, then we too may still claim, occasionally, that we have re-engaged with 'the sacred' and even maybe achieved catharsis!

(xi) One Rock

John Fox
Welfare State International frequently attempted to activate a contemporary role for the sacred in the everyday. Our artists filmed the crucifixion of Barrabas on a slag tip, hired a (reluctant) Christmas donkey from the Council in Wath on Dearne and created 'spiritual' secular sculptural installations in and around churches.

In 1974, for example, in *Homage to Meister Eckhart*, a 24-hour vigil for Birmingham International Performance Festival, we constructed a 30-metre intertwining knot of red foundry sand in the aisle of the Cathedral enhancing it with blocks of ice set on fire by a child, Icarus.

In Hereford Cathedral near Easter 2005, as part of the Good Grief bereavement awareness event, we invented our own Mappa Mundi. Constructed on the altar stage during a day (in full view of the congregation/audience) this site-specific environmental performance-sculpture featured a megalithic lime-wood urn for human ashes. Surrounding it, rippling circles of white canvas, hazel, sand and salt led to the edge of the altar space where clusters of papercuts and tiny paper boats journeyed at random. Throughout, improvised music and sounds provided a parallel universe.

The most complex of such events was, however, One Rock, an ecological triptych and site-specific installation created by a dozen people at our base in Ulverston, Cumbria, for 3000 visitors between 2 December 2003 and 31 January 2004.

One Rock, a celebration of one particular rock on the western shore of Morecambe Bay, was a time-based sculpture, using video, sound and light. Inside the Cruck Barn of Lanternhouse, artists, musicians, geologists, microbiologists and computer scientists (from the Mixed Reality Lab, Nottingham University) took three weeks to re-create the Rock and its many stories.

The actual Rock, about the size of a mini-car, is one of a family of limestone lumps left when the Ice Age retreated. Some remain in a shoreline wood of oak trees but our Rock is furthest out on the liminal tideline. As the main channel of the Bay shifts, like a sidewinder snake in slow motion, the Rock has nearly disappeared under silt and now appears as a sad hippo peering from a zoo rim of suffocating sand.

The Rock, with the tiny inland sea on its back, has been a family friend for 30 years. Our children and grandchildren have grown up with it. With dogs and daring and grazed knees they have clambered upon it. In the orbit of our dangerous and beautiful Bay, surrounded by a global environment prone to increasingly violent change, this ancient anchor is still a talisman to hang on to.

But now it is going, colonized slowly by rampant spartina grass (an old Yankee import), embryonic salt marsh and thrusting reeds.

A change to mark and celebrate.

So towards the western end of our Lanternhouse Barn we made a pond 7 metres wide to enclose a perfect life-size replica of the Rock in white plaster. Fabricated precisely by Tori Bassett using plumb lines and micro-meters, it was lit by theatre lamps with projected videos and slides so that over 7 minutes its surface trembled with clouds and sea as dawn passed to dusk.

Behind it, projected on to a cyclorama. The tide rose almost in real time. Through a wrap-around sound system wild waves and wind buffeted the walls of the Barn until suddenly all went muffled and we were underwater with eerie images of crabs and shrimps and the huge serrated moon mouth of an angel-skate.

To continue the sequence, amber runway lights in the floor led us to the centre of the spatial Barn to a 3-metre-high steel gyroscope filled with 200 bottles and jars. Here was an alchemist's incubator stinking of salt marsh and bad eggs. The glass vessels, filled with mud samples from measured locations around the real rock, were miniature worlds on heat. (They were in fact Vinogradzy columns researched on the NASA website.)

Provoked by light, water and protein (egg white) the sludge in the jars metamorphosed into unpredictably colourful and smelly planets. Behind them, on a large circular screen, sand fleas, diatoms and plankton waltzed together in a miniature ocean of creation. As if in a Kandinsky painting, our video, made through an electron microscope to 10 million magnification, revealed the inner life of the algae slime scraped from the side of the rock and the vibrant molecular culture of the soup collected from the inland sea on its back. Such bacteria are our ancestral DNA.

The mood shifted again. Nostalgic music hall, film soundtracks, echoing electronic fruit machines and shooting galleries reverberated from the east end of the Barn. Here charred vertical timbers symbolized the underneath of the burnt-out Morecambe Pier. As spectators wandered inside its labyrinth, they saw small shrines, surreal cameos of evolution. Not unlike fun-loving stations of the cross.

A nativity of the first dinosaur. A mermaids' night out with Dame Edna Everidge. The last wolf in England suckling her cubs. A psychotic Mr Punch dangling one remaining baby off the edge of the pier.

After twenty minutes the whole sequence ended with a violent interruption.The Rock melted in a firestorm. Reverting to lava in a global volcano, it glowed cinder red. The sea returned too. Finally, under a full moon we could hear the lapping of the tide and the occasional sigh of a night-heron.

Macro, Micro then Mythic. In the first part of the triptych we saw the familiar morphology of the Rock in the Bay. In the incubator, where minute life forms were revealed, we discovered what lies beyond normal human sight. Then under the pier our imaginations and genetic memories were triggered by the Mythic; sunset ballrooms mingled with 250 million years of evolution; Stan Laurel (who was born in Ulverston) met dinosaurs, wolves and Wilberforce.

So, in a spirit of play, the One Rock triptych examined ecology and what we call 'Nature'. Through transition and transformation we witnessed the graphic revelation of the symbiotic relationship between different life forms and we experienced the sacred and secular poetry under our feet.

(xii) *Wondering*
Several angles discussed by Chamberlain, Lavery and Fox are also reflected in a work-in-progress by Emily Orley, entitled 'Wondering while wandering inside spaces: approaching a method of encounter'. In it, she clarifies her interest in exploring

   installations, theatre sets and certain architectural structures and buildings. Importantly, all these spaces have the capacity to evoke a sense of wonder in the visitor. Also, they are all inside or more specifically indoors in one way or another. Literally, they are 'in-doors' in that to enter them, the visitor must pass through a doorway, or over a threshold of some kind. Indeed, the very act of crossing the threshold seems to be a key device for heightening the visitor's awareness and encouraging this sense of wonder that I wish to address. The impact of crossing this threshold may not be immediate, and often is delayed, but involves a kind of quickening and the visitor experiences a shift in perception which could be barely noticeable or, at the other extreme, overwhelming. The visitor is shifted out of his normal state and into a state of wonder. In other words, the visitor's mind is suddenly cleared of the clutter of everyday concerns that otherwise occupy her, and she is struck by the strangeness and/or uniqueness of the space she has entered. (Orley 2006)

Her first example is from Naples, where she registers the move from 'heat and dust and sweat and filth...' to 'the vast, cold marble interiors of so many churches':

You can wander into one from any of the main streets and be met with musty darkened quiet... The spatial contrast with the street world outside is immediate and physical, and your body is affected before you have a chance to think. You slow down. You become aware that you can hear your own breathing. You experience a brief – and perhaps barely noticeable – instance of wonder.

Orley traces the notion of wonder back to Plato's *Theaetetus*, where 'Socrates converses with a young aristocrat and student about the question of what is knowledge and what is the difference between knowledge and perception'; and links this to Descartes' definition of wonder as 'a sudden surprise of the soul which makes it tend to consider attentively those objects which seem to it rare and extraordinary'. Orley notes that Philip Fisher, in *Wonder, the Rainbow and the Aesthetics of Rare Experiences*, identifies wonder as 'the possibility of knowledge', which occurs 'on "the border between sensation and thought," inspiring a process of discovery in which each step includes its own moment of wonder and the rebirth of intellect.' [Lavery notes: 'I call this "enchantment"'].

For Orley,

Surprise is the trigger. The sudden change in atmosphere when you enter the cool church in Naples just off the busy street is unexpected: you lose your bearings momentarily, you are thrown. You step from the ordinary everyday-ness of the street into an unknown space. As you step through the doorway, as you cross the threshold, you experience wonder.

She analyses this as a form of époché, which

involves suspending prejudgements and assumptions and restoring openness in order to re-achieve direct contact with the world. It is about the pure immediacy of experience, when all thought and doubt has been excluded or bracketed. It involves a philosophical detachment.

She discusses another building in Brick Lane London, and goes on:

You are not simply stepping indoors from outside, but you are stepping into a different slice of time, a different environment. Your senses are called to the alert. This adjustment leaves you breathless, suspended, quiet.

Which leads her to ask:

Is wonder nothing more than a quietness, a suspended breathlessness before your response to an artwork?

To evoke a sense of wonder, how important is the role of the threshold or doorway as a device to stop the visitor before entering the work and observing it?

She speculates further that this kind of process might initiate a 'kind of theatre-of-the-invisible' (derived from Brook), thus linking it with some of the ideas explored above by Malekin.

Orley's analysis of the process occurring here breaks it into stages. The first is 'an unexpected encounter, a surprise of some sort'; this is the 'trigger' which 'propels the individual into a state of wonder', which 'in turn provokes a new response in the individual, which leads him to ask questions, think and/or imagine'. Here an immediate experience produces a shift through 'unknowing' (suspension of cognition) to the reformulation of knowing in an essentially performative sequence which we have often suggested above. Her discussion also picks up the importance of suddenness, the move across a limen or threshold, and the physiological marker of suspension of breath.

Malekin and Yarrow take up below further aspects of this suspension or surprise as it manifests in the experience of theatre.

(xiii) *Full Stops to Full Stocks*

Peter Malekin and Ralph Yarrow

Drama is direct experience... It can liberate by transmuting being, what we *are* in ourselves, prior to our *ideas* of ourselves and other associated ideas,

our mental furniture, prior even to our ground states of feeling. In the silent and magic moments of theatre we are 'taken out of ourselves' not merely merged in a collective, but experiencing the emergence of our awareness devoid, momentarily or for longer, of the limitations of the image we take upon us as 'ourselves' in the charade of ordinary life. The make-believe world of drama can transmute consciousness, which is the ground of perception, feeling and understanding, and the ground of changing self-images. [...] We can move into a moment in which 'I' is in abeyance, when there is awareness innocent of categories, including those that might apply to the drama we have witnessed.

(Malekin and Yarrow 2000)

As we go on to point out, 'the "I/we" that is predicated and suspended here is that of an audience.' Since actor-trainers from many traditions have also sought to locate this suspense-before-animation, it looks as though it can be common to both production and reception in performance.

The experience itself is simple. The moment does not abolish time, the sequence of drama and action, but it opens up within it a different dimension. The moment is a lapse into freedom, and that freedom changes the action, for dramatic action, time and freedom are all experienced in consciousness through our minds, and our minds have gone out of themselves towards that ground/groundless consciousness, towards a liberation, towards freedom. If such a freeing moment is experienced in a play, then dramatic time ceases to be self-enclosed, self-defining, whether or not there is narrative or emotional closure. (Ibid.)

Perhaps, therefore, the place of theatre also ceases to 'enclose', and instead becomes all space, the environment of Turner's 'subjunctive' mode, or even of Stanislavsky's 'magic if'.

What is the fullest level of resource for a play? It is its ability, through geste, metaphor, register, rhythm, network of relationships, visual and aural codes, to generate a dynamic of meanings.

What is the most powerful resource of the actor? It is to be many people, many shapes; and in each of these forms to tap the flow of energy, to embody the processes of their articulation.

What is the key modality of an audience? It is the capacity to intuit a 'play', to sense an organicity and to derive a coherence, from the multiple signs, sights and sounds it receives. [...]

What is needed then, is to bring performers, individually and collectively, firstly to access a state of 'neutrality, where habit and familiar patterns are suspended, where both the everyday self and its forms and roles, and any easily adopted 'actorly' personae, are put aside. A sort of waiting without expectation. Where the performer is not the everyday I, not the character s/he may adopt, only the possibility of being neither and both. Where the play, both as interaction of personae and as interweaving of text, is still unknown. It's not irrelevant then that the levels accessed here are what conventional categories of identity and meaning leave out: participants meet themselves in another guise, not as they are in everyday situations or familiar training or performance modes; they are asked to engage with what in these situations they do not know. Jacques Lecoq claimed that the most urgent need for the performer is permission to fail: to be able to become what (you think) you cannot do. Others have used terms like 'sacrifice' or 'abandonment' to describe passing through this 'failure'. What it involves is, more precisely, a temporary encounter, perhaps initially vertiginous or scary, with something like the sense that 'I can't do that; I have absolutely no idea how to do/be that; I cannot imagine what doing that would be like; I do not extend that far; if I am asked to do that I will be lost'. It is absolutely necessary to enter that loss, that absence. To rest here. To unfind oneself. To be only a readiness, a blank screen. (Ibid.)

(xiv) Coda

Ralph Yarrow

Just like Michael Chekhov's work to make actors more aware of their relationship to the space they are working in and to others working with them (also targeted by Lecoq's exercises to develop the functioning of imagination in space and in the physical sensing of elements), Núñez is concerned to enhance the performer's awareness of the extension of their physical body in space. These and other trainers aim to push out the limits of the way the body orientates and operates, to discover a wider range of ability to feel and engage; to recalibrate the sense of self and its possibilities, opening up in the body some quality which perhaps seems 'sacred' only because it has not been adequately exercised or accessed. It is only off-limits because we have accepted the limits of habit, convention or convenience. It is not the preserve of the few; there are many ways through this 'initiation', but they have to be selected and nurtured. They also, crucially, have to be acknowledged as possible, or we have to put ourselves into a situation or condition in which surprise is available. That is another reason why the range of experiences offered by theatre is particularly useful. And why we need to demystify the term 'sacred': the politics of reserving it as totemic or taboo need constantly to be challenged by reclaiming the multiple and pragmatic routes of access we have identified, revealing that the sacred is a generic capacity for particular qualities of experience, not a forbidden territory (Sellars: 'it is very important that there is a spiritual life that is simply not subject to the hijackjing of scholastic theologians' – 2005, 44).

Chamberlain's account of work with Mirecka and Núñez suggests that it does, as George proposes, 'reformat knowing', via a shift in cognitive and motoric operation. What becomes 'known' as a result is not so much a separate entity, as a modulation of the body and functioning of the knower: 'I see' is not about the object of cognition but the mode of prehension, in which the 'I' which sees and the way it perceives is experienced differently. This book has aimed to open up a number of ways in which sensing and knowing may be experienced in and as performance, both in terms of content and of form.

So the sacred for us here is a moment (in the sense that Malekin defines this, i.e. a synchronic event which is in effect a suspension, a step outside time), an incitement to a shift of frame or paradigm, a loss and a potential renewal. It occurs in and as performance, but it is not just performance; the specific quality which has caused it to be marked off as sacred is precisely that capacity of the performative to function as hiatus, as pause, to produce a void in thought. And it is available, though only in and as a kind of participation or active processing, to those who work in training or in production, and to those who receive the complexity and multiple layering of 'text' in performance. So in spite of the disadvantages of the terms 'sacred' and 'theatre', they can help to signal the distinctive features of performance in this mode and to this effect.

Notes to Part 3

1. See, for instance, the following remark by Lefebvre where he stresses the importance of performance in the production of absolute space:

   The absolute space where rites and ceremonies were performed retained a number of aspects of nature, albeit in a form modified by ceremonial requirements: age, sex, geniality (fertility) – all still had a part to play. (2004, 48)

2. Gay McAuley makes a similar point in *Space in Performance: Making Meaning in the Theatre*. For McCauley, the actual theatre building functions as a signifier, a culture frame that allows one to recognize a special site, *a theatron*, a place where fiction rules. McCauley states that 'the principal function of the primary framework constituted by the theatre building is to signal to all concerned that, once inside, we are in the realm of "denegation"'

(1999, 42). As will become apparent as my argument develops, this semiotic dimension of theatre is exactly what I am trying to get away from. In my view, signalling that one is about to enter 'the realm of denegation' is a way of denying or foreclosing the sacred.

3. David Wiles concurs:

> Brook's empty space is like the blank canvas of a modernist painter. By the end of the twentieth century it became clear that ...every canvas has a specific texture, colour and form, and an invisible label marked 'Art'. [Mike] Pearson's dismissal of the latest brilliant product of an arts centre is not just the eternal disenchantment of the creative artist, but reflects a philosophical understanding that space is never empty, and can never be a 'neutral vessel of representation'.

> I have much sympathy with Pearson's point of view – a passion for performance mixed with frustration once trapped in spatial machines that grind out predetermined theatrical meanings. (2004, 4)

> [RY: But this ('brilliant product...') sounds like a hugely patronizing remark from an established 'alternative' practitioner with Arts Council funding and a University post. Of course, you have to work against any space from one point of view. Are we not in danger here of erecting a new elite, i.e. those that turn their noses up at working in theatres? Isn't this masquerading as a new proletarianism but, in fact, setting up just the opposite?]

4. In this context, it is important to note that Grotowski abandoned theatre for paratheatre in the 1970s.

5. For those familiar with Libeskind's essay on the Bauhaus, it might seem surprising that I have made the above analogy between the spiritual and sacred. After all, Libeskind notes at one point that the Bauhaus 'declared war' on the sacred (2001, 22). However, Libeskind's concept of the sacred is limiting, and he tends to equate it with pagan violence and mystery. For me, on the other hand, the sacred, while its meaning can never be grasped, is what prevents violence. To that extent, my understanding of the sacred has, as I suggested, close similarities with Libeskind's use of the word spiritual. In both cases, the subject is compelled to confront the impossible and to open himself/herself to the Other.

BIBLIOGRAPHY

Abram, David (1996) *The Spell of the Sensuous: Perception and Language in a More-Than-Human World*, New York, NY: Vintage Books.

Agamben, Giorgio (1998) *Homo Sacer: Sovereign Power and Bare Life*, trans. Daniel Heller-Roazen, Stanford CA: Stanford University Press.

Agamben, Giorgio (1999) *The Man Without Content*, trans. Georgia Albert, Stanford: Stanford University Press.

Alexander, Charles N. et al. (1990) 'Growth of Higher Stages of Consciousness: Maharishi's Vedic Psychology of Human Development.' *Higher Stages of Human Development. Perspectives of Human Growth*, eds. Charles N. Alexander and Ellen J. Langer, New York and Oxford: Oxford University Press.

Allain, Paul (1997) *Gardzienice: Polish Theatre in Transition*, Amsterdam: Harwood.

Allain, Paul & Harvie, Jen (2006) *The Routledge Companion to Theatre and Performance*, London: Routledge.

Altizer, Thomas (1975) *Mircea Eliade and the Dialectic of the Sacred*, Connecticut: Greenwood Press.

Almond, Philip (1990) 'Mysticism and Its Contexts.' *The Problem of Pure Consciousness*, ed. Robert K. C. Forman, Oxford and New York: Oxford University Press.

Ames, Roger T. and David L. Hall (2003) *Dao De Jing: A Philosophical Translation*, New York: Ballantine Books.

Anandavardhana (1974) *Dhvanyaloka*, ed. and trans. K. Krishnamoorthy, Dharwar, India: Karnatak University Press.

Aristotle (1996) *Poetics*, trans. Malcolm Heath, London: Penguin.

Artaud, Antonin (1958) *The Theater and Its Double*, trans. Mary C. Richards, New York: Grove Press.

Artaud, Antonin (1988) *Selected Writings*, Berkeley: University of California Press.

Ashcroft, Bill, Gareth Griffiths and Helen Tiffin (2002) *The Empire Writes Back: Theory and Practice in Post-colonial Literatures*, 2nd edition, London and New York: Routledge.

Audi, Robert, general ed. (1995) *The Cambridge Dictionary of Philosophy*, Cambridge: Cambridge University Press.

Ayer, A. J. (1956) *The Problem of Knowledge*, London: Macmillan.

Badiou, Alain (2003) ed. Power/Toscano, *On Beckett*, Elinanen.

Barba, Eugenio (1985) 'Interview with Gautam Dasgupta', *Performing Arts Journal* January.

Barba, Eugenio (1986) *Beyond the Floating Islands*, New York: PAJ Books.

Barba, Eugenio (1995) *The Paper Canoe: A Guide to Theatre Anthropology*, London: Routledge.

Barba, Eugenio (2005) 'Children of Silence: Reflections on Forty Years of Odin Teatret', trans. Judy Barba, in Odin Teatret, *Andersens Drøm*.

Barnard, G. William (1994) *Exploring Unseen Worlds: William James and the Philosophy of Mysticism*, Dissertation, The University of Chicago.

Barthes, Roland (1972) 'Baudelaire's Theater, *Critical Essays*. Evanston: Northwestern UP.

Bataille, Georges (1973a) 'Le Coupable', *Oeuvres complètes*, 12 vols (V, 325–398), Paris: Gallimard.

Bataille, Georges (1973b) *L'Erotisme, Oeuvres complètes* (X).

Bataille (1973c) *Literature and Evil*, trans. Alistair Hamilton, London: Calder and Boyars.

Bataille (1987) *Eroticism*, trans. Mary Dalwood, London: Marion Boyars.

Bataille (1988a) *Guilty*, trans. Bruce Boone, San Francisco: The Lapis Press.

Bataille (1988b) *The Accursed Share*, vol. I, trans. Robert Hurley, Zone Books, New York.

Bataille (1998) 'Religion and the Sacred', trans. Michael Richardson, in *George Bataille – Essential Writings*, ed. Michael Richardson, London: Sage.

Bataille 'Expenditure and Sacrifice', trans. Michael Richardson, in *George Bataille – Essential Writings*.

Bates, Brian (1987) *The Way of the Actor: A Path to Knowledge and Power*, Boston: Shambhala.

Bateson, Gregory (1980) *Mind and nature: a necessary unity*, London: Fontana.

Bauman, Zygmunt (1997) *Postmodernity and its Discontents*, New York: New York University Press.

Bauman, Zygmunt (1998) *Globalization: The Human Consequences*, New York: Columbia University Press.

Bauman, Zygmunt (2000) *Liquid Modernity*, Cambridge, UK: Polity.

Bauman, Zygmunt (2002) *Society Under Siege*, Cambridge: Polity.

Beckett, Samuel (1964) *End Game*, London: Faber and Faber.

Begley, Varun (2005) *Harold Pinter and the Twilight of Modernism*, Toronto Buffalo London: University of Toronto Press.

Bennett, Tony (1979) *Formalism and Marxism*, London: Routledge.

Benveniste, Émile (1971) *Problems in General Linguistics*, trans. M. E. Meek, Coral Gables: University of Miami Press.

Bharucha, Rustom (1993) *Theatre and the World: Performance and the Politics of Culture*, London & New York: Routledge.

Bharucha, Rustom (2000) *The Politics of Cultural Practice: Theatre in an Age of Globalization*, London: Athlone.

Blau, Herbert (1987) *The Eye of Prey: Subversions of the Postmodern*, Bloomington: Indiana University Press.

Blau du Plessis, Rachel (1985) *Writing Beyond the Ending: Narrative Strategies of 20th Century Women Writers*, Bloomington: Indiana UP.

Blonski, Jan (1979) 'Holiday or Holiness?' *Gambit*, 33–34 (Polish Theatre Double Issue), 67–76.

Bloom, Harold (1987) 'Introduction' to *Harold Pinter*, ed. Harold Bloom. New York: Chelsea, 1–6.

Boyer, R. W. (2006) 'The Whole Creates the Parts: Debunking Modern Science of Reductive Materialism', conference presentation, Houston, July 8–10.

Brecht, Bertolt (1964) *Brecht on Theatre*, ed. and trans. John Willet, New York: Hill and Wang.

Brook, Peter (1968) *The Empty Space*, London: McGibbon and Kee.

Brook, Peter (1987) *The Shifting Point: Forty Years of Theatrical Exploration: 1946–1987*, London: Methuen.

Brook, Peter (1988/1997) 'Grotowski: Art as Vehicle', in Schechner and Wolford (eds.1997), 379–382.

Brook, Peter (1993) *There are no Secrets: Thoughts on Acting and Theatre*, London: Methuen.

Brook, Peter (1998) 'The Secret Dimension' in Needleman and Baker, eds. 1998, 30–36.

Buber, Martin (2000) *I and Thou*, New York, NY: Scribner Classics.

Burke, Kenneth (1966) *Language as Symbolic Action: Essays on Life, Literature and Method*, Berkeley, CA: University of California Press.

Burridge, Kenelm (1979) *Someone, No One: An Essay on Individuality*, Newark NJ: Princeton UP.

Capra, Fritjof (1976) *The Tao of Physics*, London: Fontana/Collins.

Chamberlain, Franc (2006) 'Ways of Working: Ten Fragments from Sixteen Years of Interaction' in Gough and Christie, eds.2006, 41–46.

Chekhov, Michael (2005) *The Path of the Actor*, Abingdon: Routledge.

Coldiron, Margaret (2004) *Trance and Transformation of the Actor in Japanese Noh and Balinese Masked Dance-Drama*, Lewiston, Queenston, Lampeter: The Edward Mellen Press.

Clarke, Chris (2005) 'The Social Context', *Ways of Knowing: Science and Mysticism Today*, Exeter, UK: Academic Imprint.

Coward, Harold (1990) *Derrida and Indian Philosophy*, Albany: State University of New York Press.

Crook, John and Low, James (1997) *Yogins of Ladakh: A Pilgrimage Among the Hermits of the Buddhist Himalayas*, New Delhi: Motilal Banarsidas.

D'Alviella, Goblet (1981) *Mysteries of Eleusis: The Secret Rites and Rituals of the Classical Greek Mystery Tradition*, Wellingborough, Northamptonshire: Aquarian.

Dawkins, Richard (2004) 'The Sacred and the Scientist', in Rogers (ed.), 135–137.

De, S. K. (1963) *Sanskrit Poetics as a Study of Aesthetics*, Berkeley: University of California Press.

De Quincey, Christian (2000) 'The Promise of Integralism: A Critical Appreciation of Ken Wilber's Integral Psychology', *Journal of Consciousness Studies*, 7.11–12: 177–208.

De Quincey, Christian (2002) *Radical Nature: Rediscovering the Soul of Matter*, Montpelier VT: Invisible Cities Press.

De Quincey, Christian (2005) *Radical Knowing: Understanding Consciousness through Relationship*, Rochester VT: Park Street Press.

Deikman, Arthur (1996) "'I' = Awareness." *Journal of Consciousness Studies*, 3.4:350–56.

Delaney, Paul (2001) 'Exit Tomàs? Straüssler, enter Sir Tom Stoppard', *The Cambridge Companion to Tom Stoppard*, ed. Katherine E. Kelly, Cambridge, UK: Cambridge University Press.

Demastes, William W. (2002) *Staging Consciousness: Theater and the Materialization of Mind*, Ann Arbor: The University of Michigan Press.

Dennett, Daniel (1991) *Consciousness Explained*, London and New York: Penguin.

Derrida, Jacques (1978) *Writing and Difference*, trans. Alan Bass, Chicago: University of Chicago Press.

Derrida, Jacques 'Living On: Border Lines', *Deconstruction and Criticism*, eds. Bloom et al., New York: Seabury.

Deutsch, Eliot (1973) *Advaita Vedanta: A Philosophical Reconstruction*, Honolulu: University of Hawaii Press.

Diamond, Elin (1988) 'Brechtian Theory/Feminist Theory: Toward a Gestic Feminist Criticism', *TDR* 8, 82–94.

Dodds E. R. (1951) *The Greeks and the Irrational*, Berkeley CA: University of California Press.

Durkheim, Emile (1979) *Les Formes élémentaires de la vie religieuse : le système totémique en Australie*, 6th ed., Paris: Presses Universitaires de France.

Dziewulska, Malgorzata (1989) 'An Analysis of the Idea of Wandering', paper presented at the 2nd Centre for Performance Research Points of Contact conference, Dartington College of Arts, April 1989.

Edwards, Paul (2001) 'Science in *Hapgood* and *Arcadia*.' *The Cambridge Companion to Tom Stoppard*, ed. Katherine E. Kelly. Cambridge: Cambridge University Press.

Eliade, Mircea (1968) *Myths, Dreams and Mysteries: The Encounter between Contemporary Faiths and Archaic Reality*, London: Fontana.

Eliade, Mircea (1994) *Aspects du mythe*, Paris: Gallimard.

Emigh, John (1996) *Masked Performance: The Play of Self and Other in Ritual and Theatre*, Philadelphia: University of Pennsylvania Press.

Esslin, Martin (1991) *The Theatre of the Absurd*, London: Penguin.

Etchells, Tim (2006) Programme note to Forced Entertainment's *The World in Pictures*.

Fennellosa, Ernest Francisco and Ezra Pound (1916), *Certain Noble Plays of Japan: From the Manuscripts of Ernest Fennellosa, Chosen and Finished by Ezra Pound, with an Introduction by William Butler Yeats*, Dundrum: Cuala Press.

Fireman, Gary D., McVay Jr., Ted E., and Flanagan, Owen J., eds. (2003) 'Introduction' to *Narrative and Consciousness: Literature, Psychology, and the Brain*, New York: Oxford University Press.

Fleming, John (2001) *Stoppard's Theatre: Finding Order amid Chaos*, Austin: University of Texas Press.

Forman, Robert K. C. (1998) 'Introduction: Mystical Consciousness, the Innate Capacity, and the Perennial Psychology.' *The Innate Capacity: Mysticism, Psychology, and Philosophy*, ed. Robert K. C. Forman, New York and Oxford: Oxford University Press.

Forman, Robert (1999) *Mysticism, Mind, Consciousness*, New York: SUNY Press.

Fox, John (2002) *Eyes on Stalks*, London: Methuen.

Frost, Anthony and Ralph Yarrow (1990) *Improvisation in Drama*, Basingstoke: Macmillan (2nd edition 2007).

Fuchs, Elinor (1985) 'Presence and the Revenge of Writing: Re-thinking Theater after Derrida', *Performing Arts Journal*. 26.7, 163–73.

Gaensbauer, Deborah B. (1996) *Eugène Ionesco Revisited*, New York: Twayne Publishers.

Gale, Steven H. (2003) *Sharp Cut: Harold Pinter's Screenplays and the Artistic Process*, Lexington: The University of Kentucky Press.

Genet, Jean (1963) *The Screens*, trans. Bernard Frechtman, London: Faber and Faber.

Genet, Jean (1972) 'What Remained of a Rembrandt Torn Up into Very Even Little Pieces and Chucked into the Crapper', trans. Richard Seaver, in *Jean Genet: Reflections on the Theatre*, London: Faber and Faber, 75–91.

Genet (1972) 'The Strange Word "Urb..."', trans. Richard Seaver, in *Jean Genet: Reflections on the Theatre*, London: Faber and Faber, 61–74.

Genet (1972) 'Letters to Roger Blin', trans. Richard Seaver, in *Jean Genet: Reflections on the Theatre*, London: Faber and Faber, 7–60.

Genet (1979a) 'Le Funambule', in *Œuvres complètes*, V, Paris: Gallimard, 7–22.

Genet (1979b) *The Blacks*, trans. Bernard Frechtman, London: Faber and Faber.

Genet (1979c) *The Screens (Les Paravents)*, in *Œuvres complètes*, V, Paris: Gallimard.

Genet (1991a) 'Note', in *The Balcony*, trans. Barbara Wright and Terry Hands, London: Faber and Faber.

Genet (1991b) 'How to Perform *The Balcony*', in *The Balcony*, trans. Barbara Wright and Terry Hands, London: Faber and Faber, xi-xiii.

Genet (1991c) 'Entretien avec Hubert Fichte', in *Ennemi déclaré: Œuvres complètes*, VI, ed. Albert Dichy, Paris: Gallimard, 141–176.

Genet (1991d) 'Les Frères Karamazov', in *Ennemi déclaré: Œuvres complètes*, VI, ed. Albert Dichy, Paris: Gallimard, 213–216.

Genet (1993) 'The Studio of Alberto Giacometti', trans. Richard Howard, in *The Selected Writings of Jean Genet*, ed. Edmund White, New Jersey: The Echo Press, 309–35.

Gergen, Kenneth J. (1999) *The Saturated Self: Dilemmas of Identity in Contemporary Life*, New York: BasicBooks.

Gerould Daniel, Bettina Knapp and Jane House (eds. 1989) *Sacred Theatre*, New York: no publisher.

Gerould, Daniel (1989) 'Iconographic Images in the Theatre of Tadeusz Kantor' in Gerould et al. 39–49.

George, D. E. R. (1999) *Buddhism in/as Performance*, New Delhi: D.K. Printworld.

Gleick, James (1988) *Chaos: Making a New Science*, New York: Penguin.

Goldman, Michael (2000) *On Drama: Boundaries of Genre, Borders of Self*, Ann Arbor: University of Michigan Press.

Goldberg, Sander M. (1988) 'Plautus on the Palatine', *The Journal of Roman Studies*, vol. 88, 1–20.

Gómez-Peña, Guillermo (1994) 'The New World Border: Prophecies for the End of the Century', *The Drama Review*, 38.1, 119–42.

Gombrowicz, Witold (1991) *Pornografia*, trans. Alastair Hamilton, London: Penguin.

Gough, Richard, Daniel Watt and Judie Christie, eds. 2006, *A Performance Cosmology: Testimony from the Future, Evidence from the Past*, Abingdon: Routledge.

Grinshpon, Yohanan (2003) *Crisis and Knowledge: The Upanishadic Experience and Storytelling*, Oxford: Oxford University Press.

Grotowski, Jerzy (1969) *Towards a Poor Theatre*, ed. Eugenio Barba with Preface by Peter Brook, London: Methuen.

Grotowski, Jerzy (1989/1997a) 'Tu es le fils de quelqu'un' in Schechner and Wolford (eds.1997), 292–303.

Grotowski, Jerzy (1990/1997b) 'Performer' in Schechner and Wolford (eds.1997), 374–8.

Grotowski, Jerzy (1995) 'From Theatre Company to Art as Vehicle' in Richards (1995), 115–35.

Grotowski, Jerzy (1998) 'A Kind of Volcano' in Needleman and Baker, eds.1998, 87–106.

Haedicke, Janet V. (1992) 'David Henry Hwang's M. Butterfly: The Eye on the Wing', *Journal of Dramatic Theory and Criticism*, 27–44.

Hauser, Arnold (1982) *The Sociology of Art*, London: Routledge and Kegan Paul.

Hillman, James (1992) *The Myth of Analysis: Three Essays in Archetypal Psychology*, New York, NY: HarperPerennial.

Hunter, Jim (2000) *Tom Stoppard: A Faber Critical Guide*, London: Faber and Faber.

Hutcheon, Linda (1989) *The Politics of Postmodernism*, London: Routledge.

Hwang, David Henry (1988) Author's Notes, *M. Butterfly*, NY: Dramatists Play Service, Inc.

Hwang, David Henry (1989) *M. Butterfly*, New York: Plume.

Ionesco, Eugène (1962) *Rhinoceros, The Chairs, The Lesson*, trans. Donald Watson, London: Penguin.

Ionesco, Eugène (1964) *Notes and Counter-Notes: Writings on the Theatre*, trans. Donald Watson, New York: Grove Press.

James, William (1960) *The Varieties of Religious Experience: A Study in Human Nature*, London: The Fontana Library.

Jeffcott, E. M. W. (1972) *Proust and Rilke: The Literature of Expanded Consciousness*, London: Chatto and Windus.

Johnstone, Keith (1981) *Impro: Improvisation and the Theatre*, London: Methuen.

Kaku, Michio (1995) *Hyperspace: A Scientific Odyssey through the 10th Dimension*, Oxford: OUP.

Kaprow, Allan (2003) quoted in Sarah Gorman, 'Wandering and Wondering: Following Janet Cardiff's Missing Voice', *Performance Research*, 8: 1, 83–92.

Katz, Steven T. (1978) 'Language, Epistemology, and Mysticism.' *Mysticism and Philosophical Analysis*, ed. S. Katz, Oxford: Oxford University Press.

Kirby, E. T. (1975) *Ur-Drama*, New York: NYU Press.

Krishnamoorthy, K. (1968) *Some Thoughts on Indian Aesthetics and Literary Criticism*, Prasaranga, India: University of Mysore Press.

Kristeva, Julia (1991) *Strangers to Ourselves*, trans. Leon S. Roudiez, London: Harvester Wheatsheaf.

Kritzer, Amelia Howe (1991) *The Plays of Caryl Churchill*, London: Macmillan.

Kumiega, Jennifer (1985), *The Theatre of Jerzy Grotowski*, London: Methuen.

Lacan, Jacques (1978) *The Four Fundamental Concepts of Psycho-Analysis*, trans. Alan Sheridan, ed. Jacques-Alain Miller, New York: Norton.

Lavery, Carl and Ralph Yarrow (2004) 'Genet's Sacred Theatre: Practice and Politics', *Consciousness, Literature and the Arts*, vol. 5, no. 1.

Lecoq, Jacques (1987), *Le Théâtre du Geste*, Paris: Bordas.

Lefebvre, Henri (2004), *The Production of Space*, trans. Donald Nicholson-Smith, Oxford: Blackwell.

Levin, David Michael (1988) *The Opening of Vision: Nihilism and the Postmodern Situation*, London: Routledge.

Levenson, Jill L. (2001) Stoppard's Shakespeare: Textural Re-visions', *The Cambridge Companion to Tom Stoppard*, Cambridge: Cambridge University Press.

Libeskind, Daniel (2001) *The Space of Encounter*, London: Thames & Hudson.

Lye, Colleen (1995) 'M. Butterfly and the Rhetoric of Antiessentialism: Minority Discourse in an International Frame', *The Ethnic Canon: Histories, Institutions, and Interventions*, ed. David Palumbo Liu, Minneapolis: University of Minneapolis Press, 260–89.

Lyotard, Jean-Francois Lyotard (2000) 'The Tooth, the Palm', trans. Anne Knab and Michel Benamou, in *Mimesis, Masochism, and Mime: The Politics of Theatricality in Contemporary French Thought*, ed. Timothy Murray, Ann Arbor: The University of Michigan Press, 282–88.

Macaulay, Alastair (1998) 'The Man Who Was Two Men', *Financial Times*, 31 October, 7.

Macy, Joanna and Molly Young Brown (1998) *Coming Back to Life: Practices to Reconnect Our Lives, Our World*, Gabriola Island, BC: New Society Publishers.

Maharaj, Sri Nisargadata (1988) *I Am That: Talks with Sri Nisargadata Maharaj* (1973), trans. Maurice Frydman, ed. Sudhakar S. Dikshit, Durham, North Carolina: The Acorn Press.

Majcherek, Janusz (1989) 'Gardzienice as a Proposition of Exit from the Land of Ulro', paper presented at the 2nd Centre for Performance Research Points of Contact conference, Dartington College of Arts, April 1989.

Malekin, Peter and Kerstin Malekin (1986) trans. Strindberg, *A Dream Play*, Norwich: UEA.

Malekin, Peter & Ralph Yarrow (1997) *Consciousness, Literature and Theatre: Theory and Beyond*, Basingstoke: Macmillan.

Malekin, Peter & Ralph Yarrow (2000) 'The Pashyanti Project', *Consciousness, Literature and the Arts*, vol. 1, no. 2 (http://www.aber.ac.uk/cla/archive/archive.html).

Marranca, Bonnie and Gautam Dasgupta (eds. 1991) *Interculturalism and Performance*, New York: PAJ Publications.

McAuley, Gay (1999) *Space in Performance: Making Meaning in the Theatre*, Ann Arbor, University of Michigan Press.

McKenzie, Jon (2001) *Perform or Else: from Discipline to Performance*, London: Routledge.

Meyer-Dinkgräfe, Daniel (2001) 'Suggestion in Peter Brook's *Mahabharata*'. Studies in the Literary Imagination, 34: 2, 117–127.

Meyer-Dinkgräfe, Daniel (2003) 'Staging Consciousness: Updating Demastes.' *Consciousness, Literature and the Arts*, vol. 4. no. 2 (July), http://www.aber.ac.uk/cla/archive/dmddemastes.html.

Meyer-Dinkgräfe, Daniel (2005) *Theatre and Consciousness: Explanatory Scope and Future Potential*, Bristol, UK; Portland, OR: Intellect.

Middleton, Deborah K (2001) 'At Play in the Cosmos: The Theatre and Ritual of Nicolás Núñez', *The Drama Review* 45, 4 (T172) winter 2001, 42–63.

Miller, G. (2006) 'Through the Wrong End of the Telescope', in *Performance and Places*, eds. H. Paris and L. Hill, Basingstoke, Palgrave Macmillan.

Mindell, Arnold (2000) *Quantum Mind: The Edge between Physics and Psychology*, Portland OR: LaoTse Press.

Mindell, Arnold (2002) *The Dreammaker's Apprentice: Using Heightened States of Consciousness to Interpret Dreams* Charlottesville, VA: Hampton Roads Publishing.

Nair, Sreenath (2007) *Restoration of Breath: A Study on Breath and Consciousness in Training and Performance with Particular Reference to South Indian Siddha Yoga*, Ph.D. thesis, Aberystwyth: University of Wales.

Nancy, Jean-Luc (1991) *The Inoperative Community*, trans. Peter Connor, Lisa Garbus, Michael Holland, and Simona Sawhney, Minneapolis: University of Minneapolis Press.

Naismith, Bill (2000) *Faber Critical Guides: Harold Pinter*, London: Faber and Faber.

Needleman, Jacob and George Baker (eds.1998) *Gurdjieff: Essays and Reflections on the Man and His Teaching*, New York, NY: Continuum.

de Nicolàs, Antonio (1976) *Meditations through the Rg Veda*, Boulder, Colorado and London: Shambhala.

Nunes, Luis Fithur (1989) 'Candomblé and Umbanda: Two Forms of Afro-Brazilian Ritual' in Gerould et al., 15–25.

Núñez, Nicolás (1991) *Teatro antropocósmico: el rito en la dinámica teatral* (2nd edition) Mexico City: Árbol editorial.

Núñez, Nicolás (1996a) *Anthropocosmic Theatre: Rite in the Dynamics of Theatre*, trans. Ronan J. Fitzsimons, Amsterdam: Harwood Academic Publishers.

Núñez, Nicolás (1996b) 'Theatre as a Personal Rite', Workshop at the University of Huddersfield, England, 26th-30th October.

Núñez, Nicolás (1999) 'Theatre and Transformation', Workshop at the University of Huddersfield, England, 6th-10th April.

Olson, Carl (2000) *Zen and the Art of Postmodern Philosophy: Two Paths of Liberation from the Representational Mode of Thinking*, Albany NY: SUNY Press.

Orley,Emily (2006) 'Wondering while wandering inside spaces: approaching a poetics of encounter', unpublished MS.

Otto, Rudolf (1973) *The Idea of the Holy: An Inquiry into the Non-Rational Factor in the Idea of the Divine and its Relation to the Rational*, trans. John W. Harvey, 2nd edition, Oxford: Oxford University Press.

Ouspensky, P. D. (1949/2001) *In Search of the Miraculous: The Teachings of G. I. Gurdjieff*, New York, NY: Harcourt Inc.

Paniker, Ayyappa K. (1986) 'The Mask-Dance of the God of Death in Patayani', *The Theatre of the Earth is Never Dead*, ed. G. Sankara Pillai, Trichur: School of Drama, University of Calicut, 1–7.

Pao, Angela (1992) 'The Critic and the Butterfly: Sociocultural Contexts and the Reception of David Henry Hwang's M. Butterfly', *Amerasia Journal*, 1–16.

Pflueger, Lloyd W. (1998) 'Discriminating the Innate Capacity: Salvation Mysticism of Classical Samkhya-Yoga.' *The Innate Capacity: Mysticism, Psychology, and Philosophy*, ed. Robert K. C. Forman, New York and Oxford: Oxford University Press.

Phelan, Peggy (1993) *Unmarked: The Politics of Performance*, London and New York: Routledge.

Pinter, Harold (1968)'*The Birthday Party*' and '*The Room*': *Two Plays by Harold Pinter*, New York: Grove Press.

Plato (1996) *The Parmenides*, trans. Mary Louise Gill and Paul Ryan, Indianapolis: Hackett.

Rabkin, Gerald (1983) 'The Play of Misreading: Text/Theater/Deconstruction', *Performing Arts Journal* 19, 44–60.

Ramachandran, T. P. (1980) *The Indian Philosophy of Beauty. Part Two*, Madras: U of Madras Press.

Rhagavan, V. (1988) *The Concept of the Beautiful in Sanskrit Literature*, Madras: The Kuppuswami Sastri Research Institute.

Richards, Thomas (1995) *At Work With Grotowski On Physical Actions*, London: Routledge.

Ricoeur, Paul (1988) *Time and Narrative III*, trans. K. Blame and D. Pellauer, Chicago, IL: University of Chicago Press.

Richman, Michèle (1995) 'The Sacred Group: A Durkheimian Perspective on the Collège de Sociologie', in Carolyn Bailey Gill, ed. *Bataille: Writing the Sacred*, London: Routledge.

Rilke, Rainer Maria (1989) *Duino Elegies*, trans. Stephen Cohn, Manchester: Carcanet.

Rimer, J. Thomas and Masakazu Yamazaki (1984) trans. *On the Art of the Nô Drama: The Major Treatises of Zeami*, Princeton: Princeton UP.

Robbe-Grillet, Alain (1965) *La Maison de rendez-vous*, Paris: Minuit.

Rogers, Ben (ed. 2004) *Is Nothing Sacred?* Abingdon: Routledge.

Ròzewicz, Tadeusz (1969) *The Card Index*, trans. Adam Czerniawski, London: Calder and Boyars.

Saint-Denis, Michel (1982) *Training for the Theatre: Premises and Promises*. London: Heinemann.

Sakellaridou, Elizabeth (1988) *Pinter's Female Portraits: A Study of Female Characters in the Plays of Harold Pinter*, Toronto, New Jersey: Barnes and Noble.

Sales, Roger (1988) *Tom Stoppard: Rosencrantz and Guildenstern are Dead*, London and New York: Penguin.

Sammells, Neil (2001) 'The Early Stage Plays', *The Cambridge Companion to Tom Stoppard*, ed. Katherine E. Kelly, Cambridge, UK: Cambridge University Press.

Scarry, Elaine (1985) *The body in pain: the making and unmaking of the world*, Oxford: OUP.

Scarry, Elaine (1999) *On beauty and being just*, Princeton: Princeton UP.

Sellars, Peter (2005) 'Performance and Ethics: Questions for the 21st Century: Peter Sellars interviewed by Bonnie Marranca', *Performing Arts Journal 79*, 36–54.

Sennett, Richard (1992) *The Fall of Public Man*, New York: Norton.

Schechner, Richard (1985) *Between Theatre and Anthropology*, Philadelphia: University of Pennsylvania Press.

Schechner, Richard (1988) *Performance Theory*, London: Routledge (2nd Edition).

Schechner, Richard (1995) *The Future of Ritual: Writings on Culture and Performance*, London: Routledge.

Schechner, Richard (1997) 'Exoduction', in Schechner, Richard and Lisa Wolford (eds.1997), 458–92.

Schechner, Richard (2002) *Performance Studies: An Introduction*, London: Routledge.

Schechner, Richard and Lisa Wolford (eds.1997) *The Grotowski Sourcebook*, London: Routledge.

Shear, Jonathan (1990) *The Inner Dimension*, New York: Peter Lang.

Simpkinson, Charles and Anne (eds. 1993) *Sacred Stories: A Celebration of the Power of Stories to Transform and Heal*, San Francisco: Harper SanFrancisco.

Slowiak, James and Jairo Cuesta (forthcoming) *Jerzy Grotowski*, Abingdon: Routledge.

Smart, Ninian (1997) *Dimensions of the Sacred: An Anatomy of the World's Beliefs*, London: HarperCollins.

Smith, Dinitia (1993) 'Face Values: The Sexual and Racial Obsessions of Playwright David Henry Hwang', *New York*, January 11, 40–45.

Snyder, Gary (2006) 'Writers and the War against Nature' in *Resurgence* No. 239 November/December 2006, 12–17.

Sorrell, Walter (1973) *The Other Face: The Mask in the Arts*, London: Thames and Hudson.

Speidel, Erich (1982) 'The Individual and Society', *Brecht in Perspective*, ed. Graham Bartram and Anthony Wayne, London: Longman.

Srigley, Michael (1985) *Images of Regeneration: A Study of Shakespeare's The Tempest' and its Cultural Background*, Uppsala: University of Uppsala.

Stoppard, Tom (1968) *Rosencrantz and Guildenstern are Dead*, London: Faber and Faber.

Suzuki, Daisetz T. (1970) *Zen and Japanese Culture* (Bollingen Series LXIV), Princeton NJ: Princeton UP.

Suzuki, D. T. (1949) *Essays in Zen Buddhism*, First Series. New York: Harper and Brothers.

Suzuki, D. T. (1956) *Zen Buddhism, Selected Writings of D. T. Suzuki*, ed. William Barrett, Garden City, NY: Doubleday.

Suzuki, David (1999) *The Sacred Balance: Rediscovering Our Place in Nature*, London: Bantam.

Tarlekar, G. H. (1975) *Studies in The Natyashastra*, Delhi: Motilal Banarsidass.

Tart, Charles T (1998) 'The Dynamics of Waking Sleep' in Needleman and Baker (eds. 1998), 116–126.

Taylor, Mark C. (1984) *Erring: A Postmodern A/theology*, Chicago: University of Chicago Press.

Teasdale, Wayne (1999) *The Mystic Heart*, Novato, CA: New World Library.

Teichert, Dieter (2004) 'Narrative, Identity and the Self', *Journal of Consciousness Studies*, 11.10–11: 175–91.

Throop, C. Jason (3) (2000) 'Shifting From a Constructivist to an Experiential Approach to the Anthropology of Self and Emotion', *Journal of Consciousness Studies 7*, 27:52.

Tsuchiya, Kiyoshi (2001) 'Nô and Purification: The Art of Ritual and Vocational Performance', *Studies in the Literary Imagination*, vol. 34, no. 2, 93–114.

Turner, Victor (1982) *From Ritual to Theatre: The Human Seriousness of Play*, New York: PAJ Books.

Turner, Victor (1987) *The Anthropology of Performance*, New York: PAJ Books.

Turner, Victor (1998) 'Are There Universals of Performance in Myth, Ritual, and Drama? *Modern*

Theories of Drama: A Selection of Writings on Drama and Theater, 1840–1990, ed. George W. Brand, Oxford: Oxford UP.

Vatsyayan, Kapila (1980) *Traditional Indian Theatre: Multiple Streams*, New Delhi: National Book Trust.

Vyas, C. S. (1991) *Buddhist Theory of Perception*, New Delhi: Navrang.

Wallace, B. Alan (2001) 'Intersubjectivity in Indo-Tibetan Buddhism', *Journal of Consciousnes Studies*, 8. 5–7, 209–30.

Wellwood, John (2002) *Toward a Psychology of Awakening: Buddhism, Psychotherapy, and the Path of Personal and Spiritual Transformation*, Boston MA: Shambhala.

Whicher, Ian (1998) *Integrity of the Yoga Darsana: A Reconsideration of Classical Yoga*, New York: SUNY.

Whitehead, Charles (2001) 'Social Mirrors and Shared Experiential Worlds', *Journal of Consciousness Studies 8.4*, 3–36.

Wigman, Mary (1974) *The Language of Dance*, Middletown CT: Wesleyan University Press

Wilber, Ken (1998a) *The Marriage of Sense and Soul: Integrating Science and Religion*, Dublin: Newleaf.

Wilber, Ken (1998b) *The Essential Ken Wilber: An Introductory Reader*, Boston: Shambhala.

Wilber, Ken (2000) *Integral Psychology: Consciousness, Spirit, Psychology, Therapy*, Boston and London: Shambhala.

Wiles, David (2003) *A Short History of Western Performance Space*, Cambridge: Cambridge University Press.

Wittgenstein, Ludwig (1961) *Tractatus Logico-Philosophicus*, trans. D. F. Pears and B. F. McGuinness, London: Routledge and Kegan Paul.

Wolford, Lisa (1996) *Grotowski's Objective Drama Research*, Jackson MS: University Press of Mississippi.

Worth, Katherine (1986) *Harold Pinter:"The Birthday Party," "The Caretaker" and "The Homecoming"*: A Casebook, ed. Michael Scott. London: Macmillan.

Wright, Elizabeth (1996) 'Psychoanalysis and the theatrical: analysing performance', in Patrick Campbell (ed.), *Analysing Performance*, Manchester: Manchester UP, 175–190.

Yarrow, Ralph (1986) '"Neutral" Consciousness in the Experience of Theatre', Mosaic XIX/3, 1–14.

Yarrow, Ralph (1994) 'Anxiety, Play, and Performance: Malte and the [post]modern' *Orbis Litterarum* 1994: 49, 216–232.

Yarrow, Ralph (2001a) 'Theatre Degree Zero'. *Studies in the LiteraryImagination, Vol. 34, No. 2: Drama and Consciousness,* ed. D. Meyer-Dinkgräfe, 75–92.

Yarrow, Ralph (2001b) *Indian Theatre: Theatre of Origin, Theatre of Freedom,* Richmond: Curzon.

Young, Dudley (1993) *Origins of the Sacred: The Ecstasies of Love and War,* London: Abacus.

Zaehner, R. C. (1961) *Mysticism Sacred and Profane: An Inquiry into some Varieties of Praeternatural Experience,* Oxford: OUP.

Zarrilli, Phillip (2001) 'Negotiating Performance Epistemologies: knowledges "about", "in" and "for"', *Studies in Theatre and Performance,* vol. 21, no. 1, 31–46.

Zeifman, Hersh (2001) 'The Comedy of Eros: Stoppard in Love'. *The Cambridge Companion to Tom Stoppard,* ed. Katherine E. Kelly, Cambridge: Cambridge University Press, 185–200.

Žižek, Slavoj (1993) *Tarrying with the Negative: Kant, Hegel, and the Critique of Ideology,* Durham: Duke University Press.

THE AUTHORS

Ralph Yarrow (also convenor and editor) is Professor of Drama and Comparative Literature at the University of East Anglia (UEA), Norwich, UK.

His teaching and research links aesthetic experience, performance practice and consciousness with reference to drama and literature in India, South Africa and Europe, with a strong current focus on theatre and development/social change. Publications include: *Improvisation in Drama* (with A. Frost) (Macmillan 1990, new edition 2007); *European Theatre 1960–90* (Routledge 1992); *Indian Theatre: Theatre of Origin, Theatre of Freedom* (Curzon 2001). Also numerous articles on the functioning of consciousness in reading and theatre, on fantasy, on Modernism; recent work on acting and directing Beckett and Genet; and a major AHRC project on Forum Theatre and development theatre in India.

Directing (in English and French, in Britain and India) includes Beckett, Ionesco, Genet, Sartre, Pirandello, Strindberg, Rózewicz, Gombrowicz, Kokoschka, Dickens, Orton, Pinter, Caryl Churchill and Habib Tanvir.

Performance includes Feste in *Twelfth Night*, Thomas à Becket in *Murder in the Cathedral*, a French homosexual speaking bad German (in Lessing's *Miss Sara Sampson*), a colonial wife (Betty in Churchill's *Cloud Nine*), a witch (in **Macbeth**), a cricket-loving Jewish godfather (Goldberg in *The Birthday Party*) and a sado-masochistic erotomaniac fantasizing as a French general (in Genet's *Le Balcon*).

Franc Chamberlain is Lecturer in Drama and Theatre Studies at University College Cork (UCC), Ireland and Visiting Professor in Performance Studies and Creative Practice at the University of Northampton, UK.

His books and articles include *Michael Chekhov*, Routledge (2003), 'Gesturing Towards a Post-Physical Performance' (2007) and 'Michael Chekhov on the Technique of Acting' (2000). He is series editor of both *Routledge Performance Practitioners* and *Routledge Companions to Theatre Practitioners* and is editing the *Decroux Companion* with Tom Leabhart for the latter series. From 1992 to 1999 he was editor of *Contemporary Theatre Review* and *Contemporary Theatre Studies* (both Harwood).

His recent productions include *My Love...* (Granary Theatre, Cork, 2006); *Telling* (Granary Theatre and Cork Midsummer Festival, 2006); Lorca's *The Public* (2005) and *Interruptions* (solo research performance, 2003).

William S. Haney II is Professor of English and Literary Theory at the American University of Sharjah in the United Arab Emirates. He has also taught at several universities in the United States, Europe and Asia.

He teaches contemporary British and American literature, postcolonial literature, cultural studies, literary theory and criticism, drama and consciousness studies in the context of the humanities.

Haney has published widely in refereed journals in the above-mentioned areas; his books include: *Postmodern Theater and the Void of Conceptions*, Cambridge Scholars Press (2006); *Cybercultures, Cyborgs, and Science Fiction: Consciousness and the Posthuman*, Rodopi Press (2006); *Culture and Consciousness: Literature Regained*, Motilal Banarsidass, Indian edition (2006); Bucknell University Press (2002); *Literary Theory and Sanskrit Poetics*, The Edwin Mellen Press (1993).

Carl Lavery is Lecturer in Theatre Studies at Lancaster University, UK. He is the editor of *Jean Genet: Performance and Politics* (Palgrave 2006) and co-author of *Walking and Autobiography: Performance Writing*, Dee Heddon, Carl Lavery & Phil Smith, ed. Roberta Mock (Intellect, forthcoming). He has published widely on various aspects of theatre and performance. He is currently working on a monograph entitled *Spaces of Revolution* for Manchester University Press. He also works closely with the poet Lawrence Bradby and has produced a number of performance texts. He is fascinated by polymorphous perversity and strives to practice that when he can.

Peter Malekin was formerly Senior Lecturer in English at the University of Durham, UK, and also taught in Northern Cyprus, Sweden, Germany and Iraq. He has translated Böhme and Strindberg and, in addition to co-authored work signalled below, has published many essays and articles on consciousness and the fantastic, chiefly in collections published by Greenwood and in *Consciousness, Literature and the Arts*.

John Fox (guest contributor) is a prolific artist, printmaker, poet, author, cultural provocateur and grandfather who works internationally. He was the Co–founder (1968) and Artistic Director of Welfare State International, the legendary Arts Collective which, after 38 years of joyous mayhem, he archived on April Fools Day 2006. Course leader (with Baz Kershaw and Sue Gill) of the MA in Cultural Performance at Bristol University.

WSI's pioneering work in celebratory theatre, site-specific events, community art, carnival, ecological installations, lantern parades and rites of passage is documented in his *Eyes on Stalks* (Methuen 2002) and in *Engineers of the Imagination* by Coult and Kershaw (Methuen 1983/90/93/95).

This book is a collaboration. The authors have worked together on the following publications and productions/performances (they are also fluent in at least six languages and competent in some four or five others):

Chamberlain & Lavery:
(2005) "Am I being Fair to Boal?" joint paper for *Interactivities*, SCUDD/SCODHE national conference, University of Northampton.

Chamberlain & Yarrow:
(2007) Ed./contributors, 'Vidya: Theatre as development', Issue 39, *Seagull Theatre Quarterly*.
(2002) Eds, *Jacques Lecoq and the British Theatre*, Routledge Harwood.
(1997) Supervising Ed./Ed.: 'Presence and pre-expressivity', *Contemporary Theatre Review*, vols. 6/4 and 7/1; includes an essay by Yarrow.
(1989) Performers/director/translator: *Sphinx and Strawman* (O. Kokoschka, Sewell Barn Theatre, Norwich).
(1984) Performers: *Oh Fair Jerusalem* (D. Edgar, dir. A. Frost), UEA.

Haney & Malekin:
(2001) Eds. and contributors, *Humanism and the Humanities in the Twenty-First Century*. Bucknell University Press; includes a chapter by each; introduction co-authored.

Lavery & Yarrow:
(2007) Ed./author 'More holes than blanket: rehearsal process as political process' in *Jean Genet: Performance and Politics*, ed. Claire Finburgh, Carl Lavery and Maria Shevstova, Palgrave.
(2004) co-authors: 'Genet's Sacred Theatre: Practice and Politics', *Consciousness, Literature and the Arts*, vol. 5, no. 1.
(2002) Director/performer: Pinter, *The Birthday Party*: Sacré Théâtre, Norwich.
(2001/2/3) Dramaturg/director: Genet, *Les Bonnes* : Sacré Théâtre, Norwich and UK tour.
(2000) Performer/director: Ionesco, *Le Tueur Sans Gages*: Sacré Théâtre, Norwich.
(1999) Dramaturg/performers/director: Genet, *Le Balcon*: Sacré Théâtre, Norwich.
(1995) Performers/director: Vinaver, *Portrait d'Une Femme*: Sacré Théâtre, Norwich.

Malekin & Yarrow
(2001) Co-authors: 'Imagination, Consciousness and Theatre', *Studies in the Literary Imagination*, vol. 34, no. 2.
(2000) Co-authors: 'Pashyanti Theatre', *Consciousness, Literature and the Arts*, vol.1, no.2, (online journal).
(1997) Co-authors: *Consciousness, Literature and Theatre: theory and beyond*, Macmillan.
(1985) Translator/director: Strindberg, *A Dream Play*: UEA (Chamberlain was a performer in *A Dream Play*).

INDEX